BY THE SAME AUTHOR

Advice from a Failure

The
Alcoholic
in
Your Life

The Alcoholic in Your Life

JO COUDERT

5B

A SCARBOROUGH BOOK
STEIN AND DAY/Publishers/New York

FIRST SCARBOROUGH BOOKS EDITION 1982

The Alcoholic in Your Life was originally published in hardcover by Stein and Day/*Publishers* in 1972.
Copyright © 1972 by Jo Coudert
Library of Congress Catalog Card No. 70-185955
Designed by David Miller
Stein and Day/*Publishers*
Scarborough House
Briarcliff Manor, N.Y. 10510
ISBN 0-8128-6121-3

for Helen Lucas
first among the two
or three friends
of a lifetime

Contents

The
Alcoholic
in
Your Life

Introduction

Alcoholism is a cruel condition. Even the casually seen body in a doorway suggests its power to shatter promise and the future, but for many of us, the evidence is disturbingly closer at hand: it is visible in the distorted or destroyed lives of acquaintances or friends or lovers or family members. We are aware of the malignancy of alcoholism, and we are well aware that, as tantalizingly simple as the remedy may seem, it is tantalizingly difficult to achieve.

With all that has been written on the subject, the alcoholic does not lack for sympathy, and with all the work being done in the field, he does not lack for places to turn for help. That the help is so often ineffective, that the therapies now available are successful with only a small percentage of alcoholics, does not mean that the answer will not be found.

But while the search goes on, what of the person who lives with or works with or befriends the alcoholic? He has been offered much less help, much less guidance, much less understanding of his difficult, involuntary plight, and yet alcoholism can be as cruel and crippling a condition for him as it is for its primary victim.

For the alcoholic there are compensations in saturation drinking, if only the negative pleasures of relief and release, and there is the magical conviction, almost universal in problem drinkers,

11

that liquor, as physically damaging as it may be to a weaker person, will not cause irreversible harm to *him,* that drinking, as emotionally and economically costly as it may be to a less nimble fellow, will not deprive *him* of love and his livelihood. And if, in the long run, he threatens to be proved wrong, why, then, in the long run, he assumes he will stop.

The one who cares about the alcoholic, in contrast, has no such illusions. He is intensely aware of the current blight and fearful of what is to come. If the drinking has gone on long enough, he despairs of its coming to an end, and yet, knowing that other alcoholics have stopped, he can never make peace with the inevitable. He cannot view alcoholism as a progressive disease, anticipate the outcome, and mourn. Nor can he, on the other hand, view it as a self-limiting disease which will run its course and be over. He must support a number of ambiguities: it is, and it is not, a chronic illness; it is, and it is not, incurable; it is, and it is not, subject to the will of the alcoholic.

These contradictions can subvert his best intentions about how he will behave toward the alcoholic. They can destroy his ability to act consistently and helpfully. They can corrupt his every good resolution to be supportive and understanding. They can undercut his own self-image as a kind and decent person. They can force him into a passive position, and because he is made to feel powerless, they can cause him pain and fear, confusion, dismay, and anger.

But the terrible carrot of hope keeps him locked in the situation, hope and love and the secret vision many of us have of ourselves as sympathetic, patient, and ultimately curative people. For myself, as someone whose life has been linked at several, prolonged points with that of an alcoholic, I think it is almost this latter that proved the strongest cement. I could not believe that there was not something I could do, or do differently, or undo, that would not be the answer. I no longer think so, but I learned much about what could be done, should not be done, and had better be left undone when one, perforce, shares the world of the alcoholic.

It is a world for which I had the deepest distaste, for my introduction to it came in my young teens, at an age when one is never more moralistic, never more unforgiving of transgressions, particularly in one's parents. It was my mother who became alcoholic then, although I did not know that it was a condition and that it had a name. All I knew was that she drank, that she behaved in ways which embarrassed me to the roots of my being, that she was alternately foolish and vicious, tearful and accusing. She brought home people she despised and drove away people she loved. She could not be trusted not to lie. She could never be trusted to be sober.

I judged her harshly then, and later, while I did all the usual things: emptied liquor bottles down the sink, hid her money so she couldn't buy more, yet went to bars with her so that there would be someone to bring her home. I took her to doctors, threatened to abandon her, cajoled her into going to A.A. meetings, moved her to another state where she said she would be happy; and all the time I loathed her, only slightly less than I loved her, for what she was doing to our lives. I did everything but forgive her, perhaps because the answer seemed so easy: she had only to stop drinking to have the nightmare end.

It did not occur to me that forgiveness was possible until an evening when I witnessed a small scene between a friend and her alcoholic ex-husband. My friend, a generation older than I, had been under such severe stress because of her husband's chronic, disastrous drinking that some months before she had had a nervous breakdown. When she was released from the mental hospital, she obtained a legal separation, their possessions were divided, and they had no further contact. But he kept a key to the mailbox in their apartment building and continued to come for his mail. On this particular evening, as we went down the walk to get into her car, he happened to be coming up it, reeling drunk, blear-eyed, mumbling. Knowing the agonies he had caused her and that she wished nothing more than never to see him again, I instinctively turned to go in another direction, but my friend went directly to him and grasped both his hands. "Hello, Ted," she said, "are you all right, dear?" He fell against her, and she steadied and held him. I knew she no longer loved him—indeed, I think she hated him—but she had not forgotten that he was a human being.

With that moment's insight, born of the compassion in my friend's voice, I began to let indignation and outrage go and made an effort to understand the person the alcoholic is. I read what there was to read, both in the lay and technical literature. I talked to people working with alcoholics. As my mother moved in and out of A.A., I got to know many alcoholics themselves. And when, again, there came to be an alcoholic in my life, I fought the alcoholism. But I did not fight the person.

Perhaps my experience of the world of alcoholism is comparable to the effort made by a writer planning a book about a foreign country. As he travels in the alien land, he struggles to keep the chitin of opinion from forming before, by an act of will, he has moved into the skins of the people who inhabit this world and has intuited what it is like to exist in this place, be subject to these influences, talk this language, see things in this light, move to these rhythms, respond to this climate. Neither native nor expert, such a traveler can return and write a description that serves a different function from the expert's analysis of facts or the native's near and emotional re-creation of his world. The book he fashions from his experience and observation is for people who may follow in his footsteps, to suggest how and where to look in order to understand, how to interpret what is there to be seen, and how to behave in ways that are appropriate and responsive.

This book, then, written by an amateur of alcoholism, is intended as a guide for the person whom, for want of a more felicitous term, I shall call the co-alcoholic. The coinage should be taken as the shorthand it is and not interpreted to mean that there is necessarily a personality type whose fate it is to become enmeshed with an alcoholic. There are certainly people like a woman I know who despised her first husband for being alcoholic, divorced him, and remarried a very nice man—only to discover him to be alcoholic too. But whether alcoholics run in some lives or whether repetitions such as this are happenstance is an open question, and the term "co-alcoholic," in this context, is meant to carry no more freight than would the word "co-worker." It simply indicates someone who is in a continuing relationship with an alcoholic.

That someone may be the husband or the wife of an alcoholic, the parent or child of one, the friend or fiancé, the employer or employee. Because the possibilities are as varied as the range of human relationships, it would be useful if the English language contained a neutral pronoun standing for either sex, but it does not, and I shall use "he" when speaking of the alcoholic, although I shall equally mean "she" unless the context rules it out. For the same reason, and because the more frequent situation is that of a wife married to an alcoholic husband, I shall refer to the co-alcoholic as "she" and place most observations in the marriage frame, leaving it to the reader to extrapolate to her particular situation.

If the reader does extrapolate and finds that my descriptions do not match her experience, that is the difficulty of such a book as this. It necessarily contains generalizations, and each should be qualified: "Most alcoholics some of the time . . ." or "Some alcoholics most of the time . . ." for not everything that can be truthfully said of alcoholics is equally true of all alcoholics.

A glance around at the attendance at any A.A. meeting is evidence enough that alcoholics come in all sizes and shapes, all levels of intelligence, from all walks of life. But are the differences more apparent than real? Do alcoholics have observable traits in common that, if added up, might shed deeper light on the surface symptom? A friend of mine, a psychologist, received a grant to study patients with multiple sclerosis, and she set about administering a battery of tests to a large number of such patients in a local chronic disease hospital. Spending hours in bleak, uriniferous wards, she marveled at the cheerfulness which the patients, almost without exception, displayed. Whether or not they had been in the hospital for years, they were pleasant and smiling; no matter their degree of incapacity and the obvious progression of the disease, they were optimistic that they would recover. So striking was this that at first the psychologist was inclined to assume that the illness in some way gave rise to a certain set of behaviors. But, as she studied the test findings, she began to suspect that the personality pre-dated the illness. The projective techniques suggested that common to these patients were deep, but deeply hidden, dependency needs, rigidly suppressed and held out of awareness by a surface display of independence. It began to seem possible to speculate that the chronic illness satisfied a basic need to be dependent, to be taken care of, while the cheerful independence displayed on the surface expressed an equally strong drive to deny this need.

Much work remains to be done in this interesting area of the link between personality and illness, but there is a public wisdom which apprehends that nice people get cancer, people who turn their anger inward and let it eat away inside rather than chew other people out; that angry people who explode at others get strokes; that the need to be loved is an itch which cannot be scratched and that the person with a skin disease may have found a way to scratch his desire. Thus, it seems worthwhile to attempt a description of the alcoholic from the physical, intellectual, emotional, and psychological points of view to explore whether the traits that alcoholics appear to have in common suggest a common genesis of alcoholism.

I shall propose a hypothesis about the roots of alcoholism which seems to fit what can be observed about the personality of alcoholics. If valid, it would explain much that appears arbitrary and self-destructive in the alcoholic's behavior. It would illuminate the reasons why alcoholism is so persistent and refractory a condition. It would indicate why the alcoholic is so difficult a person to get into treatment and to hold in treatment. And it would reconcile the many apparent contradictions in the alcoholic's temperament and actions.

The usefulness of a hypothesis is that it allows observations which might otherwise be mystifying to be organized into a coherent whole. Not long ago, at midnight on a dark country road, I sat on the front bumper of my car reading a book in the beam of the headlights. Had another car passed by, the driver would certainly have thought I was behaving irrationally unless he cast around for a possible explanation and hit upon the hypothesis that the car had a flat tire and I was reading the instruction manual to find out how to change it. If that occurred to him, what a moment before had seemed inexplicable behavior would have fallen into place as an understandable thing to be doing. In the same fashion, a hypothesis about the causes of alcoholism that seems to fit the observed facts can give the co-alcoholic a way of sorting out the alcoholic's behavior that goes beyond seeing it as crazy or careless or stupid. It provides the co-alcoholic with a sensible guess, like the guess that a tire is flat, that may allow baffling bits of behavior to click into place.

A hypothesis generated by reasoning backward, however, cannot be held with confidence until one has reasoned forward and tested whether or not it is consistent with what can be further observed. The passing motorist, for example, might have said to himself, "I couldn't see if a tire was flat, but I did notice that the trunk of the car was open and that's where the jack and spare tire are kept. If it had been engine trouble, the hood would have been up." In such fashion would he have satisfied himself that his guess was correct because the hypothesized "cause," the flat tire, had had an "effect" which was consistent with it, an open trunk. Similarly, a hypothesis about the "cause" of alcoholism that is deduced from observations about alcoholics must be tested by reasoning forward. From such a cause, what would be the expected effect? And is this effect what one actually does see in the life style of an alcoholic?

Does the alcoholic view the world in an idiosyncratic way? Does he have particular expectations of it that others of us do not? Are his wishes different from ours, his needs, his satisfactions? Is his drinking, in short, an attempted solution to a problem rather than the cause of it? And is this solution consonant with what one would expect to find in an adult who had had a certain set of shaping experiences in earliest infancy?

For a very long time, anyone who drank uncontrollably was assumed to be somehow deficient in will power. This made alcoholism a moral problem, one that could readily be solved if only the alcoholic would pull himself together and make an effort to conquer his "weakness." When it became apparent that the answer was not that simple, the concept of alcoholism as a disease was advanced. Workers in the field, anxious to move alcoholism into the realm where it could be treated rather than clucked over, made every effort to educate the public to the view that alcoholism is an illness and that the alcoholic is no more to be blamed for his condition than the diabetic is for his. It is an attractive concept for everyone involved: for the alcoholic because he cannot be held responsible for a physiological derangement, for the co-alcoholic because it shifts the responsibility of caring for the alcoholic to the professional, and for the professional because it places alcoholism in his province.

I myself am at least partially convinced that a physical uniqueness does exist in alcoholics. There is objective evidence of this in recent research that demonstrates, for example, that the liver of an alcoholic metabolizes alcohol with unusual rapidity, and I had subjective evidence in observing my mother develop a craving for chocolate and ice cream when she no longer had access to liquor, this in a woman who all her life had shunned sweets and desserts. Unfortunately, however, while the definition of alcoholism as an illness has been a helpful one in gaining greater tolerance for the alcoholic, it has not led to any decrease in the prevalence of alcoholism nor has it been fruitful in giving rise to more effective therapies. Perhaps it is time now to redefine alcoholism more accurately so that it may be coped with, by the alcoholic and the co-alcoholic as well as the professional, more adequately.

I am going to argue that alcoholism is an addiction rather than a disease. Addiction is defined as the compulsive use of a habit-forming substance, which seems an exact fit of the alcoholic state. Since many, many people, however, are able to drink without becoming addicted to alcohol, the x-factor of compulsiveness must lie in the drinker, not in the alcohol, and I am going to argue further that this x-factor is psychological in nature.

I had occasion recently to interview a neurosurgeon who had developed a method for relieving intractable pain. His patients were primarily people with advanced cancer, most of whom had been on massive doses of narcotics for months, in every instance longer than the time necessary to produce addiction. Interestingly enough, after their pain had been ended surgically, not one of the patients asked for narcotics and not one suffered from withdrawal symptoms. When I inquired about this anomaly, the surgeon commented that it was conclusive evidence, if evidence was still needed, that addiction is a psychological, not a physiological, problem.

To identify alcoholism as an addiction leads into those disquieting areas of psychology in which the only answers are the hard ones of exploration, insight, understanding, and self-awareness. It also offers cold comfort to the co-alcoholic, for addictions of any nature are notoriously difficult to cure. But, again, just as acquiring insight into the genesis of alcoholism can alter, not the fact of alcoholism, but one's way of understanding the alcoholic, so also can acceptance of it as an addiction alter one's way of viewing the alcoholic and dealing with him.

It can, for one thing, make the co-alcoholic's goals much more realistic. I am sure that no one who has tried to help an alcoholic has attempted to do anything less than persuade him to stop drinking altogether, but this may be neither a feasible nor a sensible aim. It frightens the alcoholic, and it makes inevitable the most difficult thing that the co-alcoholic has to bear: the repeated dashing of hope. If the co-alcoholic can accept the definition of drinking as an addiction, she will know that the battle will be a long one, that it will not be easily won, and that there will be many setbacks before, if ever, it is over. She may, then, instead of being desolate in times of failure, be grateful in times of success, and set both herself and the alcoholic the lesser goal, not of total abstinence, but of more frequent abstinences and turn her attention to minimizing the damage when the inevitable lapses occur.

In a book called *The New Think,* author Edward de Bono makes the suggestion that much unprofitable worrying away at problems comes from persistent thinking about them in the same terms. If you have dug and dug for an answer in the same place without finding it, he remarks that the solution may not be to dig deeper but to dig elsewhere, to start a new line of thinking by changing the initial premise. The onset of alcoholism is characteristically so insidious that patterns of reaction to it may be fixed long before, years before, the drinking behavior is properly identified as alcoholism. When it has been recognized, it is likely that the co-alcoholic will not react differently to it but only with an intensification of emotion. The content of the arguments over drinking will not change, but they will be, if anything, more heavily charged, for to her distress will be added fear and a sense of urgency. Her pressures on the alcoholic will escalate, but the rages, the tears, the resentments, and her accusations and his defenses will be monotonously the same.

I was thinking of this last night while having dinner with friends, a couple who have been married twenty-two years. Remembering back, I would guess that it was half of those years before the wife recognized her husband's drinking problem as alcoholism, another two or three years before he conceded that he was alcoholic, making nine years that they both had known it, and still she was saying the same bitter things about his drinking and reacting in the same wounded ways, and he was still being as caustic about her share in his drinking and as defensive as when I first knew them in the early days of their marriage. Year after year, the same words, the same emotional charge to the words.

It is enormously difficult not to experience the provocative, irresponsible, and worrisome behavior of the drinker as an attack, particularly if you love the drinker. You are the person closest to him, so his behavior affects you most and, you feel, reflects on you most in the eyes of other people. And it must be equally difficult, if you are the drinker, not to meet attack with attack. But how useless it is for the alcoholic and the co-alcoholic to repeat endlessly the same bankrupt refrains. Admittedly, it is the alcoholic's drinking that triggers them, but if the co-alcoholic were to dig a hole in a new place, if she saw his drinking as an addiction rather than as an assault on her peace and well-being, she might find different words and actions with which to confront the problem.

At the very least, it might permit her a new objectivity. The alcoholic does not drink because of her; he will not stop because of her. Accepting this, she may be able to make quite different decisions about how to behave. She would have a different central reference point from which to make a long-range appraisal of whether she is capable of putting up with, or willing to put up with, years of drinking. She can assess her own position, her own strengths, her own degree of tolerance of a situation that she is wisest not to anticipate getting better and that may deteriorate.

She can decide whether it is a bearable situation or whether she should get out of it.

If she decides to stay, she has a way of speaking to the alcoholic about his drinking that is less emotionally freighted. Addiction is a fact, not a personal failure, and if it is placed in this objective context, perhaps a common alliance to fight the drinking, not each other, can be made. Or if this is too optimistic an aim, she can, at minimum, look for the signs that herald a drinking bout and be prepared for it and wait it out.

So much of the emotional burden of coping with an alcoholic stems from the fact that alcoholics are masterful at displacing responsibility for their drinking. They blame other people and outside situations, and it is difficult for the co-alcoholic, who is most often the target, not to feel guilty and then not to come to her own defense, which leads to a defeating circularity of accusation and counteraccusation. If she can find ways of separating reasons from excuses by identifying the pattern of the alcoholic's drinking behavior, she can be realistic about any contributions she is making and decide how best to withhold them so as not to aggravate his drinking, and, perhaps, to alleviate it. She can begin to use herself therapeutically.

We all subscribe to the cult of the expert. When something goes wrong, we turn to the specialist; he knows how to fix the TV, repair the car, cure the illness. But alcoholism is as resistant to the specialist as to anyone else, and there is much that the nontherapist can do that is therapeutic. The co-alcoholic may place her faith in getting the alcoholic into A.A. or into a hospital specializing in the treatment of alcoholics or into individual or group psychiatric treatment. These are intelligent steps, but for reasons to be elaborated on elsewhere, it is not easy to get the alcoholic to accept treatment and it is exceedingly difficult to persuade him to remain in treatment. The usual sequence is that, after almost endless discussion and argument, the alcoholic consents to getting help and the co-alcoholic heaves a sigh of relief, feeling that her job is done and that now someone more qualified than she will take over. But it may not work this way, and she should understand why, so that she will be shielded against too great disappointment and will know how to go on from there.

Through whatever modality the alcoholic makes progress toward controlling his addiction, whether it is therapy, A.A., or an improved personal relationship, or any combination of these, there will be a series of phases he goes through, and a knowledge of these can be useful to the co-alcoholic, both as a way of enabling her to encompass setbacks without drastic discouragement and as a means of permitting her to regulate her own actions. Even if the alcoholic is receiving professional help, there is much that the co-alcoholic can also do that is therapeutic if she understands the stages he will go through; and if she has only herself to rely on because he has not accepted or will not stay in treatment, the knowledge will be of even greater value to her.

The most important thing she can know, as I shall try to make convincing, is that the only therapy is talk. The second most important thing is that the alcoholic, more than almost any other person, finds it virtually impossible to talk about his problems. Personality determinants that others of us acknowledge casually, and even find great interest in tracking down, are a closed and shunned world to the alcoholic, and it takes imaginative, subtle, patient, and intelligent effort by the co-alcoholic to stimulate the alcoholic to an exploration of the factors that lie behind his drinking. She must know what to talk about, and when, and how, if she is to succeed in by-passing his defenses.

She must also know the things she cannot do, the efforts she cannot make, the efforts that the alcoholic must make for himself. Many alcoholics feel that if they are not drinking, no more can be asked of them, but they are under no less obligation than anyone else to behave decently. Dry drunks, the times when an alcoholic is filled with all the rage and tension that he ordinarily drinks to release, while preferable to the drinking itself, are only slightly less unacceptable, and the co-alcoholic is justified in pressing for more than the negative not-drinking. Indeed, if she does not, the not-drinking may be an untenable state from which the alcoholic more or less quickly relapses. With some understanding of what the alcoholic must achieve for himself if he is to find life supportable without alcohol, the co-alcoholic can quietly hold to alternatives and indicate without rancor that there are choices to be made and acceptances to be achieved.

All of this takes time, and while a successful outcome is possible, it is far from certain. My mother is dead of chronic alcoholism. My friend's ex-husband died in jail while being detained overnight for drunken driving. There are certainly alcoholics with whom all efforts fail, and there is a point at which the co-alcoholic must give up. How to recognize that point and what the co-alcoholic can then do will be discussed, but long before that point is reached, the co-alcoholic will have had to deal with many family and social and business situations that are affected by the alcoholic's drinking, and the practical problems these entail will be considered.

Particularly is it important that the children in a marriage in which one parent is alcoholic be protected, but since it is not often possible to shield them entirely, how can they be given enough understanding without, at the same time, overburdening them with responsibility? How can the co-alcoholic explain alcoholism in a way that does not condemn the alcoholic? How can she be sure that, in attempting to help the children, she is not unconsciously asking them to help her, to side with her? It would be human to do so, but it is hurtful, and perhaps some observations can contribute to a constructive handling of the situation.

The same may be true of other family relationships and of friends. Every co-alcoholic has to make decisions about whether to try to protect the alcoholic from the consequences of his drinking, whether to try to hide the fact or bring it out in the open, whether, if it is acknowledged, she should speak of it lightly, not at all, or with the end in mind of persuading other people to share her dismay and add their urgings to the alcoholic to stop his drinking. I have seen the social problems of living with an alcoholic handled in various ways, some of which are more successful than others. Describing these ways may open to the co-alcoholic a greater number of possibilities than she has been aware of and allow her to choose among them. She cannot change the alcoholic, but she can, if it promises to be more rewarding, change herself.

It is never possible for one person to change another. But one person can make a difference to another. One person can provide the climate for change, the courage to change, and the incentive to change. How the co-alcoholic may do this for the alcoholic without distorting her own personality and perhaps even freeing herself to act less in accordance with his condition and more in accordance with her own standards is the main concern of this book. If there are elements in it that do not seem relevant to the reader's experience, I would ask only that she step across the credibility gap and continue along the path of my observation until she has seen it as a whole and can decide whether, in a sense more true than surface description, she has gained a deeper view of the alcoholic in her life.

PART ONE

The

Alcoholic

The Alcoholic

A psychiatrist of my acquaintance believes in acquiring first-hand experience of a therapy before prescribing it for patients. Accordingly, some years ago when LSD was a relatively new and unknown drug, he attended an LSD therapy session conducted by a fellow psychiatrist and, like the seven patients there, was given a cube of sugar impregnated with the drug. Half an hour after swallowing it, he was stricken with explosive diarrhea. When he was able to rejoin the group, it was obvious that the others were under the influence of the drug. He remained to observe through the eight-hour session, but at no time did he experience anything but his normal reactions. His body had rejected the drug. It was uncongenial to his chemistry, and he had been unable to retain it long enough to come under its sway.

Some number of people have a comparable experience with alcohol. For them it is a noxious substance which their bodies will not accept in any quantity. A woman I know flushes a flaming scarlet from the chest up when she drinks no more than half a cocktail, and a male friend rarely touches liquor because even a small amount causes his face to become numb. The majority of people are not as sensitive to alcohol as this and can drink in medium quantities, like my aunt, my alcoholic mother's sister, who invariably has at least two stiff drinks before dinner, three or four if it is a real occasion, and is none the worse for it. But let her go on drinking into the evening and the chances are fifty-fifty that she will become actively ill. This is the usual experience of social drinkers; they can drink some amount of alcohol with impunity, but if they exceed their customary limit their bodies reject it. Even heavy drinkers, people who drink daily in fairly large quantities, experience times when their bodies rebel, and they must cut down or abstain until their physical equilibrium is re-established. Aside from the rare drinker who persists through bouts of nausea and illness, the fact is that many of us could not become alcoholic if we tried. Our bodies, unlike that of the alcoholic, simply do not accept alcohol in the necessary quantities.

This is a question of tolerance for a chemical, which the alcoholic has or has developed, rather than a matter of health or strength or robustness. Nevertheless, it requires an impressive constitution to be alcoholic. Although alcoholics often give the impression of not being physically strong, they possess a basic toughness of fiber which allows them to withstand the continued insult of alcohol to the body. Short of the point at which the alcohol itself has produced destructive changes, such as liver or brain damage, a physical indominability is evident in their virtual immunity to colds, flu, and the other minor ailments most of us are vulnerable to. Alcoholics are rarely sick, and their absences from work are almost invariably due to drinking and its consequences rather than illness.

In a book about Alcoholics Anonymous, author Joseph Kessel repeatedly comments on the unusual vitality and aggressive well-being of recovered alcoholics he talked with at A.A. meetings around the country. Apparently, the same toughness that allows alcoholics to drink excessively reasserts itself as health when the drinking stops, and where one might expect to find sick-looking people, debilitated from years of drinking, one encounters instead rather vibrant and youthful-looking persons. Indeed, this last characteristic, that of seeming younger than their chronological age, is often present even in active alcoholics. For the ordinary person, there is nothing so aging as alcohol, as a look in the mirror the morning after a party confirms, but alcoholics seem to be immune to this aging effect. I recently took an early-morning plane back to New York in the company of a writer I know to be alcoholic; even before he had a couple of drinks on the trip, he was exuding alcohol from every pore, but still he looked fresh and rosy while even makeup was no help in hiding the haggard lines I had acquired as a result of the previous night's banquet we had both attended. That alcoholics tend to retain an air of youthfulness until their faces rather abruptly collapse into multiple wrinkles and their bodies capitulate to the long-continued onslaught of alcohol is, of course, one of the generalities to which there are bound to be exceptions, but one has only to imagine what chronic drinking would do to one's own physical being to recognize the innate resiliency of alcoholics.

As well as having a special tolerance for alcohol physically, the alcoholic must experience an emotional effect from drinking that is welcome to him. For a minority of people, alcohol is a depressant which makes them feel, not better, but worse. A greater number find the effects of drinking pleasant and relaxing but not irresistible. They do not necessarily enjoy the loss of control and the blurring of perception that an excess of alcohol causes, or if so, these effects are sought only occasionally and under special circumstances. A friend of mine who enjoys drinking wages an entirely visible fight against the onset of drunkenness when she has had too much. Pulling herself up straight and speaking carefully, she leaves her current drink untouched, refuses more, and shortly excuses herself to go off to bed. Her husband, on the other hand, a man who is possibly alcoholic, keeps on drinking past the point of coherence, past the point of being able to get to his feet. To him, the ultimate anesthetic effect of alcohol is desirable and agreeable.

In an article about drug-taking, psychologist Sidney Cohen remarked that the psychedelic experience need not be different for two persons to have them interpret it in quite opposing ways. "Identical subjective phenomena are called 'mystical union' by one, and 'depersonalization and derealization' by another. Visions and insights for one may be hallucinations and delusions for another. Very often the 'good trip' is no different from the 'bum trip' except that one person relishes loss of control and becomes ecstatic, while another becomes panicky and horrified." The same can be said for drunkenness. One need not postulate that it is a different experience for the alcoholic, only that the experience as such has a special attraction for him and that he finds it agreeable and rewarding in ways the nonalcoholic does not.

Although alcohol is commonly described as a euphoriant, enough alcoholics become surly and pugnacious when drinking to suggest that the mood-elevating properties of alcohol are not its sole enticement. An alcoholic may or may not experience a glowing warmth, a suffusion of fellow-feeling, a lift in his spirits, or he may get these effects from drinking at some times but not others. What is a regular accompaniment of drinking, however, is a lessening of control. It is this that happens to the light, medium, heavy, and alcoholic drinker alike, and it is this that may be dismaying to the ordinary drinker but welcome to the alcoholic.

Physical control over actions decreases as the quantity of alcohol in the system increases, but before this effect becomes evident—and more important to the meaning of drinking—is the relaxing of ego controls that begins almost immediately with the first drink. The ego is that aspect of the psychic economy which guards reactions and regulates responses, is self-aware and self-conscious. It can be thought of as a sentinel operating at the gateway between the inner world of the self and the outer world of others, the inner world of tensions, needs, wishes, and drives, and, as well, the repressions, the inhibitions, the critical conscience that judges and finds the self wanting, and the outer world of other people's actions, offerings, demands, needs, responses, and requirements upon the self. Often at the cost of great energy, the ego mediates between these two worlds, attempting to satisfy both, or if that is impossible, as it usually is, attempting to find compromises which will at least mollify both worlds. The ingestion of alcohol acts to relax the ego's vigilance. The sentinel goes off duty, allowing the inner world to slip through the gate and find expression in words and actions. Whether this makes the inner and outer worlds seem more in harmony or whether the greater sense of ease comes from the ego's ceasing to struggle to keep all demands in balance, the upshot is the same. With the lessening of control, the person becomes freer, less guarded, less inhibited. Tension drains away.

Lessening of control, stated in positive terms, is the release of tension, and this is the one invariable effect of alcohol that the alcoholic needs and seeks. The alcoholic may, when drunk, erupt into attack or subside into boozy friendliness, but these extremes of reaction issue from the common denominator of the release of tension.

Observation suggests that alcoholics experience more tension, and experience it more acutely, than do the run of people, and they perhaps have fewer alternative means of working it out. Although usually intelligent people, quicker thinking, more alert, cleverer than their peers in comparable walks of life, they are not intellectual. They utilize thought as a practical tool but not as a means of conceptualizing experience. Rather than mulling over events and drawing their sting by speculating about why they happened, what their own contribution to them may have been, how they might have been handled, and how, another time, they might be prevented from happening, alcoholics tend to react immediately and globally—as though the event had no history and no parallels. They are not given to reflection. They do not search to order their experience. They seek relief, a sense of rightness restored, not insight or understanding. They feel themselves a particular, and undeserved, target of events. The intellect which in other people attempts to master experience, and thus delays or varies reactions, in them plays indulgent mother to the spoiled child of the emotions. Theirs is a ready irritability, a constant sensitivity to the injustices meted out to them. Most notably, there is a low or absent tolerance for frustration. Coexisting in the hard-driving, hard-working, overly conscientious, responsible, often accomplished and sometimes gifted alcoholic is a second side that is hypersensitive, rebellious, restless, unreasonable, temperamental, and unreflective.

Are these the reactions commonly and casually subsumed under the category of neurosis, that generally used term applied to feelings distressing to the person who experiences them and to behavior that appears unrewarding and insufficiently motivated by objective events? The one constant in neurosis, no matter the form it takes, is anxiety. It is, by definition, always present. Anxiety is experienced as uncertainty about how to behave, doubt over one's capabilities and the benignity of others' motives, feelings of powerlessness and helplessness. It is made up of worry, fretfulness, insecurity, and threat, a sense of not understanding what one is driven by and of inadequacy to accomplish one's own ends. It is a state of fear, often unconscious fear, of one's own impulses. It is a sense of pushing and pulling at the self to make it acceptable and accepted, while at the same time feeling that the efforts are probably doomed to failure.

The neurotic, in his attempt to relieve his anxiety, directs his efforts at changing himself. To do this, to achieve some greater degree of comfort, he devotes an excessive amount of attention to what he feels and why he feels it. He is too self-concerned, too self-aware, and often too responsive to the possible meaning of nuances in other people's behavior. He explores his own feelings, sometimes to the degree that he is prevented from acting on them constructively. Unlike the alcoholic, he searches for meanings, for cause and effect, and however much he may wish that other people behaved differently toward him, it is himself whom he tries to change in order to persuade them to do so. He tries to make himself more acceptable, more adequate, more lovable.

The alcoholic, in contrast, tries to make the world more acceptable, more adequate to his needs, more lovable. He does this by fogging the world. As an alcoholic once described it, "When I drink, the sharp edges get smoothed out. Everything seems nicer, gentler, less threatening. It all retreats into a pleasant buzz, and nothing is coming at me."

What the neurotic feels is anxiety, and he perceives it as arising within himself. What the alcoholic feels is tension, and he experiences it as caused by factors outside himself. The neurotic looks within to find the answer to his anxiety. The alcoholic looks at the world and tells it to go away and stop bothering him. The neurotic attempts to solve his problems; the alcoholic attempts to dissolve his.

The neurotic who is experiencing anxiety will quite rightly say that he feels tense, and the alcoholic often claims that he drinks because he feels anxious. In such phrases as, "I feel tense and anxious," used by all of us at one time or another, the two words are commonly linked, and properly so because the somatic state of tension is a concomitant of anxiety—the person who is anxious holds himself tensely—and the physical state of tension may cause a feeling of anxiety, for the tense person feels himself ready to explode. But anxiety is an emotional state, and tension is a physical state.

When this distinction is made, it follows that to label the alcoholic neurotic is not necessarily accurate. In alcoholism, as in neurosis, there is maladaptation. And neurotic behavior is, as is alcoholism, an attempted solution to stress. But the source of the stress is not the same, and the coping behavior of the neurotic is not the coping behavior of the alcoholic. Alcoholism is not simply the particular form that neurosis happens to take in some people.

Neurosis may coexist in alcoholism, of course, but the fact that neurosis is not the fundamental diagnostic category can be seen in the observation that recovered alcoholics or active alcoholics in periods of sobriety are not noticeably neurotic people. On the contrary, they often function well and effectively, frequently at a level superior to the average person. Their problems of adjustment are not acute. They are not given to distortion or misinterpretation. They are loving and generous and open, not fearful or withdrawn or ill at ease. They like and go toward other people. They do not chronically dread the hurts that may be inflicted by others. To them, the world may be frustrating but it is not dangerous.

Alcoholics, when not drunk, are charming people. It is this attribute that accounts for the patience other people display toward them, an otherwise almost inexplicable patience in view of the chaos, the frights, the disappointments they cause when drinking. People, as a rule, turn on other people who are demanding and difficult, who are irresponsible, who complain and whine, who distort and blame, who indulge their own pleasure thoughtlessly. There is scarcely a category of disorder which the ordinary person, after greater or lesser efforts to help, does not turn away from. But the ability of alcoholics to elicit repeated forgiveness and second chances is legendary. Wives stay with alcoholic husbands, children are loyal to alcoholic parents, bosses are long-suffering with alcoholic employees, friends stick by alcoholic friends long past the demands of common humanity because the alcoholic is basically a warm, appealing, likable person who moves rather readily, rather easily in the world. This is the positive side of the alcoholic personality, and it wins him a tolerance that it may take him years to exhaust.

A couple befriended an alcoholic, a man in his mid-twenties, fed him, let him sleep on their living room couch, gave him a key to the house, persuaded him to join A.A., and found him a job. When he got drunk and lost the job, they supported him, and when he pawned their television set and cameras, they redeemed them and let him stay on. After some months he hospitalized himself, and they kept his belongings for him and welcomed him when he could be out of the hospital on weekend passes. Seemingly rehabilitated, he returned to live with them, but he soon started drinking again and he was repeatedly hospitalized and released, until, at twenty-eight, he had a series of alcoholic convulsions and was found dead on the street. The point is that this is neither an unusual story nor were the couple unusually gullible people. They were fond of the man, for he was excellent company when sober, sweet and thoughtful and generous. He loved their children and helped to take care of them. He thought nothing of scrubbing the kitchen floor if he saw it needed to be done; he would do the marketing, repair broken chairs, buy small gifts and flowers when he had money. He was entertaining, gregarious, and an interested, sympathetic participant in their lives. He spent their love, but he invested love in them, and they could not bring themselves to believe that this man's alcoholism made him a lost cause.

To acknowledge the winning ways of the alcoholic when sober is not to blink at other traits that are characteristically present. Alcoholics are immature, dependent people who rely heavily on other people to bolster their weak self-esteem, with a consequent vulnerability to fancied slights or seeming undervaluation of their capabilities. They feel themselves able to accomplish much, but, equally, they are prey to fears of inadequacy, and when these fears are seemingly confirmed by some implication of criticism, they are flooded with depression and resentment and they often must drink to reinstate the sense of power and autonomy and accomplishment they hunger for.

It is this overestimation of the self, coexisting with the conviction that the self is little and helpless and at the mercy of other people's acceptance, that gives rise to the chronic discontent of alcoholics. They are dissatisfied with themselves but even more dissatisfied with a world which does not provide enough recognition, enough approval, enough reward, and enough praise. They want rather special treatment: a tender appreciation of their worth and yet not to have too great demands made upon them. They want shelter and direction; they want to lean and be succored, be protected and shielded; and yet they resent authority and are rebellious and stubborn and contentious. Although they seek situations of dependency, attaching themselves to seemingly strong and reserved and competent people, they are provoked into defiance by any attempt to exert control over them.

Holding such contradictory aims—dependent but resentful of authority, undervalued but overestimated—they are tension-ridden, self-pitying and self-indulgent, and always vulnerable to their own sense of inadequacy and to affronts from others. Such conflict makes them restless and irritable, easily enraged, easily hurt, and easily frustrated.

Because the alcoholic is not introspective, he does not attempt to reconcile his inner world with outer reality. He does not ease his conflicts by compromise with the situations in which he finds himself. He does not resign himself to inevitable setbacks. He does not have recourse to humor, wisdom, or a philosophical shrug. Each frustration, however familiar it might seem to another, is greeted by him with fresh rage. Life does not teach him acceptance, and his tolerance for frustration remains always minimal. If he weathers this slight, this jolt, this disappointment, there is another booby trap just around the next corner.

If he is trying not to drink, he may negotiate one booby trap after another, surmounting what seems to him outrageous and undeserved misfortune although it may be no more than the ordinary vicissitudes of life, but the tension in him builds and he has no harmless devices for defusing it, for the alcoholic is usually a person of few interests, few resources, few pleasures, and no passions. That good mind is seldom used in any long-range pursuit. He may read, but not consistently and consumingly in one field. He may listen to music but not be a devoted opera or concert buff. He may enjoy art but take no great pleasure in museum-going. That tenacious stamina is rarely used to garden avidly, to hike, to explore the world of nature. Indeed, the natural world, to which so many of us turn to ease the disappointments of dealing with people, is largely closed to him; he finds it neither healing nor challenging. The world of sports may be somewhat more available to him, but often it is the appeal of the clubhouse after a round of golf or tennis that draws him on. I have never known an alcoholic with a hobby that intensely interested him. I have never known one with a passion for collecting or painting or do-it-yourself projects. And thus I have never known one who could dissipate his tension in constructive and satisfying activities. The boredom, the emptiness, the restlessness find no outlet, and so tension builds, and sooner or later one of the booby traps detonates and alcohol is the only restitutive agent.

Since compromise and substitute satisfactions and a degree of acceptance of the world as it is and the self as it is are hallmarks of the mature personality, there is justification for characterizing the alcoholic as immature. In truth, the alcoholic seems most analogous—in his charm, his mixture of dependence-independence, his impulsiveness, his desire for immediate gratifications, his restiveness under authority, his outgoingness, his appealing combination of strength and weakness, his stubbornness, his heart-tugging efforts to be ingratiating and helpful—to a small child, perhaps to a sturdy boy of three. It is an age at which children are at their delightful best, for they need you and yet need to be independent, they are easy and free at expressing their love and yet they attach themselves to new people with frankness and warmth, they are stubborn and yet tractable and agreeable, they are open and trusting and yet easily hurt and quick to cry, they are responsive and yet self-absorbed.

All of these things I have seen in alcoholics without ever quite identifying them as belonging to what I have come to think of as the small-child syndrome until one night I stood by while an alcoholic went from hurt and resentment to impotent rage to explosive tantrum to the taking of the first drink he had had in two months. That first drink was a water glass of vodka, and with it came relief, warmth, relaxation. He was still angry but he no longer felt helpless; he spoke grandly, and with large gestures, of where the world could go, along with all the people in it. By the end of the third glass, he was sprawled on the couch, restlessly moving his head from side to side, speaking to the ceiling in unfinished sentences that started with great energy but then trailed off into incoherence. After the fourth, he pulled himself to his feet, clinging to the couch to get his balance, took a few rubbery steps, and sat down on the floor. Striking away an offer of help, he lurched over on his hands and knees, concentrated, got to his feet, stood swaying, and collapsed again. "He looks," I thought, "like a small child just learning to walk," and suddenly I realized that what to me would have been an insupportably humiliating reversion to infancy was to him, if unknowingly, a large part of the lure of drinking.

Release from the requirements of being grown, even the physical requirement of holding oneself steady and upright, release from the requirements of rationality and reasonableness, release from discriminating and appropriate response—these things are desired by the alcoholic. He can behave as the small child behaves, be whining and winning in turn; he can be helpless and yet push away help, be obstinate and be forgiven, be protected from hurting himself and hurt others with impunity, all of this because he is drunk and people who are drunk are not responsible for their behavior. He can even avoid feeling guilty about it afterward by not remembering what he did or said. "Boy, I really tied one on," he can say the next day, and that is all the excuse or explanation he need give. He has escaped back into childhood, with all the relief from restraints this implies and with no more penalty than befalls a child who behaves childishly.

To describe the small-child syndrome is not to dismiss the alcoholic as nothing but a small child. But one of the great problems the co-alcoholic faces is dealing with the inconsistencies that the alcoholic presents. If, on the one hand, the alcoholic is a person of above-average physical and intellectual endowment, a person no more neurotic than the run of people and probably less so than most, a rather uncomplicated person who ordinarily functions at quite an effective level, how, on the other hand, are his vulnerability, his hypersensitivity, and his instability to be explained? The co-alcoholic must find a way of reconciling these contradictions lest she swing from one view to another, from indulgence to condemnation, from too few to too many demands. Temporarily withdrawing her own emotional investment from the relationship, setting aside love and hate and anger and pity, she needs to step back and gain a perspective which will allow her to hold in mind all the contradictions that the alcoholic embodies. It may be that the small-child syndrome is at least a place to begin to identify a pattern which will provide her with a consistent view of the alcoholic's inconsistencies.

2

The Genesis of Alcoholism

Not to coin a phrase but to borrow it, we are all Freudians whether we know it or not, which is to say that any number of people who mistrust psychoanalytic theory nevertheless have integrated into their view of other individuals the knowledge that the events of infancy and childhood are remarkably, pervasively, inescapably influential in determining the shape of the adult. This belief so furnishes out the consciousness of the times that it is not disputed even by those hearty people fond of recommending to a troubled person that he does not need a psychiatrist, he needs only to get busy and pull up his own socks.

Those of us who more frankly subscribe to Freudian theory (using the term generically to refer to a broad body of knowledge about human psychological development which has undergone some modification and much elucidation since Freud) are convinced, not only of the importance of childhood in determining the psychic structure, but of the major role played by early unsatisfactory relationships and traumatic events in giving rise to later maladjustment. In trying to unravel the possible causes of alcoholism, then, it would seem axiomatic to assume that alcoholics have had particularly stressful childhoods. What else but severe and frequent mishaps in infancy could account for the catastrophe of alcoholism? What else but a psychic wound so profound as to require the repeated anesthetic of alcohol could account for the self-destructive behavior? What else but damage to the personality so deep that persistent excursions into oblivion must be sought to assuage the pain could account for the courting of mindlessness?

And who else but the mother of the alcoholic could have inflicted such damage, for it is the mother who is all-important to the child. She is his world. If she does nothing to harm him, no one else truly and irremediably can. The only trouble with this assumption is that every alcoholic I know has only kind words for his mother and happy childhood memories of her. Of fathers, there are conflicting descriptions. He is remembered as weak and ineffectual and largely absent, whether actually, in that he left the family, or psychologically, in that he counted for little in it and had no great influence for good or ill on its emotional climate. Or he is remembered as strict and harsh and punitive and inconsistent in his praise and blame. But mothers are characteristically looked back to as having been unswervingly loving and kind and protective.

This view of mothers is rare, our national myths about motherhood notwithstanding. It is much more common for individuals to feel ambivalence—and to feel guilty about that ambivalence. Love mixed with dislike, demands for their interest and yet rejection of that interest as incursions upon rightful independence, longings for their approval and floutings of their wishes, intense desire that they care more and an equally intense desire that they leave one in peace—this is the more usual view of mothers. In one's own feelings, in the reminiscences of others, one senses again and again the conflictual nature of the complicated relationship between mother and child.

But not in alcoholics. The one happiness in the life of the alcoholic ex-husband of the friend I referred to earlier was his relationship to his mother. As destructive as this man could become, he never did anything to hurt her. Even when chronically drunk, he would sober up enough to visit her. He never forgot her birthday or other occasions of importance to her, and he spoke of her with unfailing tenderness. She was the one person he never blamed for his failures, the one person who retained his generous love.

So inclined is the mind to go on believing what one already believes that I dismissed this man's devotion to his mother as one more aberration in an aberrant personality, and I presumptuously took it for granted that other alcoholics were misremembering their pasts when they spoke of the goodness of their mothers. I assumed that they did not have the fortitude to admit to disappointment in their mothers, the disappointment most people feel in greater or lesser measure for not having been loved enough, for not having been given to enough. I assumed that alcoholics repressed the commonly coexisting image of the evil, ungiving, unloving mother with such force that no small representation of it could gain admission to conscious awareness. I assumed that they conveniently ignored the traumatic side of the relationship.

My obtuseness survived my having known my own mother's mother and remembering her as a sweet, gentle woman who had loved her youngest child, my mother, the best of her children. My mother's stories of her childhood often centered on willful escapades that had happy endings despite the ambiance of a strict household because her mother was too mellow at forty-odd when her last child was born to be demanding of her, too fond of the pretty thing to deny her pleasures that the older children had been forbidden, too delighted by her spiritedness to scold. Father was the ogre in the stories, but always the picture of the mother was of a loving, warm, indulgent woman, and nothing I recollected of my grandmother before she died contradicted this picture.

I was often reminded of her through the years when an alcoholic friend spoke of her own mother, a woman who, like my grandmother, had had her last child when well into middle-age. Anne, my friend, although frequently desperate about making ends meet because her drinking made it difficult for her to hold a job, always managed to send money to her mother, and she did it voluntarily and cheerfully. Whenever she got together sufficient funds, she took a thousand-mile bus journey to visit her, and she would return content, happy in the time they had spent together. She never had a criticism of the past, never harked back to a time when her mother had failed her, never expressed disappointment or a wish for something her mother had not been able to give her. Her mother was 86 when she died, an age at which a life is so indisputably at an end that it would seem difficult to mourn the death, but Anne grieved for months over her loss and the genuineness of her sorrow was not to be doubted.

Anne, who had had years of psychoanalytic treatment, and another friend whom I knew too well to question the accuracy of memories which reflected the loving warmth of his mother in contrast to the selfish cruelty of his father, finally forced me to examine the basic assumption that alcoholism must have its roots in a disturbed mother-child relationship. I continued to be convinced that the mother-child relationship must play a pivotal role because the history of each of us is that of being born into a world of which we know nothing and of having to piece together a view of that world from the experiences we undergo. In those experiences it is the mother who plays the major role, indeed almost the only role, for the infant initially apprehends nothing of the world except the being who ministers to him. Having so recently lain under the beating heart and been at one with the being who surrounds and supplies all sustenance, to be born and lie against the beating heart of the being who still is the source of all sustenance is an interruption in continuity but not, for the unknowing infant, an entirely different state. His mother remains the limits of the infant's existence. She is the world, for she is all he experiences of the world, and what he comes to know about her is what he will later believe about the world.

Perhaps this can be appreciated, as an adult, by visualizing the experience of having been severely injured in an accident. As you emerge from the deepest states of unconsciousness, you become aware only of pain, and moan and move restlessly about trying to escape it. If a nurse comes and relieves the pain, you are not aware of the injection but only, now more comfortable, slip back into unconsciousness. This climbing up from unconsciousness forced by physical discomfort and then subsidence back into unconsciousness when released from it may recur repeatedly before you gain enough strength to become vaguely aware that it is someone who comes and that it is something she does that eases the unpleasantness. With longer periods of consciousness, you realize that the nurse is a person and begin to form an impression of her by noting how consistently or inconsistently she is there when needed, how deftly she anticipates needs, how gently or roughly she goes about the actions that return you to a state of peace. And if the nurse is the only person who looks after you, it is from what you sense her to be like that you begin to imagine what the hospital as a whole is like, whether it is a place that provides excellent or grudging care, whether the other personnel are likely to be encouraging and helpful or indifferent and thoughtless, whether you will feel at home and nurtured in a protective atmosphere or be made to feel a nuisance and undeserving of more than careless and perfunctory attention. Even an adult must extrapolate from the known to form a picture of the unknown.

So, also, must the infant. His task is to form a hypothesis about what this world he has entered is like. His information is the care he receives from his mother.

Since the one instinct the infant is born with is to suck and since his primary drive is to obtain food, his earliest experiences center on the tension of hunger and the relief of being fed. Hunger causes a physical state of tension, as can be seen by the infant's being roused from sleep by it and beginning to fret and then cry. Feeding brings relief of tension, as can be seen by the relaxation that creeps over him as, his hunger satisfied, he slips back into sleep. It is likely that the infant first registers his internal tension and its relief, only later the breast or bottle that provides the tension-relieving food, and only still later the mother who supplies the breast. Although the mother soon becomes a metaphor for the world, initially the breast or bottle is a metaphor for the mother.

Roused from sleep by the discomfort of hunger, the infant kicks and cries. If the breast or bottle arrives quickly, his tension is quickly relieved. He is returned to a state of well-being before he has suffered much distress. If this is his characteristic experience, his earliest view of the world will be positive: it is a place in which he will be well cared for, nurtured, loved, made to feel comfortable, not required to wait for relief. If food sometimes arrives promptly and sometimes only after a delay, the infant's optimism will be tempered by some pessimism. He will perceive the world as usually satisfying but sometimes frustrating. If food is immediately available at some times and its arrival long delayed at others, his learning will be confused, his ultimate perception of the world contradictory. If food never arrives until his state of tension has been protracted, he will become pessimistic, perhaps lastingly discouraged about the world and the treatment he can expect at its hands.

In essence, the infant, in forming a rudimentary hypothesis about what this world he finds himself in is like, is asking a basic question: can the world be trusted? Can it be trusted to meet his needs promptly and completely, always, usually, occasionally, or not at all? Every infant answers this question for himself, and his answer is based first on the availability of the breast.

The infant does not at first distinguish that the tension he experiences from hunger is within himself and the breast that satisfies his need is outside himself. Awareness that he is a creature separate from the source of sustenance comes slowly, dimly, dimly taking shape in the fog of consciousness as he recognizes a time lag between his feeling of hunger and the arrival of food. Since his hunger is not satisfied automatically as soon as it arises, he realizes eventually that the source of satisfaction cannot be within him; it must lie outside himself. There must be two beings in the world, himself and someone who is not himself. Thus, gradually, does the breast as world expand to become the mother as world.

The infant does not, of course, understand his mother to be a person with needs and wishes of her own and with other demands upon her time and attention. He is totally self-centered, totally demanding. He does not delay expression of his needs, and he does not appreciate that their immediate gratification is not always possible. He registers only the time lag between his feeling of tension and its relief; and from whether the time lag is almost imperceptible or short, medium but bearable, or prolonged and distressing, he begins to learn whether the world is to be trusted wholly, partially, inconsistently, or not at all to meet his needs.

This early learning is indelible learning because, like a ball of soft wax, the infant's brain retains the shape of first impressions. Later experience can modify but never totally alter the basic set of the personality, partly because it builds on directions already laid out and partly because the first impressions were formed prior to conscious, evaluative awareness and thus cannot be remembered and revised in the light of further experience. Just as a house can be added on to, remodeled, refurbished, and changed almost beyond recognition, so can the personality—but the house will still have its original foundations and so will the personality. What the infant apprehends of his mother is the substructure on which his view of the world will be built.

The infant who signals his state of tension and has help arrive promptly, cheerfully, and unstintingly learns a basic trust of the world. He experiences it as a satisfying place that can be relied on to keep him contented. He can express his wants and be certain that they will be met, and he gains a positive, optimistic view of the world that, barring a disaster such as losing his mother, will be the foundation he builds on. At the other extreme is the infant who is not responded to, who cries himself into exhaustion, whose states of tension are so prolonged that he may sink into apathy. He does not learn to trust. He experiences the world as frustrating, indifferent, as a place that cannot or will not supply his needs, that will cause him pain, leave him alone and impress upon him his own helplessness. He will acquire a basic, profound discouragement about his own worth and the trustworthiness of others.

Between these extremes is a large middleground in which the experience of the average infant falls. His states of tension are relieved, not usually immediately but within a more or less reasonable length of time. From this, he learns that the world is sometimes satisfying, sometimes not. He becomes aware of his own helplessness, but not overwhelmingly so. He knows that he can make efforts to obtain what he needs and that sometimes his efforts will be successful. His answer to whether or not the world is to be trusted will be "maybe." Is it safe? Is it satisfying? Are people to be counted on? Maybe. Sometimes. Yes and no.

And this is how most of us see the world, as a rewarding and frustrating place, as a place of some successes and some failures, as sometimes providing reassurance and sometimes causing disquiet. We have more or less trust in the beneficence of other people, more or less faith in our own worth and de-servingness, more or less optimism or pessimism about the nature of the world.

What of the extremes? What issue will they have? If the infant loses hope in basic ways because his needs are met with indifference or coldness or neglect, he may, on meeting the stresses of later life, retreat from meaningful contact. With little or no faith in the helpfulness of other people and a profound mistrust of the world as a satisfying or nurturing place, he may distort or lose touch with a reality that causes him nothing but pain.

And the other extreme? What of the adult who, as an infant, learned trust because his mother provided immediate, devoted care? His expectations are, in effect, too optimistic. Having learned that he would not be required to suffer, that relief of tension was his due, that his needs would be met with little or no effort on his own part, he assumes that he can trust the world to see to his comfort. He did not learn to wait. He did not learn to accept episodes of tension and stress as part of life. He did not learn to adapt, to adjust, to compromise, to ride out adversity. He learned that a liquid in his mouth would end his tension and that it would be his on demand.

Assuming the testimony of alcoholics to be correct that their mothers were more than ordinarily loving and attentive, perhaps herein lies the genesis of alcoholism. Alcoholics expect easy and automatic gratification. They expect people to be patient and indulgent and benevolent, the world to be generous in satisfying their demands. They expect exaggerated care and tolerance. They do not have too little trust but too much. They are not too pessimistic but too optimistic. They are not too fearful but too complacent.

A man, now an alcoholic, was born in a foreign country where his father was working as an anthropologist. Their home was in a primitive village, and his mother was without real companionship, without anyone to talk to except the native servants and without diversions except reading and listening to phonograph records. When Peter was born, she felt, she said, as though she had acquired a marvelous toy. Not only did she lavish attention on him, caring for his every need almost as soon, or sooner, than he experienced it, but the servants, intrigued by their first experience of a white child and sensing how precious he was to their mistress, hovered over him, picking him up and taking him to his mother to be nursed the moment he woke.

Peter had no way of knowing that he was born into unique circumstances and that his mother was unusually devoted to him because of the special conditions of their life. The infant cannot discriminate. He does not say that this is my mother and this is simply the way she as a single and singular individual behaves. He experiences her as the world, and when he is older and gains the brain capacity to discriminate, it is too late. It is embedded in his mind that the way she is is the way the world is. Peter made his basic assumptions about life from the way his mother was, and although much in his later life has failed to substantiate them, nothing in his later life has altered them, and for most of his adult life, he has been a severe alcoholic.

Gregory Rochlin, in a book called *Griefs and Discontents,* comments that ". . . reality regularly forces us to defer a possible immediate pleasure or a respite from our discomfort for later relief that is more certain. This is the replacement of what Freud called the pleasure principle by the reality principle. It represents a profound change in the thought processes from the infantile mere wishing for pleasure to the more mature striving for satisfaction." If the infant's mother does not so behave that his trust of the world becomes salted with a degree of mistrust, this profound change does not take place, and the infant, and later the adult, orders his life on the pleasure principle rather than on the reality that respite from discomfort must often be deferred. The alcoholic continues to wish for pleasure rather than strive for satisfaction.

Reality first enters the infant's life when his awareness of the breast as an object outside himself enlarges to include awareness of the whole of his mother as a being apart from himself. He comes to understand his own crying as a signal which summons her, but his signal is not always answered promptly, and, therefore, the being who can come is also a being who can not come. Before he recognizes this, his crying is an expression of rage in response to the state of tension produced by unappeased hunger. After he recognizes this, rage over not receiving what he needs promptly may be supplanted by fear that he will not receive it at all. And this is the foundation for the anxiety that later takes many more complex forms. In what has been called the "decentering process" of the first eighteen months of life, the baby shrinks from being the all and center of the universe to being one of two, and as consciousness ripens, he grows aware that the second person possesses individual volition; he cannot summon her at will. The time lag between his summons and her arrival contains the first intimations of anxiety. He is forced to become aware of reality, to learn delay, postponement of gratification, and the bearing of anxiety until it can be relieved.

If, on the other hand, his mother is consistently there, consistently loving and responsive, the infant is not required to postpone gratification of his needs. There is no reason for him to grow anxious about her possible disappearance, her possible withholding of needed supplies. Reality is not brought home to him. The primitive feelings of tension and rage serve him well, and he is not driven, via the learning process of anxiety, to more complex and differentiated reactions. He remains impulse-ridden and tantrum-ridden, quick to appreciate any distress in himself, quick to demand relief of it, and quick to grow angry if it is not forthcoming. Tension followed by rage, the most elementary of emotions, persists as the characteristic response to stress.

Tension followed by rage is the characteristic response to stress of the alcoholic. He does not fundamentally experience anxiety but tension, and his reaction is not to adjust to reality but to seek relief. The more complex ways of achieving desired ends—waiting, increased reliance on the self, compromise, substitution of the possible for the desired—are not available to him, for reality entered his life too late. The infant who learns that the world is a good and satisfying place in which he holds a cherished central position knows as an adult, in the very fiber of his being, that it was never intended that he should suffer. The infant who knows that his distress can be and will be promptly relieved is not an adult who delays relief of his tensions or attempts to find discharge for them in circuitous ways. The infant whose rage brought response before it was transmitted into fear that the response might never come is not an adult whose anger at frustration and disappointment is soon replaced by anxiety and self-blame and self-examination. He is an adult who can find in alcohol what his relationship to his mother taught him that he is entitled to—immediate relief.

When the decentering process is not a gradual occurrence spread over the first eighteen months of life, the inevitable encounter with reality may be abrupt and shocking to the child. It will come in the second or third year of life when the child, now physically mature enough to be capable of some independent movement, ventures out from the protective intimacy with his mother and, although behaving no differently from the way he has always behaved—behaving, indeed, in the only way he knows how to behave—encounters, not gratification, but frustration from people with wills of their own and desires of their own. He comes up against "the first stranger," his father, and, as well, other children who balk his pleasure and other adults who do not consider it their mission in life to keep him happy. If his father is weak and shadowy, the child will have further psychological evidence that the world is a pushover and he himself is powerful; this coupled with the unavoidable physical evidence that he is actually small and vulnerable will provide him with his lifelong split view of himself as both mighty and helpless. If, on the other hand, his father is strict and demanding, particularly if the father decides that the child is in danger of becoming spoiled and that it is time he learned he cannot always have his own way, the child will too abruptly learn that he is not all-powerful. Because his father is physically much stronger, psychologically can deny him approval, and intellectually can cut him down to size, his inferiority and vulnerability will be borne in on him suddenly rather than gradually and his self-esteem will be ferociously assaulted. He cannot give up the grandiose appraisal of his place in the world his mother has endowed him with because it is too deeply engraved, but neither can he reconcile it with the message he receives from his father. Thus, again, he will possess two contradictory pictures of himself: he is a person of infinite worth; he is a person of no worth; he is all-powerful; he is helpless. And this dichotomous view of himself will persist throughout his life. He will feel himself capable of everything and nothing; he will be strong and weak; nothing can touch him and anything can destroy him. From this will stem his great but extremely fragile self-esteem, a self-esteem that drives him to accomplishment but that shatters at the slightest blow, and also from this will come his difficulties with anyone in authority over him.

Rather than having an integrated and cohesive picture of the world, he will have a dual, shifting, and contradictory picture. Instead of appreciating it as rewarding *and* unrewarding, satisfying *and* frustrating, he will experience it as rewarding *or* unrewarding, satisfying *or* frustrating, swinging between these views almost as chance or luck would have it since events will seem capricious rather than consequent upon his own actions. When the world frustrates him or disappoints him or refuses to accord him special treatment, it will not cause him anxiety but tension, a physical feeling of being tied in knots, and he will be angered by the malevolence of fate.

These, then, are the alcoholic's basic assumptions about life, assumptions made on the evidence provided by his infancy and early childhood: That the world is a good and satisfying and nurturing environment. That he cannot be expected to suffer. That he is entitled to instant relief of uncomfortable states of tension. That the vehicle of relief will be intake of a substance which provides warm relaxation and a reinstituted sense of well-being. That he is the center of the world and that his comfort is all-important. That he is simultaneously powerful and weak, a being of whom much can be expected but nothing asked. What he has not learned from his childhood is a steady sense of his worth, a self-esteem of realistic proportions. He has not learned to postpone gratification, to substitute attainable goals for wish-fulfillment. He has not acquired the means of handling stress or frustration. Not having had to learn to support anxiety, he is a person in whom the less differentiated states of tension and rage remain strongly operative.

He is, in sum, a person whose positive view of the world is often dismayingly and incomprehensively contradicted by his treatment at its hands, which invariably surprises and angers the alcoholic and prompts him to turn to the one sure solace he knows.

3

The Life Style
of the Alcoholic

Since infancy provides the ground against which the later figures in our lives move, we are all products of our infancy and alcoholism is an outcome like any other outcome. The alcoholic with his belief that the world is bountiful and indulgent misconstrues the world to no greater extent than, for example, the man whose infancy implanted in him the view that other people cannot be relied on to do tasks for him with the celerity and attention to detail he thinks proper and who accordingly has become an expert do-it-yourself-er. His archaic view of the world is, to him, a self-evident truth, and he acts upon it unquestioningly, turning himself into an industrious, self-reliant, accomplished person. This redounds to his credit, but perhaps he is not justified in accepting credit, for his determined independence is an outcome, just as the alcoholic's drinking is an outcome. Is the alcoholic, by the same token, equally justified in not accepting blame? In this context, yes, but it is obvious that some outcomes are more personally rewarding and socially constructive than others. Since each of us is responsible for his behavior as an adult, if that behavior is deviant in personally damaging and socially destructive ways, the individual has little choice but to search for sufficient understanding of its sources to release himself from automatic bondage to them. The alcoholic had a fortunate infancy, but its unfortunate outcome makes it necessary that that infancy be reconstructed and examined for its ramifications in the present, in the same way that the neurotic, if he is not forever to be the prisoner of his misconceptions, must exhume his formative experience and learn from it what it is that he believes he "knows."

While the munificent infancy of the alcoholic has led to the disaster of alcoholism, it has had positive outcomes as well. Having learned that the world is a good place and that the people in it are generous, supportive, and available, the alcoholic is trusting in his relationships and hopeful about his prospects. Presuming other people to be as giving as his mother was, he is gregarious, outgoing, and appealing. He attaches himself easily to other people and looks to them for supplies of affection. More attracted to people than objects, he is friendly and warm and interested. He is, in short, a very likable person.

But, since the world is not an effortlessly supplying and protective environment and people are not always kind and supportive, a person with these expectations is constantly open to disappointment. Thus the alcoholic lives in an almost perpetual state of discontent and frustration. Restless and irritable, he is harried by poorly controlled rage, ridden by tension, preyed on by frustrations he feels fall to his lot unaccountably, and bedeviled by a sense that he is being cheated of the recognition and reward that should rightfully be his. This is not the neurotic living in a state of anxiety that he will be found wanting; this is the alcoholic living in a state of irritability over finding the world wanting.

The basically positive attitude toward life that makes the alcoholic such a nice person, not small and mean and withholding but expansive and responsive and energetic, gives him unrealistic expectations which are again and again thwarted. Other people have known from their earliest days that life is full of disappointments, but to the alcoholic each setback is an unexpected personal affront, calling into question his entire worth as a human being, making him doubt his value and making him quite certain that he is the particular target of fate, that malign forces are at work expressly to disappoint him. My mother's favorite and reiterated phrase was, "Everything happens to me," although, in actuality, nothing happened to her that would occasion surprise to another person. To objective eyes, it would seem that she had a rather easy and in some ways desirable life. But the slightest swell in the sea was a storm; anything but fair weather was a cruel affliction specifically manufactured to try her soul; the most trifling of mishaps was a catastrophic misfortune from which it was doubtful that she could recover. An unpaid bill was bankruptcy. An ache was cancer. A failure to meet her wishes was the death of love.

In the customary way of alcoholics, she felt life's blows to be undeserved, and thus she could not be expected, she could not expect herself, to keep from seeking immediate balm. "I deserve a drink," she would tell herself. And why not? Nothing in her infancy had taught her to postpone relief of unpleasant feelings. Nothing had taught her the patience to wait for better times. Nothing had taught her to contain anger at a world that treated her unfairly. Nothing had instilled in her anxiety over the possible consequences of her own actions. She knew only irritable and retaliatory defiance, and defiantly she would take a drink. She had infinite pride, but no self-pride; infinite self-will, but no will; infinite strength, but no self-control. When the world failed to supply her with mothering, she supplied herself, on demand, with the bottle that relieved her distress.

After a drink or two, she grew expansive, whole again, and queenly forgiving. A certain largeness entered her gestures, and she was prepared to be tolerant of other people's failure to appreciate her enough. She felt herself impervious, out of the reach of attack. The world that had brought her low could now nip at her heels, and she grandly ignored such a minor matter. From being a small, helpless, skinned victim, she puffed to lofty size and calmly held the world at arm's length. Her equilibrium was restored.

But it was the equilibrium of the infant who has been returned to a state of well-being because his tension has been relieved, not the equilibrium of the adult who has won through to confidence in his own ability to handle his life and its problems. It was the omnipotence of the infant who has raised his voice and had his needs served and so can dismiss the world as no longer needed, not the realistic appraisal of the adult who is prepared to renounce needs that cannot be fulfilled, who is able to say, if not now, later; if not today, tomorrow; if not tomorrow, then it is not to be. The adult, by his own effort, achieves well-being. The alcoholic, by means of the bottle, returns to it.

All of us have a tendency, when under stress, to revert to an earlier level of development, to become dependent and seek care and protection. A small incident is illustrative of this. A house guest (not an alcoholic), feeling ill, excused herself after dinner and went upstairs to bed. Half an hour later she called to her husband to come and take her to the bathroom because, being extremely near-sighted, she could not find the way without her glasses. He went to her and she put her hand in his, docilely, trustingly, as though she were a small child, and he led her along the hallway. Had she not been ill, she would have done the obvious thing, that is, reached for her glasses on the night table beside her, put them on, and found her own way, but with the stress of feeling sick, she regressed to the status of helpless child who is entitled to ask for solicitous care.

For this woman it took only transient illness to cause regression from mature modes of behavior, while in another person stress would have to be much more severe and prolonged before there was a retreat from independence and a falling back on childhood patterns of behavior. An elderly man of my acquaintance, the most mature man I have ever known, was critically ill for four months, but not until two days before he died did he cling to his wife and blindly plead, "Help me. Please help me." This is not to say that it is immature to ask for help— to be adult is to be able to rely on others when it is appropriate as well as to draw on one's own strength while reserves of strength still exist—but to indicate that each of us has a point at which we are overwhelmed by stress and that this point varies from person to person.

For the alcoholic, more of life is stressful and the point of intolerable stress is more rapidly reached than for the nonalcoholic. Not having been subjected to stress in infancy, when for

others it occurred in small, manageable, indoctrinating incre-
ments, the alcoholic acquired no immunity to it. He is as vulnerable to stress as a child raised in a sterile environment is
vulnerable to contagious disease when he ventures forth into the
wider world. Unvaccinated by exposure, the alcoholic has few or
no defenses. He cannot shake off episodes and events that to
others would be nonpathogenic. He finds life difficult and demanding and frustrating to a degree that others of us, toughened
and tempered by the mishaps of infancy, do not.

With his excessive need for approval and support, for affection and protection, the alcoholic encounters stress at every turn,
and it quickly escalates to unbearable proportions, filling him
with the tension and rage from which he must get relief. The
regressive tug, back to the undemanding satisfactions of infancy,
becomes irresistible. He knew a happier time, a time when tension
did not have to be borne, when his needs were effortlessly supplied, when peace and contentment were his for the asking, and
he has discovered the means of returning to it. Complexity of
thought, differentiated appraisal of alternatives, adaptation, compromise, modification of drives, judgment, logic—all the functions of the mediating intelligence that ordinarily governs behavior—are swept away in the undertow of regression, and the
pleasure principle becomes overriding.

Although an intense desire for relief of discomfort is characteristic of alcoholics, it is by no means unique to them.
Avoidance of pain and achievement of a pleasurable state of
well-being are unexceptionable goals commonly pursued. No one
willingly supports insecurity, dread, loneliness, fears of abandonment, and a cracking sense of self. We all long for relaxed
comfort, ease, safety, stability, esteem and belongingness, and
therefore we are all subject to the pull of regressive forces. We
have all experienced a time of oneness with another, a time of
simple comfort and safety, and it remains a magnet in the unconscious, drawing us back when stress grows too great.

Regression, however, does not have as strong an allure for
the nonalcoholic as the alcoholic, for most infancies were not a
period of unmixed bliss. There were the uncomfortable waits
before relief came; there was the dawning awareness of de-

pendency on the whims of others; there was the birth of anxiety; there were defenselessness and constriction. Thus, it was not entirely unwelcome later in childhood to begin to learn a degree of mastery over the self, to learn that the self could be trusted and that independence from not always reliable others could be achieved. It did not replace the security of oneness, since apartness, too, has its terrors, but it set an opposing drive to be separate against the need to merge, setting the stage for an ambivalence that is seldom entirely resolved in a lifetime.

Andras Angyal, the author of *Neurosis and Treatment,* has described this ambivalence as the dual, coexisting drives toward homonomy and autonomy, homonomy being the wish for closeness and dependence, autonomy the need for distance and independence. These two opposing drives are reflected in most of one's relationships in life. One searches for persons to be unquestioningly accepted by, to be cherished and sheltered, loved and protected, understood and guided by. But no sooner does a dependent situation present itself as attainable than one begins to assert one's independence, establish one's right to act in individual ways, to think unpredictably, to make decisions without interference. In friendship and love, one searches to become part of another, but because this presages a loss of the self, one equally pulls back and insists on the prerogatives of individuality. Dependence carries the threat of domination, of the swallowing up of one life by another; independence carries the threat of isolation, of loneliness; and so one maneuvers between these two poles, seeking to bring people close, but not too close, seeking to hold people at a distance, but not too distant.

When life is going well, feelings of autonomy are in the ascendance; the self is appreciated as strong, in charge, able to meet challenges; there is a confident joy in one's own powers. When setbacks are encountered, on the other hand, one seeks borrowed strength; having stumbled, one longs to be caught and sheltered in the arms of another. Usually, however, one continues to steer a course between the two poles even while veering closer to one or the other, for both are appreciated as containing some dangers. Homonomy means loss of self, autonomy loss of others, and neither extreme is acceptable.

The dual goals broadly apparent in all lives, the search for merger and the insistence on separateness, are particularly evident in the life of the alcoholic, and he, almost more than anyone else, comes closest to touching the extremes in his swings between them. When things are going well, he is touchy about accepting advice, direction, or help; he is stubborn, independent, and jealous of his autonomy. Let him encounter a rebuff, however, a blow to his hopes or to his self-esteem, and he is doubly subject to regressive forces: stress is more intolerable to him than to others, and homonomy is more enticing. Two people were so pleasurably one in his infancy that regression is not the tender trap which frightens as much as it beguiles the rest of us. For him, it fulfills a deep longing rather than activates a deep fear. If others of us welcome a brief respite from too sharp awareness of the demands and difficulties of life, we nevertheless pull back from letting ourselves go entirely because, as much as we long to be enveloped in a warm cocoon of protection, equally strongly do we push toward freedom and self-determination. We have struggled to achieve control of our destinies, and an undermining of that control can make us profoundly anxious.

This is not true of the alcoholic. Loss of control, threatening to the average person, is desirable to the alcoholic. He is not drinking for the reasons other people drink: to feel relaxed, to have a good time, to release inhibitions, to court intimacy. He is drinking to achieve regression to the earliest state of being. He drinks, as the infant sucks, to induce the peace of satiety. And thus he drinks to the point of "passing out," to the state of unconsciousness. He cannot stop at a sensible amount, as other people can, because his need, unlike theirs, is for insensibility.

In drinking, the alcoholic runs the reel of his life backward, becoming first as gay and expansive as a child of eleven or twelve before the complexities of puberty set in. A preteenager is usually alert, outgoing, interested, and responsive. He likes people and makes friends with them readily, but he is quick to be offended and quick to become petulant and truculent when crossed. Compare this to the behavior of an alcoholic at a party or in a bar. Although he may have been on the edge of panic when he entered, nerves strung tight and single-mindedly concentrated on getting a drink, after the drink is down, he relaxes, looks around, and begins to relate affably to whoever is near. As his drinking progresses, he becomes more willful, self-centered, more responsive to his own promptings and less differentiated in his response to others. Now, like a child of three, he is little aware of other people as individuals playing starring roles in their own life stories but appreciates them only as supporting cast on his stage. He desires attention and applause, and he is displeased if restraints are placed on him, becoming stubborn and argumentative if balked. He cannot pursue a line of thought very far, but he holds on to it perseveratingly, boring and exhausting his companions. When he walks, his balance will be no steadier than that of a toddler, but he will be just as adamant as a child in insisting on his prerogative to negotiate on his own two feet. With still more alcohol in him, he loses comprehension, except fitfully, of the world around him, and his talk is words on the air, like the very young child talking aloud to himself or to imaginary companions. The boundaries of his perception contract to the circle of himself, and he mumbles and mutters in the solipsistic fashion of the one-year-old babbling in his playpen. To reach for his glass takes the same concentration the baby exerts in picking up a toy and bringing it to his mouth, and his locomotion, if he attempts to move, is just as slow and unsteady and subject to sudden collapse as is the baby's. The entrance of someone else into his ken is greeted with emphatic but short-lived reaction, loud affection if the entrant is smiling and playful, howls of rage and impotent blows if the person is there to put an end to pleasure. And with the final drinks, the alcoholic's head goes down on his arms, consciousness seeps away, and he is as an infant again, asleep, unaware of the world, lost to it. Regression is complete.

It is this state that the confirmed alcoholic drinks to achieve, which means that there is not simply a quantitative difference in the alcoholic's drinking but a qualitative one. He receives the same rewards along the way back that the medium or heavy drinker does: increased social effectiveness, tranquillization, relaxing of inhibitions, release of aggression and hostility, and a congenial lessening of the distance between himself and others, but these are only way-stations on the road and he cannot stop, as other people do, because his destination, unlike theirs, is oblivion. Once started on drinking, he must retrace the whole route. Hence, the compulsiveness of his drinking, the repeated drinking to unconsciousness that can be so mystifying to the co-alcoholic.

The co-alcoholic is often not unsympathetic to the alcoholic's obvious need for a drink. She recognizes his tension, and she knows the relief that drinking grants. What baffles her is that, having gotten relief with two or three drinks, he does not stop. She would have no objection to the two or three drinks, any more than she would deny a hungry person the right to eat, but just as she would think it stupid and wrong for a person to stuff himself to the point of stupor and illness, so does she lose patience with the alcoholic who does not stop at satisfaction but goes on to satiety. She makes the assumption, understandably, that relief is the alcoholic's goal, but it is a deeper, hidden, irresistible goal that compels him, and once he sets foot on the road back, nothing less than traveling to the beginning is the answer to his need.

The alcoholic himself cannot explain this to her, for it is no more known to him than to the outsider. It is his firm intention to drink sensibly. The most familiar refrain he hears from himself is that he will have only a couple of drinks, just to get over this hump, just to relax from this strain, just to pick himself up at this trying moment. He genuinely plans to take no more, and he is startled and discomfited to find that his resolution has been subverted, his will has been washed away, and he searches for outside factors to blame his insatiability on. It must have been, he decides, what he was drinking, so he switches from scotch to bourbon or gin to vodka or substitutes beer and wine for hard liquor. Or it must have been where he was drinking, so he determines not to go to that particular bar again. Or it must have been his convivial companions, so he decides to drink alone, or it was because he was drinking alone, so he decides to drink only in company. Or it must have been because it was the weekend, so he decides to drink only during the week, or it was because of the pressures of his work, so he decides to drink only on weekends. He tries every permutation of drinking behavior in a process that may go on for years until he comes up against the ultimate wall of the fact that he cannot drink as other people do, and where or how or what he drinks does not alter this.

This is the point at which alcoholics, co-alcoholics, and professionals alike turn to physiological explanations. The alcoholic knows, and observers can adduce, that defective will power cannot be the sole explanation, for the alcoholic has often exerted more will power in staying away from a first drink than most people are called upon to summon up in a lifetime. Therefore, it is assumed, there must be an x-factor that overrides conscious will and decision, and this x-factor must be concerned with the individual's physical being—a lack of some substance that the body craves, a defect on a metabolic level, a malfunctioning system complex—but such an explanation, if it cannot be ruled out entirely, is nevertheless made unnecessary if alcohol is understood to be a thoroughly effective vehicle of unconsciously longed-for regression.

As a vehicle of regression, alcohol has one great asset. Were it a substance identified with children, were it, for example, literally the milk that children drink, the alcoholic might feel great shame in drinking it, for it would too clearly label his need as infantile. No more than do other people does he wish to appear childish. Indeed, the compulsive independence so visible in the surface behavior of alcoholics in their refusal of offers of help, in their insistence on doing things their own way, in their stubborn pursuit of their own directions suggests how strongly they defend themselves against recognition of their dependency needs, and if alcohol revealed them, it might be difficult for the alcoholic to indulge in this method of solace. But alcohol is singularly identified as a substance only an adult drinks, and, culturally and socially, drinking is identified as an adult activity. More than that, to drink is to be sophisticated, worldly, quintessentially adult.

I was thinking of this on a recent Sunday while listening to one of the members in a party of canoeists complaining of his monumental hangover. While ostensibly deploring the fact that he had no idea where he had been from the previous midnight on, no notion of how he had gotten home or in bed, there was an undertone of bragging. He was conveying to the rest of us, people he had never met before, what a man of the world he was. He mentioned off-handedly that he had four times cracked up his car and only the past Saturday had driven it off a bridge into the very river we were canoeing on. Obviously, he did not expect censure, only an amused shaking of heads and some envy of the sophisticated, devil-may-care, man-about-town life he led.

If the world viewed drinking as damning evidence of immaturity, this man might have had great trouble in explaining and excusing his behavior to himself. He might have been so deeply embarrassed by it that he would make an enormous effort to control it, and he might have had to view it as inescapable evidence of pathology. Instead, he got from drinking not only the primary rewards of the drinking itself but the secondary benefits of seeing himself as manly, strong, and courageous to the attractive point of foolhardiness. Had one of his listeners called him a reckless idiot, he would have laughed and agreed and found approval in it. Had one of us belittled his behavior as infantile, he would have bristled and then dismissed the comment as coming from a prude too timid to enjoy life.

Because drinking is thought of as an adult activity, this conceals, both from the drinker and the world, its essentially infantile nature. The world is indulgent, and the drinker can indulge himself without destroying his self-image as a free-wheeling adult until he is in danger of destroying his life. The drinker is not entirely wrong in thinking himself envied, for, just as we envy the freedom of children from constraint and responsibility and care, so also does something in us identify with the escape mechanism of the drinker. We wish we were able to find the same surcease from care, and we do not judge him too harshly. We are tolerant, as tolerant as we are of a naughty but spirited child whose insouciance wins him repeated reprieves from ordinary demands and restrictions.

The alcoholic has much in common with the child. He elicits nurturing and protective behavior from the people around him, strangers as well as the people close to him, for his vulnerability is patent. He is shielded, insofar as it is possible to be, from the consequences of his heedless behavior. He is allowed to prattle on, and nothing he says is taken too seriously, even if it is rude and insulting. He is cleaned up after, undressed, put to bed, his clothes hung up. He is solicitously urged to eat. Excuses are made for him, lies told for him. His irresponsibility is repeatedly forgiven. Despite his frequent states of helplessness, he almost magically avoids coming to grief, like an alcoholic friend who, after an evening of heavy but not obliterative drinking at home, lurches forth into the streets of New York and walks until dawn, stopping frequently at bars but moving on again after one drink. A sober person hesitates to walk the streets of New York at night, but this man has not been robbed in all the years he has followed this pattern, has never been hit by a car, and has only once fallen so severely as to break a bone. His luck will not always hold, of course. He will end up in an accident ward, like another alcoholic friend who was found dreadfully beaten in an alley one night, or in a morgue, like the mother of a friend who, drunk, burned to death in bed when the cigarette she was smoking set the mattress on fire. The wonder is not that such things happen eventually but that for so long the alcoholic gets away with their not happening.

Because the co-alcoholic can envision some such fate as a very real possibility is one of the reasons she stays with the alcoholic. To abandon a person who often is in no condition to look after himself would be like abandoning a child. The wife of my wandering friend has many times been on the verge of leaving him, but the spectre of his roaming the streets night after night if he had no family to anchor him at least part of the time makes her resolution falter. I myself was once angry enough at an alcoholic friend who arrived staggeringly drunk for a dinner party that I turned her out of the house, but I could watch her reel down the street for only half a block before I became so concerned about what might happen to her that I went after her and brought her back.

As with a child, one's heart softens because of the alcoholic's defenselessness, and as a child knows how to win forgiveness with contriteness, promises, and charm, so does the alcoholic. Were the alcoholic only defenseless and dependent, one might shuck his care early in his alcoholic history, for it would be an intolerable weight, a stone dragging one down in a sea of anxiety for his safety, but he is the same compelling mixture of dependence and independence as the child is, with the same appealing combination of responsibility and irresponsibility. One hovers between despair and rage at the child who disappears for hours without a single word as to where he is and whom he is with, and then he reappears tired and dirty and one melts, and he does something thoughtful like tidying up his room without being asked to, and one has hope. Similarly, the alcoholic disappears for hours or days without warning, but then he reappears and is too pathetic to be scolded, and when he struggles out of bed to get to the office the next morning, hope again comes to life.

Alcoholics have the reputation of being bad employees, and as a generality it is undoubtedly correct, but the overconscientiousness that is the other side of the coin of their irresponsibility is often most manifest in connection with their work. When the alcoholism is advanced, they may not be able to function well enough to hold on to a job, but before that point is reached, work, rather than family or social relationships, is the area they make the greatest efforts to keep intact. My wandering friend, even when at the edge of exhaustion, makes it to the office in the morning, and his employer has given no indication of suspecting that he is an alcoholic, nor has the boss of another friend, a periodic drinker who, ashen-faced and trembling, nevertheless continues to go to work during the first days of a drinking bout, where he carefully sets the stage for the attack of flu that purportedly will be his reason for staying home the rest of the week.

Perhaps the alcoholic senses that family and friends will put up with more than will an employer. Perhaps he senses that, because he can readily find companionship of a sort, their rejection will not be as catastrophic as loss of his livelihood. But perhaps most of all he need to conceal from himself the childish connotations of drinkings To hold a job is man's work. A child plays; an adult works. The job the alcoholic performs is evidence he can point to in refutation of the accusation that he is irresponsible, and in this way he can preserve his self-image. It is also his best defense when taken to task for his drinking. Many an alcoholic answers angrily, "So what if I drink? It's not interfering with my work, is it? I've never lost a job because of it. If I'm an alcoholic, how come I get to work every day?" Example after example comes to mind: a vice-president of a bank, advertising director of a magazine, a fashion editor; not one of them admits to being alcoholic, to himself or to others; each hides behind the defense that, were he really an alcoholic, he would not be able to function in the workaday world.

The alcoholic often behaves with absolute irresponsibility within a carefully maintained framework of responsibility. In this way, he can simultaneously deny and satisfy his deep desire for dependency. He can communicate, by his drinking behavior, his need to be the recipient of care and devotion without ever having to acknowledge it. By the agency of alcohol, he wipes out the otherness of other people. He achieves his own centrality. He reinstitutes the oneness, the rightness, the wholeness of infancy, while at the same time clinging to his franchise as an adult. The capacity of alcohol to facilitate regression and dissipate tension satisfies his permanent nostalgia for the simplicities of peace in the comforting guise of an adult pursuit.

4

The Incurability of Alcoholism

On the early road to alcoholism there is little to differentiate the potential alcoholic from other drinkers. He perhaps responds to alcohol with more release and relief than the average person, but this is unremarkable in the eyes of others and no alarm is sounded. Drinking, even repeated heavy drinking, has an accepted place in the present-day culture; it is socially sanctioned and often is actively encouraged in that it is difficult to spend an evening with friends or to have dinner in a restaurant without being under pressure to drink. One can stop smoking and receive nothing but congratulations, but when a person refuses a drink, the comment is likely to be, "Come on, be a sport. One drink won't hurt you." To offer a drink is a mark of hospitality, and to pour strong drinks is the mark of a generous host. Even when a guest has obviously had too much, it is the rare host who does not refill the glass, and I can recall only once hearing someone, very politely but very firmly, refuse another drink to a guest in his house.

Alcohol is expensive, and no one wishes to be thought stingy. Too, open-handed hospitality to friends and strangers alike is a tradition in this country, as is manly, two-fisted drinking, and thus the person on his way to becoming alcoholic not only does not meet with negative sanctions on his drinking but receives active boosts to speed him along the road. Only when drinking begins to interfere seriously with his functioning do the people around him, and often no more than one or two of those, such as his wife and his employer, begin to suggest to him that it is time he thought about cutting down, and for the alcoholic the admonition comes too late.

He may follow it, but he does so in the spirit of demonstrating that his drinking is not out of control rather than in an attempt to curb it as a long-range effort. He stops, and having proved he can stop, he starts again. He makes a great show of going on the wagon, so that when he resumes drinking, he can reassure himself that it is by choice, not compulsion, and he can refute any attempt to label him alcoholic by pointing to this or that period of time when he did without liquor. This sequence, which may be oft-repeated, so muddies the picture that it can be years before the alcoholism is identified as such.

The alcoholic puts up an intense struggle to resist having the label of alcoholism attached to his drinking, for if he accedes to it, he will have to admit that he is powerless to stop drinking—and that is anathema to him. It connotes weakness, which no one likes to acknowledge. It implies that he is not in control of his own life, which is a disturbing notion. And it carries the implication that he must stop drinking and never drink again, which is an intolerable prospect. Thus, he will stubbornly and with great tenacity counter all arguments that he is alcoholic. "Sure, I like to drink," he says. "Who doesn't?" Or, "Sure, I got falling down drunk last night. Who doesn't once in awhile?" And he will cite the times he swore off, the fact that he continues to hold a job, the occasions when he has stuck to beer and refused anything stronger—any shred of evidence he can dredge up to keep the label of alcoholic from adhering to him.

The co-alcoholic has an equally strong investment, however, in attaching the label to the drinking behavior; for if the drinker is not alcoholic, if he chooses to drink excessively rather than being powerless not to, she must view the harm that drinking does to their life and their relationship as a deliberate choice, and to accept this makes the relationship untenable and herself a fool for enduring it. The only means by which she can tolerate the destructiveness of the drinking is to consider it beyond the drinker's control. But her belief that the problem drinking deserves the name of alcoholism gives rise to a curious paradox. On the one hand, she is saying, "Because you cannot stop drinking, you are an alcoholic." On the other hand, she is saying, "Because you are an alcoholic, you must stop drinking." The communication: "You are an alcoholic," contains two messages, each of which contradicts the other. If the drinker cannot control his drinking, he is by definition alcoholic and must stop drinking. If he can control his drinking, he is not alcoholic and why, therefore, does he not control his drinking?

The alcoholic is placed in a double-bind. He can go on drinking, which confirms the diagnosis of alcoholism. Or he can stop drinking, which demonstrates that he is not an alcoholic and is entitled to drink by choice, which he proceeds to do and thereby proves that he is an alcoholic. The paradox in the statement, "You are an alcoholic," engenders the further paradox that the only way the drinker can prove he is not alcoholic and accordingly need not accept prohibitions on his drinking is by not drinking.

To remark on this paradox is not to imply that the co-alcoholic is misguided in insisting that the drinker recognize that he is an alcoholic. It is the necessary beginning of any attempt to cope with alcoholism. But it is only a beginning, for when the drinker finally capitulates and agrees, "All right, it's true, I am an alcoholic," he immediately adds, "Therefore, you can't expect me not to drink because if I could control it, I wouldn't be an alcoholic."

Now it is the co-alcoholic who is in the double-bind. She has persuaded the drinker he is alcoholic because he has no control over his drinking. She cannot then demand that he exert control over what he has no control over. The customary escape from this dilemma is to define alcoholism further as an illness. But in what sense is it an illness? Is the person with an allergy to strawberries ill? Only if he eats strawberries. He is perfectly well until he swallows the substance which has a deleterious effect on him.

When an attempt is made to equate alcoholism with illness, the comparison most frequently made is with diabetes, but the parallel is inexact on several scores. Diabetes is a chronic disease that is due to a physiological malfunctioning. It is present quite apart from anything that the diabetic does or does not do. He can exacerbate his condition by not avoiding certain foods, but even the strictest adherence to a prescribed diet will not correct his illness, nor will it necessarily prevent its progression. Total avoidance of liquor, on the other hand, is the answer to alcoholism, and there is no progression of the condition if the alcoholic does not drink. The diabetic, because he has insufficient endogenous production of an essential hormone, must take insulin for his body to stay in equilibrium, but no deficiency has been demonstrated in alcoholism, and there is no replacement therapy that renders the alcoholic capable of drinking normally. As is true of the individual with an allergy to strawberries, the alcoholic need only avoid liquor to remain symptom-free.

An analogy between diabetes and alcoholism is seductive because it conveys the chronicity of alcoholism, the fact that the drinker, no matter how long he abstains from alcohol, is not cured of alcoholism and that the "illness" is immediately reinstated as soon as he takes a drink. This is true, but he must *take* the drink. And taking or not taking a drink is in the realm of will power, which makes alcoholism subject to voluntary control in a way that diabetes is not.

This is both fortunate and unfortunate for the alcoholic— fortunate in that he does not suffer from a condition about which he can do nothing, of which he is the helpless victim and against which his most responsible efforts may be unavailing, but unfortunate in that there is no prescription that can be given him, no medicine he can take to right his problem. Proscription of alcohol is the single anwer. But to ask the alcoholic to accept this is to ask him to accept a cure for *his* cure. He is drinking to relieve tension, to regress to a state of peace, to rid himself of pesky assaults on his sense of well-being. Since it is his inability to withstand stress that is at the root of his alcoholism, it is this, if anything, that is his illness, with alcoholism being his attempted cure.

Can a most satisfying infancy be called an illness? Perhaps it can, in the same sense that schizophrenia has been termed an "environmental deficiency disease." The schizophrenic, in his infancy, received too little care, too little love, too little mothering; his environment was deficient in qualities as essential to healthy growth as vitamins and sunshine, and so, as an adult, he displays symptoms as pathognomonic of early lacks in his psychological supplies as rickets or poor teeth are of faulty nutritional supplies. By comparison, the alcoholic—well-mothered, nurtured, protected, and catered to as an infant—displays the symptoms, as an adult, of an environmental surplus disease. His growth was distorted, not by a lack, but by an excess, just as a tree planted in too rich soil makes rank, rapid growth, grows tall and seemingly flourishes but soon succumbs to cold and wind and snow because it has not been stimulated to develop the sturdy strength that would allow it to weather adverse conditions.

Illness is not a useful definition of alcoholism because it implies that alcoholism is an intrapersonal condition, an internal malfunction, whereas, in actuality, it is an interpersonal condition, a state arising from the relationship of the person to his environment. The alcoholic has flawed expectations of his environment, unrealistic expectations engendered in him by his particular history. When his expectations are inevitably frustrated, he attempts to compensate for his disappointment by means of alcohol. His drinking is a symptom that something is wrong, not the thing itself that has gone wrong. It is an indication and a communication.

It is fashionable in psychotherapy, particularly in family therapy, to remark that the patient has come by his symptoms honestly, meaning, for example, that the schizophrenic patient has not manufactured his symptoms out of whole cloth; they arose in the family in specific response to the particular family constellation and they have utility in preserving a certain malign equilibrium. By the same token, the alcoholic has come by his symptoms honestly. If he misperceives the world, if he views it unrealistically, he has come by his misunderstanding unintentionally. He was taught what he knows, and it is not surprising that he acts on his knowledge in an attempt to preserve his equilibrium.

If alcoholism is not a physical illness, is it more accurate to call it a psychological illness? More accurate, yes, but still not a sufficiently inclusive description, for it does not take into account the physical dependence on alcohol present in the alcoholic. Alcohol is a chemical agent, the repeated use of which produces a physiological need for the drug. There is cellular habituation to the presence of alcohol in the body, and the alcoholic, by drinking, is satisfying not only a psychological but also a physiological craving.

And a craving that is both psychological and physiological is properly termed an addiction.

An addiction is neither physical illness nor mental illness but a category in itself, one characterized by emotional *and* physical dependence on an intoxicating agent. The alcoholic is emotionally dependent on alcohol for the exquisite relief of tension it provides, and he is physically dependent on it because his body has become accustomed to its presence. Since addiction encompasses both these aspects of the condition, physical and psychological, this inclusive definition elucidates alcoholism in a way that partial descriptions do not, and thus it is by far the most accurate and useful of possible explanations.

With alcoholism understood in the dual light of addiction, it becomes apparent why a treatment approach aimed at only the physical or only the psychological side of the problem may come to naught. Very often, the family of an alcoholic places great hope in getting him to accept hospitalization for detoxification, only to find that when he is released from the hospital, cured for the moment of his physical reliance on alcohol, he nevertheless returns to drinking. This was the case with a man of my acquaintance, a chronic drinker of decades' standing whose binges had become so frequent that the large corporation for which he worked gave him the alternative of being fired or agreeing to three months of hospitalization in a private sanitarium. He acceded to the latter and dutifully underwent detoxification, emerging from the hospital in robust health and seemingly firmly established on a regimen of Antabuse to reinforce his newly gained will power to stay away from liquor. His wife grew complacent, secure in the knowledge that, even if he was occasionally tempted to drink, the daily dose of Antabuse would prevent him from succumbing to the wish, and his superiors felt safe in entrusting important work to him because there would now be no sudden, week-long absences from the job. But quietly, two weeks before his birthday, the man stopped taking Antabuse, carefully flushing one pill down the toilet each morning so his wife would not suspect, and on his birthday he began a "celebration" that, to the best of my knowledge, is still continuing some months later.

While in the hospital this man was seen weekly by a psychiatrist and attended group therapy sessions and A.A. meetings. This typical supportive treatment approach was intended to give him an appreciation of the fact that he is not alone in his problems with alcohol, that other people also use it as an escape, but that it is self-defeating and self-destructive. What was treated was the symptom of alcoholism, with treatment being a combination of education, exhortation, and example, plus tranquillizers, occupational therapy, and physical rehabilitation, to all of which this man responded well.

What was not attempted, however, was an uncovering, exploratory type of therapy designed to give him insight into the problems underlying his symptoms. Undoubtedly, this was because of several considerations, one being the practical matter of insufficient time. Psychoanalysis is an extended process and it cannot be hurried, for it is not a question of the analyst's coming to understand the life history of the patient and then feeding back to him a series of interpretations that illuminate why he behaves as he does. The patient himself, by ranging backward and forward over his life, must discover consistencies in his feelings, thoughts, attitudes, and behavior that are not in events or in other people but in himself, and from these consistencies gain insight into the way in which he unconsciously structures his experience of the world. In this process of bringing what is unconscious into consciousness, the analyst acts as companion but only in a special and limited sense as guide. It is as though the two, analyst and patient, were traveling in a wilderness, with one, the analyst, familiar with the terrain but the other, the patient, choosing the paths in order that he too may make the territory his own, not merely follow blindly along. The patient must wander, explore, circle, and probe at any one level until he knows it thoroughly before he can afford to push on into deeper regions. The analyst is by his side to encourage and support him, but he can give only occasional suggestions of alternative paths the patient has overlooked and now and again call his attention to similarities that indicate they have been over the ground before. Were he to do otherwise, were he to lead and the patient to follow, the patient would simply have made a journey in someone else's footsteps, and when it was over, he would have a jumbled impression of trees and rocks and mountains and ravines but scarcely increased ability to find his way unaccompanied among them. He would not have taken possession of the terrain of his life so that he could henceforth choose his course confidently, immediately recognizing paths that led nowhere or that brought him to the edge of an abyss or that ended in insurmountable obstacles.

If an individual is to function autonomously and exercise intelligent and discriminating control over his life, the knowledge of how he has come to be as he is must be gained by him; it cannot be given to him. Briefer therapies can educate the alcoholic to the futility of drinking as a problem-solving device, can reinforce his will power not to drink, can sensitize him to the situations in which he is likely to drink, can encourage him by the example of alcoholics who have learned to live without liquor; they can, in short, foster repression of the urge to drink. But they do not end the urge, and the resolution not to drink must be renewed each morning when the alcoholic opens his eyes and faces the world. At best, such approaches cap the bottle, but the pressure remains and there is always the possibility that the lid will blow off, as it did for my acquaintance who was hospitalized. His hospitalization gave him weapons to fend off the need to drink, but it in no measure lessened the need.

Only insight into the causes of his drinking might have

done that, but, in addition to the time involved in the arduous process of unearthing the source of the alcoholic's unusual vulnerability to stress, to frustration, there is a second factor that makes psychoanalytic treatment of the alcoholic a very difficult undertaking. The instrument of psychoanalytic therapy is words, and the alcoholic has no liking for words, not the words that probe his feelings and needs and drives and motives. He may be highly verbal. He may make his living as a writer or editor or publisher or actor or speaker. He may be an engaging conversationalist and story-teller. But words are a practical tool to him, a means of communicating with, and often manipulating, others. They are not instruments he uses on himself. He does not conceptualize his feelings; he acts on them.

The alcoholic has a lifelong, entrenched pattern of acting out, not talking out, his problems.

This is a crucial difference between the alcoholic and others. If his self-esteem is wounded, the alcoholic acts out his hurt by drinking. If he feels rejected, if he feels depressed, if he feels criticized, if he feels ashamed, if he feels angry, he does not explore his feelings but acts to rid himself of them by drinking. The dialogues he holds with himself are designed to justify his reasons for drinking, not to obviate them. Nor will he sit down with another and attempt to explain how he feels and the possible reasons for his feelings. Indeed, after some such terse explanation as, "You made me feel like a fool in front of those people," or, "They don't appreciate me at the office," he is through with speech, and if prodded to go on, he grows impatient and angry. "What's there to talk about?" he demands. "I felt like a drink so I started drinking. Why make something complicated out of it?" Shame and defensiveness play some part in his refusal to explore his behavior, but there may be other reasons as well. For one, he senses that no explanation will be sufficient to excuse the destructiveness of his drinking. For another, any invitation to explore the reasons he drinks carries the implication that he should talk instead of drink, and he does not wish to be made to give up drinking. Words cannot offer the immediate relief that drinking does; they are not soothing, tranquillizing, ego-building. On the contrary, they threaten more pain, more distress and discomfort. But on a deeper level, and even more influential, is the fact that the alcoholic's drinking stems from a time when there were no words, from infancy.

He has no recollection of his infancy, and if he did, what could he say of it? That it was a happy time, that he was well taken care of? That seems irrelevant, since we are accustomed to tracing our problems and attitudes back to traumatic events, and, in any event, there is a reluctance to probe what was good and satisfying. What is he being asked to face? That he has unrealistically positive views of the world? It is far easier to persuade the neurotic that his pessimism about ever feeling loved and cherished and wanted is unfounded than it is to lead the alcoholic to an understanding that he is unreasonably optimistic and that his search for the common goals of life, love, and security must be tempered.

The following, from Hinsie and Campbell's *Psychiatric Dictionary,* is a definition of oral dependency: "The unconscious wish for maternal protection, to be encompassed by the mother, to regain the peace, protection, and security of her sheltering arms. This stems from the original intense and forgotten gratifications of the infantile nursing period, when the infant's prehensile mouth anchored it to the mother's nipple and breast. To the child, to be fed means to be loved, i.e., to be protected, ergo, to be secure." The alcoholic's dependency on the bottle is unquestionably oral dependency, and to require him to explore it is to ask him to plumb the most inaccessible reaches of his unconscious, accept by deduction what he cannot verify by memory, and identify the pervasive wish of all people for peace, protection, and security as his particular undoing. It is a very large demand.

What can psychoanalysis offer him in return? He is not the neurotic plagued by anxiety, paralyzed by depression, insecure in his relationships, and dogged by a poor sense of his own worth for whom psychoanalysis holds out the promise of a better way of life. He is not the schizophrenic with whom he shares the therapeutic difficulty of having the roots of his problems buried in a preverbal time. Alcoholism is as refractory to treatment as schizophrenia, but the alcoholic is even less motivated to seek cure, for his world is not as frightening, he is far less cut off from other people, and his symptoms are not as disturbing; thus, he has much less to gain from treatment.

Treatment cannot even hold out the promise of enabling him to drink rationally, for his addiction to alcohol is physical as well as mental, and even were he to come to understand the psychological necessities involved in his drinking, this would in no way guarantee that his physical dependence on alcohol would not be reinstated if he started drinking again. What treatment would offer are the rewards of insight, of being a fully conscious human being, but this is not an enticing prospect for the alcoholic, who is the least introspective of individuals. Having all his life acted on what he felt—more specifically, having acted to rid himself of what he felt—he fears and mistrusts self-exploration.

I have sometimes thought of the alcoholics I have known as anti-intellectual intellectuals, that is, highly intelligent, they nevertheless misprize reason as a means of governing a life. I once asked an alcoholic if he had observed that particular occasions gave rise to his drinking. He was aghast at the very notion of self-observation. "Good heavens," he said impatiently, "I don't spend time sitting around watching myself." He thought it an odd and narcissistic pastime to examine one's own behavior, that it was in some way self-indulgent, although, in fact, it was his unexamined behavior, his drinking, that was self-indulgent.

Since psychoanalysis is a treatment in which the patient must not only watch himself but take an active part in exploring himself, it further does not commend itself to the alcoholic because of his passivity. Having been indoctrinated in infancy to the passive recipient of the care that relieved his tension and distress, and having perpetuated this posture in later years by using alcohol to wash away uncomfortable feelings without effort on his part, the alcoholic who finally surrenders to the need for treatment expects and seeks a treatment in which something is done *to* him. His idea, and ideal, of treatment is based on the medical model in which the parental figure of the physician administers pills or injections and rights the condition with the acquiescence but without the participation of the patient. The alcoholic has a marked preference for physical treatment, for rehabilitative measures, for an outside agency to intervene and make him comfortable, as his mother once did. He wants to be the passive recipient of care and attention and a specific set of therapeutic maneuvers that will relieve him of his problems, which is why alcoholics, when their lives are in disarray, often welcome hospitalization. The alcoholic in a hospital has achieved a dependent situation, a structured situation in which authority figures are now responsible, in his eyes, for his care and cure. He waits, as a child waits, for measures to be taken. He says, in effect, "All right, I'm here. Now it's up to you to fix whatever's wrong."

But this is just half the story of the alcoholic's approach to treatment. Not only is the child's attitude toward authority, his faith and reliance and realistic dependence on adult figures, duplicated in the alcoholic, but also the child's rebelliousness, his need to thwart authority in covert ways, to test the firmness of the limits that have been set, to be defiant in order to exert his autonomy. In the professional literature describing treatment programs for alcoholics, passive and rebellious are the two adjectives most frequently used. The burden of many such papers is the perplexing question of how alcoholics can be motivated to take an active part in their own treatment. Apparently cooperative, they will, for example, dutifully attend group therapy meetings, but in the sessions they talk endlessly of their drunks and fall silent when the therapist tries to lead them into the murkier waters of the reasons behind their drinking. They make fun of recreational and occupational therapy, claiming it is childish to make leather belts or take part in ping-pong tournaments, or, conversely, they throw themselves into activities with such fervor and completeness that they have no time or energy left for introspection. A friend of a friend of mine, for example, when denied his heavy supply of tranquillizers and urged to make more constructive use of his time in the hospital than simply lying in bed, took up sculpting and spent sixteen hours a day at it, until finally his therapist was reduced to forbidding him to work at it at all because it was proving just as effective as sleep in enabling him to avoid coming to grips with his problems. By overcompliance with the suggestions of a therapist, the alcoholic expresses his hidden defiance. His plea, "Cure me," is actually the challenge, "Cure me if you can." He does not, of course, want to stop drinking. At best, he wants to *want* to stop drinking, but he assumes it is up to someone else to bring about this change in him. With his passive, dependent orientation, he truly feels that he has done all that can be expected or required of him if he puts himself in a position to be treated. The notion that this is the beginning, not the end, of treatment is antipathetic to him.

Outside of a hospital situation, this same attitude obtains, with the alcoholic looking to the therapist to produce some magic formula that will relieve him of his necessity to drink compulsively, preferably by means of some pill but, in any event, by some agency that can work on him, as it were, behind his own back. While this makes therapy difficult enough under any circumstances, in the private setting it is further compromised by the alcoholic's ready access to alcohol. For anyone in psychoanalytic treatment, the attempt to unravel the complicated strands of a life, to bring to light the unconscious determinants of behavior, to expose failures, to resurrect painful memories, to admit to inadmissible wishes, to face fears, and to acknowledge the childish and irrational in oneself is an enterprise beset with chagrin and frequent misery, and the temptation to abandon the effort when it becomes particularly grueling is great. For the alcoholic, to whom flight from stress is a well-nigh automatic reaction, it is virtually irresistible.

If therapy is to be of help to the alcoholic, however, he cannot be permitted to take flight from its difficulties. Thus, the first requirement therapy will impose on him will be that he not drink, and again the disturbing circularity in the problem of alcoholism surfaces. The alcoholic needs treatment to help him stop drinking, but he cannot be treated unless he stops drinking, unless he foreswears, in the stressful situation of therapy, his habitual response to stress. He, not without reason, feels that this is comparable to asking the person who is severely anxious to master his anxiety before he enters the treatment that, if it is successful, will help him to master his anxiety. What the alcoholic expects to hear if he seeks treatment—indeed, what, in essence, he does hear—is, "Alcoholic, heal thyself. Only then can thou be healed."

With alcoholism characterized, as it is, by a lifelong propensity for acting out problems rather than thinking them through, by a deep distrust of the efficacy of reason as a means of achieving desired relief of stress, by a habitual response of flight rather than fight, by passive avoidance rather than active grappling, it is obvious that the condition itself conspires against its curability. As long as the alcoholic himself does not feel alienated from life, from other people, from his own self, as long as his wishes are not incongruent with what it means to be a human being, he is not motivated to go against his own grain and undertake an endeavor antithetical to his own nature.

That a percentage of alcoholics conquer their addiction is incontestable, however, and this suggests a change in some factor in them sufficient to set them apart from other alcoholics. It is an A.A. tenet that the alcoholic who recovers is the alcoholic who has "hit bottom." Perhaps the alcoholic who finds himself in severe trouble, whose life, family, friends, job, and future are in jeopardy, is experiencing a new element in his psychic equation. For the first time, he is having the threat of isolation and alienation, of aloneness and rejection thrust upon him. And for the first time he is experiencing profound anxiety, existential anxiety. If he grows anxious to the degree that the long-range goal of avoiding intolerable anxiety takes precedence over the immediate aim of relief of tension, the reality principle enters his life, and he is motivated to examine that life. His concern over what he does, which is drink, shifts to a concern over what he is, which is alcoholic.

The pivot of change hinges on the supersedence of tension by anxiety, for when this occurs, the pleasure principle, which has heretofore been controlling, must give way to the reality principle. The reality principle, unlearned in the infancy of an alcoholic, comes late to his life, but when he is forced to its recognition by anxiety, the necessary ground is established for the fight to break the addiction.

PART TWO

The

Co-Alcoholic

5
Identification of Alcoholism

If alcoholism is the end result of a particular set of shaping experiences in infancy, the sober cannot, in good conscience, congratulate themselves on their ability to handle liquor wisely, for they did nothing to insure their temperance. By the same token, those who are alcoholic need not castigate themselves because of their vulnerability to alcohol, for they did nothing to insure their immoderate response nor to set in motion their inordinate need. But the sober can try to understand the alcoholic, and the drunk must try to understand his alcoholism.

Because drinking, however pain-producing and problem-causing it may seem to a bystander, is nevertheless extremely rewarding to the alcoholic, it is the co-alcoholic who will be motivated to seek understanding far in advance of the alcoholic. Even so, it is likely that some years will have elapsed before the co-alcoholic recognizes that the situation she is confronted with is addiction to alcohol. No more than other people is she accustomed to thinking of alcohol as a drug. Where she would have no hesitancy in identifying dependence on marijuana or Demerol or heroin or barbiturates as addiction if their use occurred frequently and compulsively over even a short period of time, she cannot be so clear-cut about alcohol. Too many people consume it socially and casually to have addiction be a frightening spectre whenever a glass is lifted, and there is no boundary a drinker crosses that distinguishes him beyond a doubt from the world of nonaddictive indulgers. The co-alcoholic, witness to the inroads that drinking is making upon the life of the drinker, may suspect the presence of alcoholism, but as long as the alcoholic continues to deny it, she has great difficulty in obtaining objective confirmation of the diagnosis.

A friend of mine, married to a man who drinks compulsively and excessively, hopes fervently each year that the medical examination his company requires will reveal him to be an alcoholic so that pressure additional to her own may be brought on him to do something about his drinking, but it never happens. The examining doctor asks how much he drinks, he replies, "As much as anyone else in my line of work," and that is the end of it, for he has not yet developed the signs of physical damage that would alert the physician to probe his drinking habits, to pin down the amounts, the times, and the frequency.

A simple test can determine that a person has been drinking, but it establishes only alcohol consumption within the previous twenty-four hours; it does not differentiate the man who has been drinking heavily for one year from the man who has been drunk only this one day in the year. And such a test is without prognostic value; it does not indicate which man will be drunk again tomorrow and which will not drink for another year. Even the presence of cirrhosis of the liver, the most common physical consequence of inordinate drinking, does not warrant a presumptive diagnosis of alcoholism, since it can have other causes as well, which is equally true of tremors, polyneuritis, delirium, and unconsciousness, each of which can be, but is not necessarily, a sequel of drinking. Polyneuritis, for example, can be arsenic or diabetic as well as alcoholic in origin. Likewise, Korsakov's psychosis, a brain disorder characterized by disorientation, suggestibility, faulty memory, and hallucinations, although usually presumed to be associated with chronic alcoholism, may arise from other conditions.

If the co-alcoholic, desperate for a neutral diagnosis of the drinking problem, persuades the alcoholic to agree to a joint visit to their family physician, she, almost by necessity, sounds querulous and exaggeratory if the alcoholic chooses to be offhand about the extent of his drinking. And the result would be no different if a psychiatrist or psychologist were consulted. The drinker himself must describe his drinking honestly, must acknowledge his craving for alcohol, must admit his dependence on it, must concede that his drinking is out of control before either physician or psychiatrist can say authoritatively that alcoholism is present. In short, if the alcoholic avoids trouble with the law and frequent public drunkenness, he must admit that he is alcoholic before he can be objectively diagnosed as alcoholic.

Even friends, curiously enough, are not likely to lend their support to the co-alcoholic's suspicion that alcoholism is present. While they may readily agree that the alcoholic drinks too much, they are inclined to minimize the seriousness of the problem, dismissing the co-alcoholic's fears with some such comment as: "Sure, he hits the bottle pretty heavily, but he can handle it." In addition to a laudable reluctance to sit in judgment on a friend, there is the fact that the drinker is a ready companion who is always available if one feels like stopping off for a drink or two on the way home from work or going out on a Saturday night. He is convivial, agreeable, and available. After the drinks on the way home or after the party, the friend waves good-bye and departs, or if the alcoholic is in no condition to get home by himself, he deposits him at his front door. The friend is not present for the last drinks that pave the descent into incoherence, falls, and unconsciousness. He is not witness to the glass of whiskey the alcoholic takes to bed, the restless, thrashing sleep, the morning drink. He is an occasional viewer, not a night-after-night, day-after-day observer of the extent of the drinking and the inroads it is making on the drinker's ability to function. He can afford to be tolerant because he is not intimately involved. His safety, peace, security, and sanity are not threatened. He can laugh and say indulgently, "Well, old George has done it again." And when old George has done it once too often, the friend can drift out of his life.

This lack of support and confirmation from friends that the drinking warrants the name of alcoholism can be more disheartening to the co-alcoholic than the fact that professional help is so difficult to get without the alcoholic's willing admission of alcoholism. At least, in dealing with my mother, it was this that caused me the most despair. No one was with her constantly, as I was, and in the company of people whom she saw frequently, she could often enough pace her drinking so that only occasionally was it visibly out of control. They did not see her late at night or the following morning, and when with her, they looked at her casually. They were not sensitized to the dilation of her eyes that indicated she had been drinking before company arrived. They had not a thousand times heard the plausible, "Excuse me while I look at the roast. Excuse me while I check to see if a window is open upstairs. Excuse me while I go to the Ladies' Room." They did not know that the vitamin bottle in her purse contained whiskey, the perfume bottle in the bathroom, the first-aid kit in the car. They took at face value the explanation that she had a bad back and that this caused her difficulty in getting out of a chair and walking steadily. If I commented, "She walks that way because she's drunk," the answer was an incredulous, "But she's only had two drinks," which was indeed all she had had in public view. Thus, no friend's voice was added to mine; no pressure was put on her to admit to her problem with alcohol; and by the time her alcoholism was unmistakable, the friends were gone, alienated by her irresponsibility, her unpredictable behavior, and her tearful demandingness.

Some part of why friends are reluctant to intervene may be due to the feeling that they are in no position to throw the first stone, some further part to the apprehension that if they do throw the first stone, it will be rocketed back by the alcoholic, who, with his propensity for rage, surges to the attack if his drinking is mentioned in terms which he interprets as critical. Since there is no clear line of demarcation separating the alcoholic from the heavy drinker, a friend may feel unwarrantedly presumptive in proposing the label of alcoholism. If he accepts the co-alcoholic's description of the extent of the problem, there is the delicate situation of being drawn into a domestic fight. More elusive, but also inhibiting, is a general tolerance of pleasure-seeking behavior; the alcoholic may be secretly envied his escapism. Most inhibiting of all is embarrassment, the same embarrassment that counsels the tactful overlooking of a physical disability. At a school reunion of mine, there was present a class-mate with an exotic ailment evidenced by his enlarged head, distorted features, and affected sense of balance. He twice fell down and was solicitously helped to his feet without comment, although there was lengthy speculation away from his presence about the nature of his illness. Had he spoken of his disability, he would have gotten a sympathetic response, but since he did not, delicacy dictated a matching silence. It was probably no favor to support his denial that anything was amiss, but it was a human reaction. And it is a reaction common in the presence of alcoholism. We are uncomfortable in calling attention to a disability. We shrink from the prospect of sitting down with the drinker and talking to him with the intention of forcing his problem into the light. Is it our business? Must we become involved? Why incur his wrath? It is easier to indulge his pretense that all is as it should be until the day when the evidence to the contrary mounts into final proof, and then it is easier to turn away, still silent.

In recent years, I have become good, although not intimate, friends with a couple who are poised, intelligent, charming, somewhat reserved people, close enough friends so that we exchange dinner invitations fairly often and occasional weekend visits. Despite my high index of suspicion concerning alcoholism, it was more than a year after knowing them that I suddenly added up the clues that suggested the husband was an alcoholic: his near-stupor at the end of an evening not accounted for by the number of visible drinks he had had, his insistence on being helpful in the kitchen (near the source of liquor), his trips to the cellar to check on the furnace or outside in the summer to check on the lawn sprinklers, his solitary walks to admire the scenery (there is a tavern a mile from my country house). Certain that he is an alcoholic, am I now to sit down with him and say, "Look, Paul, I know you're an alcoholic"? I cannot. Only if he spoke of it could it be talked about.

Or if his wife spoke of it. But that is another dilemma bedeviling the co-alcoholic. She loves this person. She is reluctant to expose him to ridicule or contempt or ostracism. She shrinks from revealing what seems like a mortal softness of character. She is humiliated by his behavior when drunk, and she would prefer it not to become common knowledge that the affable fellow everyone knows can metamorphose into a vicious, foul-mouthed, and occasionally physically violent drunk. It is a widespread assumption that people do not drink excessively unless there is bitter unhappiness in their current lives; in talking about his drinking, then, what would she inadvertently be saying about the wormy heart of their relationship? For such reasons of shame and protectiveness, the co-alcoholic becomes the co-conspirator of the alcoholic in masking his problem. She, the person with the most to gain from exposure of the alcoholic, is often the person with the most to lose from doing so.

She will, of course, have talked to the alcoholic about his drinking, but because alcoholism is a slowly developing condition, surprising stretches of time may go by before she identifies it with certainty, years in which she is no more convinced of the inexorability of the drinking than is the alcoholic. And she does not want to become convinced of it, so she accepts the alcoholic's excuses and assurances. Indeed, it would be premature of her to label heavy drinking, or even frequent drunkenness, alcoholism if, as is so often the case, drinking is an integral part of their social life and his business life. She would seem an alarmist, a spoilsport, a nagging wife. Thus, her first concerns about the drinking are usually expressed tentatively. Her husband agrees that he should cut down, that he is drinking too much and too often, and that the last bout did cause him to go a bit overboard. For as long as his resolve lasts, the co-alcoholic is lulled into complacency, and even when the alcoholic next shows up drunk, she is likely to say little, feeling that a slip now and again is excusable. But repeated slips cause her to bring up the subject again, often in terms of, "But you promised," and the alcoholic, feeling guilty, grows defensive. He accuses her of exaggerating how much he drinks, of overreacting, of making a mountain out of a molehill. Often, he effectively silences her with the accusation, "You're driving me to drink by harping on it so much."

As their life deteriorates and the co-alcoholic cannot escape the conclusion that silence and forebearance are, if anything, less effective than speech, she attempts again and again to discuss the drinking. And the fights start. It is impossible for them not to.

The alcoholic must protect his addiction, and must equally protect himself from recognition of his addiction. Perhaps unaware himself that his drinking is out of control, and in any event desperate to avoid such an admission, he diverts attention to problems other than his drinking: their relationship, her personality, his job, his boss, their children, their friends, his frustrations and disappointments, any spindle on which he can skewer his tale of blame. And because there are always things wrong with any relationship, any job, any geographic or social situation, there is a plausibility to his arguments. If there is not, or if one or more of the conditions he is blaming for his drinking get righted, he switches to another argument. The alcoholic is not a fair fighter; he is slippery and transilient; and with so much at stake for him, he is diabolically cunning at shifting blame. The co-alcoholic, attempting to be fair-minded, can seldom stay on the track of his drinking as the central problem; she is constantly derailed into a discussion of the areas he blames for his drinking and diverted into haring off after elusive solutions to these secondary problems. Still persuaded that rationality is somehow involved in the drinking, her weapon is reason, and she either loses every fight or, if she wins, the payoff comes in the guise of promises which will soon be broken.

Often, the promises simply force the alcoholic into ruses to conceal the amount of his drinking: sneaked drinks and hidden bottles. The co-alcoholic hesitates to accuse him of drinking secretly because this either enrages him or causes him to say in discouragement, "See, it doesn't matter what I do, you always assume I'm drinking." Eventually, of course, the co-alcoholic grows so attuned to the signs of his drinking that a glance at his face as he enters a room or no more than a word or two on the telephone is sufficient to give him away, a fact that no alcoholic can quite believe and that increases his sense of being sorely persecuted. Alcoholics cling to the consoling fiction that even after several drinks they are still behaving perfectly normally and conversing in ordinary, sober fashion, that gum or mints or mouthwash hides the smell of liquor, and that a flushed face or a glazed eye does not betray them. Since it is almost impossible to remark on the fact that the alcoholic has been drinking without sounding accusatory, the co-alcoholic may not comment, which convinces the alcoholic that he is getting away with his drinking and allows him to retreat into martyrdom when the co-alcoholic is driven to speak of it again. He demands that she name the occasions, and when she complies, he argues them, and the attempt to discuss his drinking quickly degenerates into a bootless dispute over dates and times.

The binge drinker, on the other hand, the drinker whose ordinary life stops for days or weeks while he gets and remains sodden, cannot deny his drinking. But neither can he be made to discuss it because he is in no condition to talk about it while on the bender, and when he sobers up, he is likely to be so sick that it would be inhumane to flog him with words. The co-alcoholic postpones discussion until he has returned to normal, at which juncture the alcoholic waves aside the event with airy assurances that it will not happen again and the co-alcoholic does not grow insistent for fear of disturbing the so-recently restored calm.

This is the case with an acquaintance of mine who enjoys an excellent law practice in a New England town and for months at a time maintains an unblemished record of abstinence, until a day comes when he does not return to his office after lunch. Two, three, or four weeks later, his wife is notified that he is in a Boston hospital, and she journeys there to fetch him home. He has no memory of the intervening weeks. He simply wakes up in the hospital where the police have deposited him after retrieving his unconscious body from some side street. Choked with apologies, mortified at the worry he has caused, baffled to account for the 3-D amplitude of his binge, he assures his wife with ardent conviction that it will never happen again. What is there for her to say? She knows by now that it will happen again—she even recognizes the signs of increasing tension and short-temperedness that presage its happening—but if she betrays her skepticism, it will bespeak a lack of confidence in him and perhaps precipitate the next episode.

Another acquaintance is married to a third type of drinker, a chronic, day after day, heavy drinker who makes no bones about how much he drinks and no attempt to conceal it from her, although he is rather more circumspect at his office. He arrives home each evening, far from sober but not yet staggering, and proceeds to drink until he passes out. If she attempts to talk to him, he does not answer, or he snarls her into intimidated retreat, and on weekends, when, out of an obscure sense that he is proving mastery of his drinking, he touches not a drop, he is much too splenetic for her to dare the subject.

Because he holds a job, an unusually responsible job, because they engage in a degree of social life, because he continues to function and is far from being a skid-row alcoholic, this husband was not recognized to be alcoholic by his long-suffering wife until after a lustrum of egregious drinking. While he continues to rail against the designation, she can be quite certain that it is so because of several factors. The first is his craving for alcohol. Although he would deny that craving is present by citing his abstinence on weekends, his melancholy, his nervousness, and his short temper when sober reveal his body's need. The second is his lack of control over his drinking. While it is true that he abstains on weekends, for five days of the week he is unable to stop drinking short of unconsciousness, and weekend abstinence no more absolves him of alcoholism than do the months of sobriety of the lawyer between binges. A third confirmation is his nightly amnesia for the events of the evening. The fourth is his high tolerance for abnormal amounts of alcohol.

These four signs: craving, inability to stop drinking short of drunkenness, blackouts, and a high tolerance for alcohol, are pathognomonic of alcoholism. However, the presence of just one indicator, craving, is sufficient for a presumptive diagnosis. The secret, steady drinker does not always imbibe to the point of unconsciousness, and many an alcoholic, particularly one of longstanding, exhibits a very low tolerance for alcohol. My mother, for example, eventually had the same reaction to one drink that she had formerly had to a fifth of whiskey, and a friend recently described a mutual friend who "goes crazy" on two bottles of beer, a person who some years ago was alcoholic, had stopped drinking with the help of A.A., and has now, under stressful circumstances, resumed what would be for another person a negligible consumption of alcohol.

Some authorities, recognizing that it is not the literal amount drunk nor the degree of deviant behavior that is conclusive, have broadened the definition of alcoholism to include any drinking that gives rise to persistent problems in the personal, social, and/or economic realms. Unless the co-alcoholic is the rare person so inordinately opposed to drinking that she overreacts to social drinking and overinterprets it, she is doing the drinker no injustice by defining him as alcoholic if his drinking cannot be reasonably discussed, or if discussed and promises made, it still remains a threat to the quality of his life. As a rule of thumb, if the person closest to the drinker suspects that alcoholism is present, it almost certainly is, for the suspicion of alcoholism does not find fertile ground until it is already apparent that the drinking cannot be controlled.

In the literature about alcoholism, a period of seven to fifteen years from the start of drinking is cited as the average time before alcoholism is identified. In those years, the co-alcoholic watches the drinker progress from an early point where two drinks will produce the glow of friendship and conviviality to the necessity for four drinks before the drinker begins to unwind. She sees the monthly drunk give way to the weekly and the weekly to the daily. She sees the before-dinner cocktails become augmented by the before-luncheon cocktails and the after-dinner highballs. She sees the start of the morning pick-me-up drink. She sees liquor become an essential lubricant to the drinker's handling of social situations. She becomes aware that any stress or distress calls for a drink before it can be faced. And she finally becomes convinced that the drinker is dependent on alcohol, quite independent of his excuses and the rationalizations he gives for his drinking.

At this point, the alcoholism she may have long suspected becomes a certainty in her mind, and this certainty brings a curious sense of relief. The drinking behavior has a name. It is a recognized condition. It is not perversity on the drinker's part. It is not careless destructiveness. It is not aggressive indifference to her peace of mind. It is a medical, legal, and social entity. She can speak its name and other people will hear it with the same referents as she.

To know names is a very human necessity. The first thing

one asks about another person is his name. The first words one learns in a foreign language are the names of objects. The first questions asked on a walk in the country are the names of trees, birds, and flowers, even by people who have little interest in such things. To have a name, whether for an object or a condition, is to have a way of thinking and speaking about it. As an example, I have a friend whose husband, over a span of several months, grew more tired, more cranky, more depressed, more and more unlike his usual self. His physician, detecting nothing wrong, prescribed rest, tranquillizers, vitamins, a change of scene, a new job. Nothing helped, and as his condition deteriorated, so did their marriage. The wife, despairing and feeling their relationship must be somehow to blame, considered leaving him. But deciding on one last effort, she made a list of every way in which her husband was presently different from the way he had been a year before, every physical and psychological deviation, no matter how slight, and she took the list to his doctor. He read it and said, "These are the symptoms of subacute bacterial endocarditis," and that is what it proved to be. The diagnosis had grave implications, and, indeed, the husband was critically ill for months and ultimately required heart surgery, but nothing was so difficult for this man and wife again once they had been given a name for his condition. They were no longer dealing with the unknown but with an entity that had a name, a name that allowed them to communicate with others about his condition, a name that automatically told them what they must do and what they must expect.

When the co-alcoholic finally says to herself, "This is alcoholism," she experiences the same sort of reaction. It is an uncheerful realization because of its implications; nevertheless, it is a great relief to recognize that the drinking behavior has a name. She is no longer dealing with the gratuitous but with a delimited condition. She has a road map for her circling thoughts and a glossary for speaking them. She can plan. She can seek information and advice. She can say to the alcoholic that his drinking behavior is alcoholism and thus locate that behavior within the framework of a known condition. She is no longer blaming him or criticizing him or pleading with him or fighting him. She is expressing her awareness that he drinks, not willfully, but addictively. The pinpointing of his condition takes him off the spot, she feels, and she assumes that now they will be able to discuss the problem and together decide on steps to take to handle it.

Alas, her relief at having finally labeled the problem will not be shared by the drinker. However little or much he knows about alcoholism, he knows one thing: an alcoholic is someone who under no circumstances can drink normally. The diagnosis of alcoholism, to his ears, is tantamount to an order to stop drinking and never drink again, a horrendous prospect for someone whose coping mechanisms are almost entirely bound up with alcohol. Pleading guilty to alcoholism entails a mandatory life sentence of imprisonment within his panics, fears, tensions, inadequacies, and vulnerabilities, with no prospect of escape or parole, no means he can envision of dealing with them in other ways. It threatens him with relinquishment of his means of righting his world when it dips alarmingly, the elixir that makes him grandly invulnerable, the magic potion that slips comfortingly into his bloodstream and makes him run warm with well-being. Never again to feel the glow that allows him to be magnanimous toward others. Never again to retreat into the pleasant blur that silences the importunate world. Never again to vanish into a misty landscape where nothing is threatening, where all is soft and distant and muffled. Never again to retreat into original oneness. It is an intolerable future. It is, at this usual point in the alcoholic's life, inconceivable.

The truth, finally uncovered and embraced by the co-alcoholic, is anathema to the alcoholic. Where she welcomes it as liberating them from the malefic and recriminatory arguments over his drinking, he senses in it only intensified threat. Where she sees its heuristic advantage, he appreciates its menace of closure. Where she feels that she has taken a giant step forward in understanding, in sympathetic acceptance that the problem is beyond his control, he hears the snap of the trap. She means only to release him on safer ground; he would chew off his own leg to preserve his freedom to drink. She, safe in rationality, finds him retreating further into irrational, frantic denial.

Expecting a scene of subdued reconciliation and joint resolution, the co-alcoholic sets off, instead, a round of unanticipated fire. It is as though Jane F., the wife who provided the clues which led to the diagnosis of endocarditis, returned home and said to her husband, "Look, Alan, it's not good news, but at least we know now what's wrong," and he, instead of being grateful for her loving persistence, turned on her in wrath and excoriated her with: "So you've been going behind my back, making me out to be some kind of monster just because you don't like the way I behave! Doesn't the doctor realize that you're the one who's sick, that you've got a sick mind, that nine-tenths of the trouble is in your imagination?"

Jane would, of course, answer: "But, Alan, I'm not making all of this up. You can hardly get out of bed in the morning. Lots of times you can't even make it to the office. And look at how often we quarrel. Think of how long it's been since you enjoyed life.

And Alan might reply: "You're exaggerating just like you always do. Sure, we fight. Who doesn't? Sure, I hate to go to work. So would you if you had to work for my boss."

"But, Alan, you could die of this. We have to do something. You have to have treatment."

"Look, Baby, you take care of yourself, and let me worry about me. I know what's wrong with me, and if I think anything needs doing, I'll do it."

"You've got to have help!"

"Don't tell me what I have to have! I'll look after myself!"

In the circumstances of physical illness, this a wildly improbable dialogue. No one with a life-threatening disease would bury his head in the sand and stubbornly insist that nothing was happening to him, that he was perfectly all right, that all he needed was to pull himself together. But alcoholism is a life-threatening condition and this is the dialogue, or some variation of it, that is likely to ensue when the co-alcoholic attempts to sit down with the alcoholic and say: "This is what we're up against. We're not dealing with your intransigence and my unreasonableness. We're dealing with a specific problem. You're an alcoholic. Now what are we going to do about it?"

The alcoholic's response, stripped of its surround of verbiage, gestures, sighs, silences, and explosions, will essentially follow the lines of an old joke in which a housewife accuses a neighbor of not returning a borrowed pan and gets the following argument: "In the first place I never borrowed your pan. In the second place it had holes in it. In the third place I returned it yesterday." The alcoholic will claim: "In the first place I'm not an alcoholic. In the second place there's no cure for alcoholism. In the third place I'll cure myself." Funny or not, it is terribly true. I have never battled with an alcoholic in an attempt to make him face his drinking problem without having him break from one to another of these positions in such wily fashion that it is almost impossible to pin him into the ultimate corner that he is an alcoholic and that he must do something about it.

If the improbable dialogue between Jane and Alan F. had actually taken place and the gift of clarity she had held out in optimism and relief had withered in her hands, what might she have decided to do? Would she leave him because she couldn't bear to watch his downhill course? Would she make up her mind to stay with him but say nothing more and simply wait until his worsening condition made it impossible for him to deny its seriousness? Or would she look after him energetically and fight daily to urge the truth upon him?

These are the choices that confront the co-alcoholic. She can leave the alcoholic. Many co-alcoholics do, and it is sometimes the sensible course. But often the diagnosis of alcoholism is perversely riveting. The condition has been so insistently defined as an illness that to walk out on an alcoholic appears equivalent to abandoning someone sorely sick, and this goes counter to the co-alcoholic's decent instincts. Whether she conceives of it as an illness or not, the remedy for the condition is so tantalizingly apparent that the co-alcoholic tends to live on in hope, either patiently waiting for the events that will force the alcoholic to recognize his jeopardy or vocally attempting to storm his wall of denial. Too, the alcoholic is masterful at manipulating those who love him with mea culpas, resolutions, new starts, demonstrations of helplessness, threats of total collapse or suicide, and the painful tears of shame and guilt. Thus, bound by her own hope and the alcoholic's claims on her love and tolerance, the co-alcoholic, when she is confident of the diagnosis of alcoholism, usually finds herself up against the next problem: not of how to separate from the alcoholic, but of how to live with him in such fashion that she may eventually be instrumental in helping him but in the meantime will not collaborate in the destruction of her own life.

6

Acceptance of Alcoholism

The person who stays with the alcoholic does so out of hope, hope that someday the drinking will end, the nightmare will be over, and life will resume its normal course. It is this hope that sustains the co-alcoholic. She believes that without it she could not go on, that if she were to give up hope, she would be defeated and life with the alcoholic would be intolerable. But hope can be a terrible trap for the co-alcoholic.

She hopes against hope that the alcoholic's promises will be kept. They are not. She hopes that he will live up to his good resolutions. He cannot. She hopes that a miracle will take place. It does not. Over the years, freshly wounded each time her hope is crushed, the co-alcoholic may become a deadened mass of scar tissue, like a friend of mine who, once alive and zestful and curious and interested and intelligent, now has a burned-out quality as though her life has lost its richness and meaning and purpose and she is merely existing. Only occasionally in conversation does her old spark flare and does the person she once was shine through. Only very occasionally is she goaded by her husband's drinking into an independent action like standing up and walking out of a restaurant before her husband is ready to permit himself to be taken home. For the most part, this co-alcoholic's life is blanketed in apathy, the apathy born of repeated frustration of hope.

Another wife does not seem to have lost hope in that, almost incredibly, after thirty years of life with a drinker, she still whines and scolds and cajoles and pleads, but the monotonous voice in which she pays out her worn phrases suggests that she is speaking out of long-entrenched habit rather than out of any persuasion that she will be heeded. Although it is a cruel judgment, the fact is that she with her droning has become as tiresome as her husband with his drinking.

Both women, in clinging to hope, have lost themselves. They have endured, but alcoholism has prevailed. They live on in defeat, empty shells where once they were sensitive, responsive, fully alive human beings.

For every co-alcoholic who endures, there is another who convulsively breaks free when the repeated scything of her hope finally shrivels its roots and optimism cannot rise again. An acquaintance of mine, in love with a man whose wife had left him because of his drinking, was not so incautious that she would marry him, but she lived with him, hopeful that her imaginative caretaking would make the difference in straightening him out. He was a pediatrician, and invariably by mid-evening he would be too drunk to answer the telephone, forcing her to take calls from worried mothers, relay their description of symptoms to him, and then repeat his instructions into the phone. One night, after a two a.m. call, she hung up the phone and thought, "What am I doing? A child could die because I'm trying to protect this man." As she gazed at his sprawled body with its lolling head, the conviction that he could be saved suddenly seemed quixotic, and hope hemorrhaged from her, leaving her cold and empty. The next morning she left him, and two weeks of uninterrupted drinking later the man himself was dead.

This woman had believed she could be curative. All of us who are co-alcoholics secretly pin our hopes on this. We are a self-appointed Salvation Army. We harbor the ego-building fantasy of being the instrument of the alcoholic's reform. Altruistic, self-sacrificing, even a bit noble, we expect praise, appreciation, and eventual triumph, and when, instead, we are repeatedly dealt blame, rebuff, and failure, we may finally turn on the alcoholic, pronounce him incurable, and abandon him.

But perhaps it is hope itself that defeats us. Perhaps, rather than being the staff which supports us, it is the rod with which we are beaten down. Take the instance of Maria M. She told me over lunch that she had gone so far the day before as to wait outside her husband's office with the notion of persuading him to go directly home instead of to a bar as he customarily did. He, with a look of frozen fury, had brushed past her and that night had lurched home only long after midnight and far more disastrously drunk than usual. "I suppose it was the wrong thing to do," she admitted, "but I've tried everything else and nothing has worked."

I was having lunch with her at the request of a woman in Mr. M.'s office who had heard, through a mutual friend, that I was engaged in writing this book. Although quickly certain that I wouldn't be able to tell her what she wanted to hear, I had no objection to listening to her story, which was a familiar one in outline if not in detail. She and Rafe, her husband, both born and raised in a Central American country, had come to the United States eight years before when he was appointed manager of an import-export company. Always a man who liked his liquor, Rafe had enthusiastically embraced the American custom of conducting business over the three-martini lunch. Soon, to counteract the afternoon letdown, he was leaving his office early and settling himself in a corner at his favorite bar for some serious solitary drinking. At whatever time he made it home, he demanded his dinner, ate it in stupefied silence, and either crawled into bed or tapered off with cans of beer in front of the T.V. set.

Maria had, of course, made uncounted attempts to talk to Rafe about his drinking. When she found that these efforts led only to growled rebuffs or noisy fights, she switched to forbearance, but this was no more influential than talk, so she tried emptying his whiskey and beer bottles and hiding his money, but this propelled him out of the house to a bar where he had credit and condemned her to evenings of cold sweat as she imagined him struck by a car or rolled by muggers. Hearing of A.A., she asked for help there, only to find that they could offer none unless the drinker himself was ready to accept it. They did refer her to Al-Anon, however, and she attended a few meetings before Rafe discovered where she was spending her evenings and, incensed both that she defined him as alcoholic and, as he said, discussed their private life in public, threatened to walk out on her if she did not withdraw.

What Maria wanted from me was some new hope to cling to. But was her problem the question of how to keep on hoping, or was it the fact that she continued to cling to hope that was the source of much of her agonizing? Their move to New York had originally been full of promise because she was intensely interested in becoming a painter and this was her opportunity to study with accomplished teachers. After one semester, however, she had dropped out of her classes because, in casting about for reasons which might explain Rafe's escalating drinking problem, it had occurred to her that Rafe might be resentful of her absorption in an endeavor he could not share. And after an incident in which Rafe had, whether intentionally or accidentally, damaged a painting she was working on, she had retired her canvases to a closet and not touched them again.

A companionable person, she had begun in this country to establish a circle of friends, but, again on the supposition that Rafe might be jealous, she had withdrawn from social contacts. Some part of her withdrawal was prompted by reluctance to expose her friends to her husband's drunkenness, but she was also proving her loyalty to Rafe by demonstrating the sacrifices she was willing to make for him. Although Maria did not describe the scenes between them, it took little imagination to picture how often she had bravely displayed her stigmata and reconstruct her gentle voice saying plaintively, "Rafe, tell me what more I can do? I've done this and this and this, and nothing seems to make any difference. Tell me what it is you want. I'll do anything to make things right for you." Having listened to enough co-alcoholics and remembering my own pleas in similar circumstances, I know that Maria could not help but sound like the long-suffering mother of a wayward child who says: "Look at all I've done for you. Look at how I've sacrificed my own life." What none of us adds but all of us imply is: "You owe it to me to reward me by behaving as I want you to behave."

Like the hapless child, the alcoholic wants to shout, "I didn't ask you to!" Like the child saddled with guilt for the misbehavior he seems perversely driven to, the alcoholic bristles with defensiveness. His remorse for the disappointment he causes is matched only by his resentment at having to carry such a heavy burden of responsibility for someone else's unhappiness. He longs to be left in peace, but since he cannot do without his protector, he drinks to still his own conscience and the echo of the sad voice pleading with him to be good.

And when he drinks, what is he met with? More patience, more forbearance, more sighs of stifled blame. Whatever the co-alcoholic's literal words, the message behind them is: "See how hard I try. See how reasonable I try to be with you. How can you let me down this way?" And back to drink he goes, and the alternating current of drink, sacrifice, drink, pleas, drink, forgiveness continues.

Why? Because the current is energized by hope. My mother did not drink because of anything I did or did not do, and I could not right her world, any more than Maria can right Rafe's world or my friend could have righted the pediatrician's world. All our self-sacrificing efforts only perpetuate the problem they are meant to solve, but hope, until it dies, condemns us to repeat them. Why, then, do we struggle so to hold on to hope? Perhaps because we cannot think of anything else to do.

A co-alcoholic who found an alternative was a woman I shall call Ellen Gunther. As a child, I knew about Richard Gunther's drinking. It was impossible not to, for he went on ten-day binges during which he was obscenely drunk night and day. Ellen often took refuge with my parents, and Richard would come looking for her, weaving up the front walk to our house and shouting curses as he pounded on the front door demanding to be let in. If my father could not persuade him to go away, the police would have to be called, and he would be hustled off to jail until he sobered up.

Between binges, Richard Gunther was a pleasant man with a sense of humor and a capacity for the simple pleasures his wife enjoyed, such as picnics, drives in the country, and bridge games with friends. This coupled with the fact that he was such a first-rate salesman that his employer tolerated his drunks and he never lost his job, made it not entirely mystifying why Ellen stayed with him. She loved him, and he was sober enough of the time to feed her hope that someday his drinking would end. It never did. Eventually, Richard died during a drinking bout from an inadvertent mixture of sleeping pills and liquor. But long before that, his binges had grown infrequent, their internecine wars had ended, and Ellen no longer fled the house to escape him. There were long stretches when Richard did not drink at all, and when he did relapse, Ellen did not lose the serenity, the composure, compassion, and stability that had come to replace her former fearfulness, fault-finding, and depression and that grew to be strikingly characteristic of her.

At the time, in the way of a child, I did not wonder at the change in her and at the difference in her relationship to Richard. But years later, I asked her about it. It was not an idle question, for again I was involved with an alcoholic, again, as a friend, incredulous that I had not learned from experience, remarked, I was "back doing business at the same old stand," pouring love and support into a drinker and hoping against hope that he could be changed.

"How did you manage?" I asked Ellen. "How were you able to go on?"

"I stopped hoping," she said. She spread her hands as if to say that the answer was as simple and complete as that. And in a way the answer *is* as simple and complete as that.

"In the early years," she said, "the years you remember, I didn't think I could go on. Richard was thirty-eight when we married, and he was a heavy drinker, I knew that, but I thought it was because he was a bachelor and a salesman, and, like a foolish schoolgirl, I thought I was going to be the one to reform him. I thought all it was going to take was a loving wife and an attractive apartment and a good dinner to come home to every evening. I think even he believed it might be the answer. But it wasn't, of course. It never is. No alcoholic drinks because he doesn't have these, and no alcoholic stops because he does.

"But I didn't know that then, so I kept on hoping. Richard was a great one for promises, as what alcoholic isn't, and I wanted to believe him, so I listened after each drunk when he said it was his last. And if he stayed sober for any length of time, I was convinced that our troubles were over. I would grow foolishly happy. But no drunk was ever the last. Sooner or later, he would lapse, and I would be shattered. I felt it as a terrible betrayal, really the most crushing blow, and finally I couldn't take it any more. I made up my mind to leave him."

Ellen described how, with her suitcases packed and ready at the door, she made one last circuit of the apartment to see if she had forgotten anything. Unbidden, there arose the picture of Richard's return home. He would sit in his armchair and drink until he passed out. That was nothing new; he would do that even if she were there. But what of the morning? Would he reach for the bottle of orange juice—or the bottle of whiskey? Would he swallow some food to get him on his feet—or some pills? Without her there, would he drink past the point of no return? Would this be the drunk he did not come out of? She hesitated at the door, suspended between, "How can I leave him?" and the equally despairing, "How can I stay with him?"

"I stood there with tears running down my face," Ellen said, "telling myself there was no hope, he was an alcoholic, he'd never be anything else, and I couldn't live with that. But I was also remembering that he was my friend as well as my husband, that he was a kind and decent and loving man as well as a drunk, that there were good times in our life as well as the horrors. He was the only man I'd ever known that I wanted to spend my life with, and, to be perfectly honest, I didn't want to be alone, I didn't want not to have a husband. All I wanted was the impossible: Richard and a life that did not include his drinking.

"If I stayed, it would have to be Richard *and* his drinking, I knew that. Then I had a funny thought." Ellen looked at me half-apologetically, as people do when they are afraid they might be laughed at. "It was one of those silly sayings: As you go through life, keep your eye upon the doughnut, not upon the hole. I said to myself, 'Well, Girl, you sure got the hole,' and I picked up my suitcase and opened the door. But I couldn't walk through it. I went back and sat down and lit a cigarette, and that idiotic sentence kept coming back. Finally, I really began to think about it.

"Was there a doughnut? Richard was a drunk, yes, but he wasn't drunk all the time. There were the sober times, too. Except that I spoiled these because I fretted and nagged and cried and tried to force promises from him. I never took my eye off the hole. I acted as though the hole was everything, the doughnut nothing. In a way, I was as responsible for the ruin of our life as he was. Because I insisted he had to stop drinking. Because I had to have hope to live on.

"Suppose I didn't insist? Suppose I accepted that he would always drink? I had survived his drunks up until now. Why couldn't I go on surviving them if I knew—if I really made myself know—that there would always be a next time? Always before, I had said that I would stay with him if. . . . If *he* stopped drinking. Now I said I will stay with him if. . . . If *I* can make myself give up hope that he will stop drinking."

The condition she had made was not for Richard, but for herself. The promise she had exacted was not from Richard, but from herself. She stayed, and in the end, it was the doughnut that had mattered, not the hole. The hole was always there, but as it shrank in importance, there grew between them a rare gentleness and generosity, a respect for each other as persons, a quality perhaps best described as an affirmation of each other. Ellen, in freeing herself of hope, had freed herself of dread and Richard of the inevitability of failing her.

If the co-alcoholic is not to abandon herself to apathy and defeat or, alternatively, if she is not to abandon the alcoholic, perhaps it is hope that she must give up. Perhaps she must say: So be it. He is an alcoholic. So be it. I cannot cure him. So be it. He may always drink. So be it.

In the place of hope, what is there? *Acceptance*. Acceptance not just of the concept of alcoholism but of the specific, realistic fact of the drinking. All of us who are co-alcoholics pay lip service to the idea of alcoholism. We acknowledge that it is a condition in which, by definition, the drinker has lost control over his drinking, but then we turn right around and say, "Stop it. Stop it for my sake. Stop it because you love me." The difficulty is, of course, that, almost unconsciously, we are making a distinction between alcoholism, a condition not subject to voluntary control, and drinking, an activity the person willfully engages in. Because the liquor does not go down the alcoholic's throat unless he raises the glass to his mouth, we assume an intermediate stage of purposefulness. We believe he is sick, but sick by his own hand, sick by virtue of an act he can desist from, and thus we make it a contest of wills between ourselves and the alcoholic. We put our lives, our welfare, our happiness, and our ego, that ego which says we can, we must, we *shall* be curative, on the line, and we announce that these are the stakes we are playing for.

How unrealistic we would think ourselves for doing this if the person had, for example, arthritis, if every flare-up of the condition we took as a personal attack, an indication that the person was heedless of our peace of mind, was indifferent to our wishes, was defiant in the face of our threats. We would think ourselves ostriches if we did not expect relapses and take them in stride. We would think ourselves children not to be able to absorb disappointment, not to be able to accept a situation as it is, because it is. We would think ourselves fools, or worse, if we bet our lives and happiness on the absolute, perfect control of the condition. But, in dealing with alcoholism, this is the trap that hope baits.

To avoid the trap, to remain buoyant in the face of setbacks, to protect the quality of her life with the alcoholic, the co-alcoholic must accept the drinking as well as the alcoholism. She must accept that there will never be a certain end to the drinking. She must tell herself that it will recur, that another drunk is always around the corner, any corner, that it can come at any time. She must make herself believe this, as truly and as deeply and with as much conviction as she has ever believed anything, believe it in her bones, her heart, her brain, every recess of her being. She m st root out all hope. If she finds herself whispering, "Maybe this time . . . ," she must quash the treacherous phrase and replace it with the stern, "No. No, not this time. Not ever. He is an alcoholic. He will drink again."

To live with an alcoholic requires an act of faith—faith, not in the alcoholic, but in oneself, faith that one has the stamina to weather disappointments, the humor to preserve perspective, and, most of all, the courage to deny oneself the luxury of hope. To live without hope. What a spirit-shriveling phrase that is if one does not think it through. Maria M. seemed to grow smaller in the chair across the lunch table when I broached the possibility. "Oh, no," she said. "Oh, no, I couldn't do that. I *have* to believe he will stop." She reached for her pocketbook, the check, her gloves, fumbling in sudden anxiety to be gone. "No, what I'm going to do is write to the president of his company and ask him to fire him," she said. Her voice became firm, as though, by suggesting the unthinkable, I had crystallized a slowly growing resolve in her. "Then we'll have to go back to our own country, and our families will help me to get him straightened out."

As we said good-bye and I watched her walk away, I thought of how vulnerable all of us who are co-alcoholics are to the puppeteer effect. We attempt to manipulate, guide, restrain, and control the alcoholic, never realizing that the strings that run from us to the alcoholic run from the alcoholic to us as well. We slacken and tighten the strings, make an adjustment here, a maneuver there, hoping to stumble upon the tug that will make it come right, and all the time we are being controlled by the alcoholism just as inexorably as is the drinker. And perhaps just as destructively.

I might have told Maria M. a homely anecdote of something that had happened that morning. My neighbors had gone away for a few days, leaving their large dog in my care, which was a bit of a nuisance because the dog was strong and always strained at the leash. In the course of walking him, I had stopped at the laundromat where I collected three bundles of heavy washing and then wondered how I was going to get both dog and load home. Expecting gloomily that my bundles would land in the gutter, I started out, and, surprisingly, the dog walked sedately at my heels, brushing against me at each step as if to reassure himself that I was there. I found out why when we arrived at the front door. In picking up the bundles, I had inadvertently dropped his leash, and, far from dashing off, without me to control him, he had grown anxious and controlled himself.

Would Maria's Rafe, released from restraint by her acceptance of his drinking, have grown anxious and controlled himself? Perhaps not. But Maria, in freeing him, would have freed herself—to paint, to make friends, to turn her own life into a going concern. And that is all the co-alcoholic can do. She cannot change the alcoholic. She can only prevent herself from being changed by him. She cannot make the alcoholic behave well, but she can prevent him from making her behave badly. She cannot control his life, but she can regain control over her own. She can hold on to initiative and courage, sanity and strength, and she can protect their joint life by accepting his alcoholism and refusing herself the illusion of hope that cannot help but cause her to grow embittered.

The co-alcoholic who tries to impose her will on the alcoholic is condemned to a life of resentment, hostility, and despair. The person she is becomes lost in a set of reactions to someone else's actions. Each disappointment makes her a little more worn, a little more eaten by rancor, a little more painfully aware of the futility of her efforts. But if she can give up hope, if she can accept that alcoholism is a chronic condition not subject to her will or her wish, the problem falls into a different perspective. No longer is it one person battling the weak or callous or destructive behavior of the other, but two people faced with a common problem. No longer is it one person attempting to dominate another, but two people trying to make a life together despite a common enemy. No longer is it one person acting as judge, jury, and potential executioner of the other, but two people released to make the choices each alone can make.

The alcoholic may never make the right choice. He may never stop drinking. So be it. The co-alcoholic cannot force him to. She can only leave him room to make the choice, not simply because ultimately everyone must make his own choices but because the alcoholic is the only person who can make this one—and make it stick. The co-alcoholic's choice does not concern the drinking; it is only whether to stay or whether to go.

If the co-alcoholic gazes down the corridor of time and finds herself shrinking from the prospect of a life in which there will never be a final end to the drinking, if she cannot conceive of living without this hope, she should give up and get out. If the doughnut is insignificant in relation to the terrible hole, she should cut her losses and go, for in the end, even if the alcoholic should stop drinking, there will prove to have been little worth saving anyhow and it is best that she save herself the benumbing journey. But if there is much that is valuable in the person and in the relationship, she must find what Dag Hammarskjold, in his book *Markings,* spoke of as the "strength to say Yes . . ." to one's fate, whatever life decrees that fate to be.

Looking around at other people's lives uncomplicated by the cruel burden of alcoholism, the co-alcoholic may want to cry out, "Why me? Why should I have to be the one to live with alcoholism?" It is a very human plaint, but there is a very simple answer. A doctor to whom I was talking recently gave it when he remarked that the most frequent question he heard from his patients was: Why? Why have I been the one to have a stroke or get cancer or break a leg in a fall? His impulse, he said, was always to answer: Why not? It is bound to happen to someone, why not you? And, indeed, why not? No one is immune from the vagaries of fate, and if a particular fate seems arbitrary and undeserved, as that of living with alcoholism so often does, it is nevertheless real, and defeat at its hands can only be avoided by acceding realistically to those things about it which cannot be changed.

I was lately thinking of this in another context while listening to the discontented voice of a friend on the telephone describing the latest in her series of trips undertaken with the intent of finding herself a husband. Unable to accept her fate of singleness, with each passing year she grows more querulous, more panicky, more absorbed by her search. Life, she feels, is passing her by, and, of course, it is, for she enjoys nothing she has in her preoccupying quest for what she does not have. In contrast, I had just read a charming article by a writer who, at thirty, had faced the fact that her chances of marrying were slight and had set about making her single life completely viable and enjoyable by filling it with friends and work and cats and her absorbing hobbies of amateur musicianship and photography. Now, at 51, she was writing of the totally improbable and deliciously upsetting event that had happened to her: marriage to an attractive man of worth and accomplishment.

There is wisdom in the paradoxical observation that you will never be happy until you know you will never be happy. My friend defines happiness as marriage, and she rushes through life, bitterly unhappy, in search of it. Ellen Gunther once defined happiness as her husband's sobriety, and she was bitterly unhappy until she recognized that she would never be happy. Richard Gunther remained an alcoholic until his death, but Ellen Gunther was not diminished by his drinking. She did not grow small and mean and dispirited. She became every inch the person she had the potentiality of being, and she lived, in decency and dignity, with the man she loved. By accepting her fate as a co-alcoholic, she transcended it.

Acceptance of the fate of being a co-alcoholic does not imply resignation. It does not mean passive submission. It is a long, clear look at the circumstances of one's life and the simple acknowledgment, made without dread or distaste, of the specific circumstances that one is powerless to change. When one can say to the drinker, "From now on, it is your choice whether to drink or not. I cannot stop you and I shall no longer try," it is not a sentence but a parole. In freeing the alcoholic, one frees oneself to become a person in one's own right.

And the alcoholic may become unexpectedly less free. I laughed aloud when the alcoholic to whom I said the choice to drink was his, that I would no longer try to stop him, was silent for a moment and then remarked plaintively, "But I could kill myself with all this drinking." I had spent months and years arguing that people die of alcoholism, that it is a devastating insult to the body, that sooner or later it destroys, and always the answer had been: "Other people, not me. It won't get me." In a sense, by worrying, by arguing, I had acted as the repository of his fears, and in me, they could be ignored. But when I refused him the arguments, suddenly they were inside his own mind. When I dropped the strings, he had to hold himself upright if he was not to go smash. When I let go of the leash, he had to rein himself in if he was not to be lost.

He drinks far less frequently now, and he has been able to do what for him is an extraordinary thing. Always before, once the drinking began, he could not stop until it had run its course, until, that is, he was too ill and debilitated and exhausted to go on. But lately he has been able to stop after a few days of heavy but not catastrophic drinking, and lately he has begun to speak, almost confidently, of being able to envision a time when he will not wish to drink at all. I say very little, not only because I want to protect both of us from becoming trapped again in hope, but because it genuinely makes very little difference to me. I would be pleased if it proved to be so, but the one week out of every eight or ten that he drinks does not seem that important any more.

On one of the infrequent occasions when we have spoken of his changed pattern of drinking, he asked if I knew what had made the difference. "It was your saying that I would drink for the rest of my life," he commented. "It made me mad. I said to myself, 'How does she know? I don't have to if I don't want to.' And that made me think for the first time that I really do have a choice, that it really is up to me."

In psychoanalysis, it is said that the analysis is over when the patient realizes it can go on forever. It is tempting to say that, in alcoholism, the drinking is over when the alcoholic realizes it can go on forever. But alcoholism is an addiction. It is a difficult, stubborn, often intractable condition, and all that can be said with certainty is not that the drinking will end with the co-alcoholic's acceptance of alcoholism but that she will be able to go on.

7

Co-Alcoholism

Acceptance of alcoholism is not an easy answer to the problems of dealing with an alcoholic. Perhaps only the co-alcoholic who has exhausted her repertoire of tricks, traps, and threats—and is no longer able to hide from herself their ineffectiveness—will be able and willing to consider it. But even she must be careful not to embrace this approach too hastily, for it can readily be skewed to provide a rationale for old ways of behaving instead of a stimulus for new.

Just how readily this can happen became disconcertingly apparent when I explored with two very different co-alcoholics, both intelligent and imaginative women, the tenet that a frontal assault on alcoholism more often fails than succeeds. Both women felt that acceptance of alcoholism was possible and feasible. Both welcomed it as a fresh approach that held promise of releasing them from their sterile struggles. Both were utterly sincere in putting it into effect. And both found their situations perceptibly worsened by it.

Christine D., one of the two women, an articulate, forceful, strong-willed person married to an alcoholic who admires and adores her but suspects she despises him as he despises himself, had been handling her husband's alcoholism by a stubborn, bland facade of denial. She kept the two of them involved in an extremely active social life, and never once did she permit his drinking to interfere with it. They regularly attended the theatre, opera, and ballet, and the heavy breathing that indicated Evan was asleep within five minutes of the curtain's going up went unacknowledged, with Christine, at intermission, discussing the performance exactly as though Evan had absorbed every nuance of it. In a social gathering when, as the evening wore on, Evan became too befuddled to speak coherently, she nevertheless included him in the conversation as though he were a contributing member of the group, and I have seen him at dinner parties of their own, although almost too drunk to stand, propelled to his feet by her quiet statement to a woman guest, "Evan will see you to a taxi." A current of will passing from Christine to him animated Evan just sufficiently to keep him staggering through the social motions.

Persuaded that it may be more fruitful to accept alcoholism than to battle it, Christine shut off that current of will. She continued to ignore Evan's drinking, but additionally she began to ignore Evan as well. Where before she had acted as though the drinking did not exist, now she acted as though Evan did not exist. One small but epitomizing incident was her purchase of two season tickets to the opera, as usual, but then her prompt gift of the second ticket to a friend who shared her passion for music. When Evan questioned his exclusion, she informed him that for years past he had spoiled her pleasure in the performances and that now she intended to go without him, as, indeed, she now intended to do a great many things without him. What she conveyed to Evan, in acting on what she understood acceptance of alcoholism to mean, was that she had to put up with his drinking but that she did not have to put up with him. A hands-off attitude about the drinking resulted, in practice, in a writing-off of the alcoholic, and this, understandably, so frightened and dismayed Evan that he promptly lost the last semblance of control over his drinking.

The second woman, Judy P., also listened to the whole of my reasoning and heard only a part, that part which seemingly lent theoretical support to her already characteristic manner of coping with her husband's alcoholism. A quiet, patient, unassertive person by nature, Judy took acceptance of alcoholism to be akin to acceptance of God's will, as though her husband's alcoholism was a tribulation she must bear in stoicism. Long on the verge of leaving her husband Douglas, she decided instead to accept his alcoholism and made the immediate mistake of telling him so and of her resolution to make a normal life for them. The most apparent form her resolution took was a reversal of her previous stand against inviting guests to their home because of Douglas's boorish behavior when drunk. Now she promised herself to carry on normally, neither commenting nor cringing no matter how humiliating his behavior.

The effort this cost her was apparent on an evening when I had dinner with them. Since one of Douglas's traits when drunk is a maddening insistence on being helpful, Judy had been accustomed to leaping up almost in the middle of a meal to forestall his clumsy attempts to clear the table, but on this occasion she sat on, talking unconcernedly and taking no notice of him as he fumbled and lurched between dining room and kitchen. A heart-stopping crash in the kitchen made her turn white, but after a weak joke about the last of the heirloom Spode, she picked up the thread of conversation. Douglas peered shamefacedly at her when he returned, but when she said nothing, he straightened and grew contemptuous. "Look at her," he taunted, "sitting there so well-bred, just like the good little girl her mother taught her to be. She thinks I'm a pig, but she hasn't got the guts to say so." Much of the evening went like that, with Judy carrying on as though nothing was amiss and Douglas goading her with more and more outrageous taunts.

Like Christine, Judy had adopted a hands-off attitude toward her husband's drinking, but, whereas it had led Christine to write off her husband, it led Judy to write off herself, with unhappy consequences in each instance. Given the personalities of the two women, perhaps this was not surprising, but it was not necessarily inevitable. Had either of them made an effort to analyze her characteristic behavior and then explored the idea of the acceptance of alcoholism for the clues it offered to new and different behavior, she might have made a fresh start instead of using the concept to legitimize old and bankrupt approaches. Christine, for example, had she identified her propensity for handling a problem by refusing to recognize its existence, might well have bought two tickets to the opera but, rather than making a unilateral decision that she would attend without Evan, talked it over with him and offered him a choice. It would be his option to drink if he wished on the designated evening, but she would reserve to herself the choice to invite someone else to accompany her if he was not sober. In the instance of Judy, had she recognized that she had already exhausted every dodge of patience and forbearance, how much better if she had stated her intention to reinstitute a normal life for them but with the proviso that she would unhesitatingly cancel all plans if Douglas came home drunk. He could drink if he wished, but if he did, she would exercise her option not to be forced to undergo an evening of embarrassment.

There is no attribution of blame in either of these courses. There is no attempt to control. There is no coercion or pressure or abrogation of prerogatives. There is only sensible acknowledgment of the right of each person to make his own choices. But perhaps it is exactly this right that the co-alcoholic does not wish the alcoholic to have. Accustomed to thinking in terms of ways of chivying the alcoholic into remaining sober, the co-alcoholic is likely to go no further in her acceptance of alcoholism than the use of it as one more ploy in a long campaign, as these women did. The approach was different, but the intent remained the same: to pressure the alcoholic into behaving differently. Each wished the alcoholic to make a choice—but only the choice she wished him to make.

In an article * essentially describing how difficult it is to leave it to individuals to make their own choices instead of insisting that they must want what one wants for them, the American psychologist Harold N. Boris fashioned a telling analogy to the foreign policy of the United States:

> In the national sphere there is on the one side the fervor of the Foster Dulles, Dean Rusk position, with its difficulties concerning neutrality and its missionary attitude toward cultural differences. This establishment, if it

* Boris, H. N.: "The 'Seelsorger' in Rural Vermont." *International Journal of Group Psychotherapy,* 21:159-173, 1971.

can be called that, appears to have in mind certain goods —self-determination and autonomy—which it wants for the world, so much so that it seems at times to such critics of the establishment as Senator Fulbright that in the name of fulfilling what it takes to be universal aspirations, it positively wishes to impose these goods. The anti-establishmentarianists hold that to want these goods for our sister nations really means wanting things *from* them, thus constituting, in Fulbright's phrase, the exercise of an arrogance of power. They observe that to enforce self-determination is a contradiction in terms, while to impose autonomy constitutes a usurpation of it.

Although Mr. Boris goes on to extend his analogy to a quite different sphere from that of alcoholism, it has many points of validity for the co-alcoholic. The co-alcoholic has a foreign policy, so to speak, which she pursues with missionary fervor: that of reforming the alcoholic into a sober, conscientious, upright member of society. Since society views self-determination and autonomy—that is, dominion over one's own behavior and the pattern of one's life—as a universal aspiration, she ostensibly wants these desiderata *for* him, but, in reality, she wants to impose self-determination and autonomy on him because she wants certain things *from* him, to wit, a changed style of life and a responsible standard of behavior. In the exercise of an arrogance of power, she decrees his self-determination, a contradiction in terms, and she insists that he assume autonomy, a usurpation of it.

Just as the United States, in attempting to guarantee the self-determination and autonomy of South Vietnam, has inadvertently abolished them, so the co-alcoholic, in attempting to force the alcoholic into asserting control over his life, has unwittingly preempted control of his life. It can be argued that South Vietnam, internally weak and externally beset, is in no position to exercise self-determination and autonomy. True. It may be argued that the alcoholic, internally weak and externally beset, is in no position to exercise self-determination and autonomy. Also true. But the incontrovertible fact remains that, however laudable the motives for interference in the conduct of the affairs of another country or another person, the interference itself subverts the aims it is intended to achieve. One may intervene to help, to protect, to support, but one cannot intervene to bring about self-determination and autonomy. These, by definition, exist only when the interested partner pursues a strict policy of nonintervention.

Christine attempted to impose autonomy on her husband by going her own way, but, by denying him any part in the decision, she usurped his autonomy. If he did not have a choice between behavior which would lead to his going to the opera or staying home, he did not have a choice, and without the latitude to make choices, there is no autonomy. Judy, for her part, attempted to impose self-determination on her husband, but, by assuming he would use it in ways she had already determined, she denied him self-determination. If he could not choose to behave badly just as freely as he could choose to behave well, his behavior was not self-determined. Both women, believing that they were presenting either/or situations, were, in actuality, saying either/and. Christine did not communicate to her husband: Either you stay sober or you stay home, but: Either you stay sober and you stay home. Judy was not saying: Either you drink or we entertain, but: Either you drink and we entertain.

The alcoholic, if he is to appreciate himself as an individual of free will whose fate is in his own hands, must recognize that he has options. And the option not to drink does not exist unless it is coupled with the option to drink. For him to have a choice, the co-alcoholic's foreign policy toward the drinking must be one of neutrality, and it is this that acceptance of alcoholism is intended to permit her. Accepting that the alcoholic drinks, that he may always drink, she must set about living with his drinking in ways which make it clear that the choice of whether or not he will drink at any given time is up to him. She must grant him true alternatives and leave the choice between them to him, genuinely accepting his choice to drink so as to give him the genuine choice not to drink.

A decision to adopt a policy of neutrality toward the drinking does not mean, of course, that the co-alcoholic will cease to harbor intense feelings about it. Anger, irritation, and anxiety will still be present, and the co-alcoholic must not try to rid herself of these feelings. Indeed, perhaps she can only be neutral toward the drinking and leave off her attempts to control it—and the alcoholic—if she first candidly and forcefully brings into consciousness the entire range of emotional response the drinking engenders in her.

Because no one who lives with an alcoholic has not flared into rage or screamed in denunciation or wept in frustration and hurt, it can be argued that the co-alcoholic has all-too-ready access to her feelings. But outbursts have a way of appearing to be isolated responses to extreme provocation, and often the co-alcoholic remains essentially unknowing of how deep is her anger, how pervasive her frustration, how enveloping her hurt. This was true of a woman I shall call Mary Edwards. With the exception of occasional crying jags, Mrs. Edwards had lived quietly and patiently with her husband's drinking for some years until one night, to her horror, she found herself snatching the glass from his hand and hurling it at him. Aghast at the realization that what she really wanted to do was grind the glass in his face, she stood transfixed for a moment. But then the last of her control deserted her, and she snatched up every movable object in the room and sent it crashing—at him, at the walls, through the windows. In a frenzy—screaming, laughing, sobbing—she rushed out into the street, where the police, called by alarmed neighbors, finally subdued her, summoned an ambulance, and bundled her off to the psychiatric ward of the city hospital.

Mrs. Edwards emerged from her psychotic storm, only to lapse into a severe depression which necessitated a series of shock treatments before she was accessible to psychotherapy. In treatment, she gingerly explored the field of rage and resentment which had spread in darkness far below the surface layers of composure and fortitude she had maintained for years, and eventually she came to accept these feelings as legitimate and allow them their justified existence. Had she been able to acknowledge them long before, however, and given them at least sporadic vent, they might never have built to the point of explosion.

Unacknowledged and unexplored feelings forcibly held out of consciousness are haunting and damaging. Even if they never erupt, they can corrupt the positive emotions and rob all of life of ease and enjoyment. The co-alcoholic who attempts not to be angry blunts her capacity for love and affection; only if she recognizes there is hate in her is she able to go on loving. The co-alcoholic who attempts to deny her pain undermines her capacity for pleasure; only if she reconnoiters the desolate landscape of her hurt is she able to respond to calmer pastures. The co-alcoholic who disowns her desire to retaliate lessens her capacity to relate sensitively to the drinker; only if she acknowledges her vengeful side can she appreciate the drinker as an individual with more than one side of his own.

If buried emotions are to be brought to consciousness, the first requisite is simple identification of how one characteristically behaves, which is not particularly difficult. Judy P., for example, were she to ask herself how she handled her husband's alcoholism, could readily answer that it was with patience and forgiveness and the awarding of innumerable second chances, and Christine D. would have no trouble in identifying her active pursuit of a facade of normality. Each, however, would have a problem in going on to deeper awareness, for it is a very human failing to agree with one's own behavior. Although too sophisticated a woman to voice pride in her ability to carry on, head high, tongue held, Christine would not think to question that the admirable way of handling problems is with unshakable good manners and a well-bred refusal to admit to the presence of ugliness. Nor would Judy be less than certain that a supplicating, undemanding approach which makes trouble for no one is commendable and desirable. Each woman approves of her respective attitude; it accords with her personal view of appropriate behavior; and, therefore, it does not occur to her to examine it further.

But a psychological truth having virtually the status of a law is that any trait strongly evident in the personality is so emphatically present in order to prevent the emergence of its opposite. In the light of this, if self-approval can be temporarily suspended and the possibility considered that the dominant behavior, however praiseworthy it may be in itself, is a defense against being driven to act on contradictory but coexisting feelings, some hint of those repressed feelings may be gained that, with a little effort, allows them to be teased into awareness. Judy, for instance, recognizing her patience but setting aside her approval of it, might catch a glimpse of the anger underlying her passivity, and Christine, acknowledging her propensity for active denial, might coax out the depression concealed behind her conscious impatience.

Since emotions are not repressed unless one feels them to be unbecoming, even reprehensible, certainly at odds with the general cast of the personality, one is disinclined to relax one's guard sufficiently to allow them to seep into consciousness, but hypothesizing the opposite of what one knows to be true is not a particularly threatening exercise and it can be unexpectedly revealing. If the fact is: I hate his dependence on me, the hypothesis becomes: I like being the stronger of the two of us. If the paramount complaint is: I always feel frustrated because I can't make plans, the hypothesis is: I'm glad of this excuse for not managing my life more sensibly. As outrageous as the hypothesis seems, if it is entertained for a few minutes, it may begin to gleam in the dark with some faint ray of truth.

If self-pity takes shape behind the pity, impatience behind the patience, intolerance behind the tolerance, the strong probability is not that one is true and the other false but that both are true. The conscious mind is disturbed by contradictions, but the unconscious mind has no objection to them at all. One is not only capable of harboring conflicting feelings; in nine out of ten instances one does. One loves and hates, is frustrated and gratified, is independent and dependent. And who would be more likely to inspire ambivalent reactions than the alcholic, with his seductive charm and outgoingness and loving nature and his equally evident demandingness and irresponsibility and self-centeredness?

The point of discovering buried feelings is not to downgrade an accepted feeling because at a deeper level its unacceptable opposite is also present but to allow both a place in consciousness so that a variety of behavior becomes possible. Judy P.'s situation would not be improved if she became chronically angry rather than chronically depressed, nor would Christine D.'s if she let her depression take over rather than galvanizing herself with anger. But if Judy recognized her anger and expressed it appropriately, as, for instance, when her husband baited her, she might be far less depressed, and she would validate that she was presenting her husband with genuine choices since she would be able to react appropriately if he came home drunk instead of being immobilized by the feelings of helplessness bound up with her depression. In similar fashion, Christine, recognizing her underlying depression and allowing it to appear in her voice and manner, would no longer have to flee from it in actions which, rather than giving her husband alternatives, deprived him of them.

As it was, failing to understand their buried feelings, both women simply redoubled their previous efforts. They did not, they could not, try new directions because they were driven by the same old feelings, a portion of which were unknown and unacceptable to them. There can be no flexibility of approach until hidden feelings have been exhumed and granted a place in consciousness, even an occasional release in behavior. It is sometimes necessary to be patient and forgiving and understanding, and it is sometimes appropriate to be angry and discouraged and rejecting, but it is never relevant to display one or another of these reactions in every situation. A blindly repeated response to a variety of provocations rigidifies the interaction between alcoholic and co-alcoholic, locking each in petrified positions which preclude change.

If there is to be a possibility of change in the alcoholic, the relationship must be opened up sufficiently to provide room for options, and since the co-alcoholic cannot force different behaviors upon the alcoholic, the only way in which she can crack apart the chronic mold of their interaction is by varying her own habitual reactions. To dredge up alien emotions and face them in all their bitter, mean, and narrow proportions and their startling intensity is initially dismaying, but the consequences can be rewarding, not only for the effect it may have in shaking up the alcoholic but in the unexpectedly greater ease and spontaneity the co-alcoholic can display in dealing with the alcoholic.

Indeed, a sense of increased ease, spontaneity, and flexibility is the test of whether or not the co-alcoholic, in attempting to put herself in touch with her buried feelings, has struck pay dirt. Making an effort to delineate the broad lines of her behavior and attitudes and then hypothesizing the presence of opposing emotions against which the behavior and attitudes are a defense is the tool for digging, but confirmation that she has uncovered some additional, contradictory but simultaneously present truths is obtained if awareness of them allows her to behave differently. For example, my own habitual stance is to be relentlessly understanding and tirelessly cerebral in coping with alcoholism, and it was inconceivable to me that somewhere behind the patient effort to understand might lie buried a cache of anger. The law of opposites was an entering wedge that pried my defenses apart just sufficiently to give me a hint of its presence, but still I was inclined to discount any significant amount of anger until I returned home one day to find a besotted body and heard myself shouting, "I don't give a damn what happened! I'm sick of your drunks!" Ordinarily, I would have spent hours delicately probing for the small, cumulative frustrations, disappointments, and ego blows which had necessitated the anesthetic and antiseptic application of alcohol, but this time, given the small crack to escape through, my anger had surfaced, and instead of engaging in my usual hand-holding exercise, I turned on my heel and went slamming out. Postulating that I might be angry had allowed me to behave differently, and the freedom to behave differently confirmed the presence of the anger.

In the circumstances, it was appropriate to be angry, far more appropriate than to sit in patient denial of my own feelings and choke back boredom and irritation as I listened to the excruciatingly familiar, rambling, unconvincing tissue of excuses. It was appropriate to go to a movie, for what need was there for me to spend a dreary evening just because the alcoholic had managed to fall from grace yet again? By the time I emerged from the movie, I could say, "Oh, well, I know he's an alcoholic. I know there are always going to be times like this. It's not so earth-shaking," and thus my own ability to accept alcoholism was strengthened.

This is not to say that, from then on, I always reacted angrily. As it happened, on the next occasion, I was as understanding as at any time in the past, but that was because I had seen the drunk coming, knew the reasons for it, and thought they were as "justified" as such reasons can be. What I had done, however, was add another string to my bow, seen there were alternative ways I could behave, and, in effect, given myself a choice. One of the very discouraging aspects of dealing with the alcoholic is the sense that the alcoholic can behave as he chooses, while, for one's own part, one is forced to take it, but that is not really true. An habitual type of reaction is not enforced by the alcoholic but imposed by the co-alcoholic on herself. If she recognizes this and enlarges her range of available responses, she feels freer, less dominated, more of an individual, and the alcoholism itself becomes a less discouraging fact because it is no longer so apparently all-controlling.

With the co-alcoholic liberated to choose between a variety of reactions, being sometimes tolerant and sympathetic, some-times enraged and accusing, sometimes indifferent and amused, sometimes impatient and irritable, the alcoholic cannot predict his reception when next he turns up drunk. He cannot be certain of what the co-alcoholic will do or say, and he cannot push all the familiar stops he has relied on in the past to restore the modus vivendi. If, for example, he has known that he will be greeted with harsh silence and that the silence will last until he has progressed through a set of ritualistic apologies and promises, he will be exceedingly disconcerted if the atmosphere is affable and his attempts at apology are waved aside. Similarly, if he is accustomed to understanding but is instead greeted with a screech of vilification, he is startled and must find different ways of his own to cope. When I returned home at midnight, for instance, I found not an unconscious alcoholic, as would ordinarily have been the case that far into the night, but a half-sober and thoroughly alarmed one. I had behaved unexpectedly and, in so doing, had forced him into uncharacteristic behavior. From that time on, he could not, perhaps more or less unconsciously, think, "If I drink, she will do so and so, and I know how to get around that." The safety in being able to predict my behavior was gone. If I could walk out and go to a movie, could I walk out and be gone for a week? Could I walk out and be gone forever? The possibility was there, and his certainty of what I would do if he drank had necessarily to turn into a nagging question: "If I drink, what will she do?" My having given myself choices was the beginning of making it clear that he had to think about his choices, not simply act characteristically in the confidence that I would react predictably.

In any situation, in all relationships, one is inclined to understand the other's behavior but not accept it and to accept one's own behavior but not understand it. It is no casual endeavor to amplify this customary approach by extending acceptance to the alcoholic and turning one's understanding on oneself, but, then, no one ever said it was a simple matter to live with alcoholism. If it is to be managed in decency, dignity, and full acknowledgment that each partner is a person in his own right, the co-alcoholic must try to understand her co-alcoholism so that she moves away from stereotypy into flexible, discriminating, self-selected and self-determined behavior. Confirming her own autonomy in this way, she may perhaps find that she has affirmed the autonomy of the alcoholic, which is to say that she genuinely accepts his alcoholism, not in passive, defeated acquiescence, not in dogged, self-perpetuating battle, not in flight from it, but in concerned neutrality, and thus, *pari passu,* has opened up options for the alcoholic by the very act of exercising her own.

8

Coexistence

"Life is easier to take than you'd think. All that is necessary is to accept the impossible, do without the indispensable, and bear the intolerable." These words, an observation made by Kathleen Norris, might have been written for the co-alcoholic, who must accept the impossible—alcoholism; do without the indispensable —hope; and bear the intolerable—her envenomed emotions. A heavy order, but, withal, the best prescription for coexistence with the alcoholic.

Few are the problems encountered in life that do not appear soluble by the simple expedient of having someone else change his behavior. This is, of course, a particularly seductive belief in relation to the alcoholic. The solution—to have him stop drinking—is so obvious that it is difficult to look elsewhere for answers, but since this solution is impossible to impose, the co-alcoholic must look elsewhere. She must look to herself. Her behavior is the only behavior she can control. Her part of the interaction with the alcoholic is the only part she can determine. She can only change herself, not the alcoholic. She can set goals, but only for herself, and she can meet those goals only if they are realistic. If her exclusive aim is to reform the alcoholic, the odds are against her, but it is within her power to become more honest and objective about the drinking, to achieve a kinder, less abrasive relationship with the alcoholic, and to insure her own self-preservation as a reasonably well-functioning individual.

Concerning her honesty and objectivity, it is a curious fact that so all-important a matter as the alcoholic's drinking is seldom referred to other than in euphemisms. The alcoholic himself speaks of being bombed, stoned, smashed, fried, boiled, oiled, plastered, loaded, gassed, or tanked, of being high as a kite, tight as a tick, or three sheets to the wind, of being on a binge, bash, or bender. And too often the co-alcoholic falls in with the use of these light terms, allowing the alcoholic the comfort of pretending that his drinking is merely a peccadillo. Since this is far from the way the co-alcoholic views it, however, she should require herself to be blunt and call the drinking by its rightful name of alcoholism. Where she has been circumspect in alluding to the drinking for fear of arousing the alcoholic's defensive wrath, she should be frank in speaking of it as alcoholism. Where she has been discreet to avoid wounding his sensibilities, she should be matter-of-fact in terming him an alcoholic. Where she has been subtle in deference to his pretenses, she should be direct and refuse him the comfort of sham.

She should do this for her own sake because, by using the words "alcoholic" and "alcoholism," she reminds herself of what she is up against. To speak of "your drinking" or "your problem" is very different from speaking of "your alcoholism." The latter connotes severity, chronicity, and intractability, and as often as the co-alcoholic hears herself use the terms, just so often is she delineating the limitations on her own abiilty to influence or control the condition. The words "alcoholic" and "alcoholism" serve as a constant reminder of the realities of the situation. They may seem aggressively tactless, but they are a necessary antidote to wishful thinking and the sneaking rebirth of hope. They are descriptive, they are objective, they are inclusive, and as bare and as bleak as they may ring at first, they are ultimately consoling because they at least ring true.

Invariably speaking of the drinker as alcoholic and his drinking as alcoholism whenever it is appropriate and natural to do so, the co-alcoholic can use the words simply and easily while taking care to keep them free of a pejorative flavor. No imputation of blame or judgment should cling to them; they should merely issue as accurate and relevant. Above all, they should not be used reductionistically in the sense that, while ostensibly saying, "You are an alcoholic," the co-alcoholic appears to be conveying, "You are nothing but an alcoholic." Her intention is not to indict the alcoholic but to identify the nature of his drinking.

The alcoholic will not let the words go unchallenged, of course. The last thing he wants is clear identification of his drinking for what it is, and he will buck, twist, turn, squirm, and attack to shake off the hated labels. He will demand definitions—and point by point refute them. He will insist on evidence—and damn the evidence in the course of demolishing it. He will lure the co-alcoholic into citing chapter and verse—and triumphantly dismantle her arguments. He will prove to his own satisfaction that the co-alcoholic is unfair, unreasonable, and if not actually deluded, at least foolishly mistaken. But the co-alcoholic should stick to her guns. That he is an alcoholic, that his drinking is alcoholism justifies her use of the words. She is not trying to change the alcoholic. She is not trying to put a stop to the drinking. These are not her prerogatives. But it is her prerogative to call a spade a spade.

She can afford to insist on it, but she cannot afford to argue it, for the alcoholic is masterful at skewing any discussion into a no-win fight over side-issues, and the co-alcoholic who lets herself be drawn into debate will find herself bested at every turn. To avoid defeat, she should avoid discussion, an odd admonition in this era of emphasis upon communication when the explication of points of view is touted as the panacea for problems in human relationships; but if discussion leads only to argument and argument to bitter polarizaton, there is no point in engaging in it.

Denial is the alcoholic's strongest line of defense. He denies the nature, the extent, and the seriousness of his drinking by speaking of it in terms that make it seem tame. Attacking that denial directly by attempting to argue him into an admission that he is alcoholic only drives him into more impassioned defense and more imaginative rationalizations, but the co-alcoholic can chip away at his denial by so calmly and matter-of-factly using the words "alcoholic" and "alcoholism" that they lose their threatening quality. Since the sting of even the most loaded words is drawn through repetition, there is a good chance that the alcoholic will eventually cease to question them. There is even a chance that he will slip into using them about himself, and the clarity that cannot be produced by argument may come into being through attrition.

Because the words speak volumes about both the past and the future of the alcoholic's drinking, when the co-alcoholic uses them, she may find that they are sufficient in themselves to account for what has happened and what will happen again. She can listen to the alcoholic's excuses in the wake of a drinking bout, for example, and rather than feel compelled to drive home to him the magnitude of her hurt, the extent of the damage he has done, she can perhaps say no more than, "That's how it goes with an alcoholic." And when he makes fervent declarations that it will not happen again, that he has definitely decided to reform, rather than her pointing out, in rancor and rage, the emptiness of his promises, she can perhaps say no more than, "You're an alcoholic. You can't make promises," and in such fashion spare them both the abrasive fights that threaten to tear the relationship apart.

Lacerating scenes are an inescapable part of life with the alcoholic only because each partner feels compelled to explain and excuse his behavior. Under the guise of elucidating his difficulties, each enumerates them, shifting responsibility and attributing blame as he does so. Neither wishes to understand, but to make the other understand. Each tries to paint the other into a corner, and each struggles, viciously if need be, to exculpate himself. Let the words "alcoholic" and "alcoholism" be used, however, and there is a third entity present, an impersonal entity that accounts for the situation. The partners need not look to each other for fault and failure, and little needs to be said, for it is all said in these words.

The alcoholic will not be entirely grateful for an end to argument because the battles, in a twisted way, have been one of the means whereby he grants himself permission to drink. He has cast the co-alcoholic in the role of heavy, a self-righteous figure of moral rectitude whose pleasure it is to deny other people pleasure. Persuading himself that he is duty-bound to fight back, he escapes into drink defiantly. He does it to prove that he is his own person, that he cannot be coerced, that he is an untrammeled spirit whose wings must not be clipped. And when he sobers up and these arguments are not quite as convincing as they sounded when he raised his glass, the ensuing battle is a means of obtaining absolution. Forced to feel guilty by the co-alcoholic's heaping of blame, his genuine guilt is relieved. Required to express remorse by the co-alcoholic's listing of his egregious sins, his genuine remorse is exorcised. If he has caused the co-alcoholic suffering, she in turn has exacted suffering from him by putting him through an ugly scene. He has paid for his peccancy, and he feels obscurely, without ever quite formulating it to himself, that they are even; she has had her retribution, and he, having atoned, is released to go and sin again.

As unpleasant as the fights over his drinking may be, for the alcoholic they are cathartic. So sorely may he need them that if he is denied them by the co-alcoholic's retirement to a neutral corner, he may try to tempt her back into the fray by offering some such bait as: "I suppose I behaved pretty badly." Or, "You must have been upset when I didn't show up." Or, "Look, I know you're mad, so why don't you just say so and get it over with?" As inviting as these openings may be, if the co-alcoholic can spurn them and let the fact that he is an alcoholic speak for itself, she immediately alters their interaction to a degree far more profound than the most prolonged quarrel could bring about.

No one is comfortable when the person with whom he shares a life steps out of their customary pattern of interaction. Least of all will the alcoholic be. He knows the old rules of the game. What are the new ones? His first question is likely to be whether the co-alcoholic has stopped caring, to which she can make the realistic reply: "I care about you, and, yes, of course, I care about your drinking, but I cannot and will not do anything about it. It's your problem." While not implying that her concern for him has in any way diminished, she has made it clear that she is less than his policeman and more than his opposition. The alcoholic will undoubtedly press for a definition of how he is to behave, and when he learns that he may behave in any way he likes, he may rush to drink like a starved dog to his dinner. He may drink more, and more drastically, to test whether the co-alcoholic means what she says. So be it. The co-alcoholic, knowing that it is through no failure of hers that he drinks, can afford to wait.

What is she waiting for? The alcoholic's own imagination to take over. Imagination is a faculty that feeds on the absence of information. To illustrate, I once saw a rehearsal of a play starring Arlene Francis. The director, after describing the set briefly, went on to explain that Miss Francis, when she made her third-act entrance in the actual performance, would be wearing a magnificent ballgown, and we, the audience, would have to imagine this in place of the rehearsal slacks she actually had on if the dialogue that followed was to be intelligible. As one member of the audience, the minute Miss Francis came on stage, my mind's eye clothed her in a radiantly beautiful dress, and I was satisfied that she looked as stunning as the other characters pronounced her to be. After the play opened in New York, I went to see it again, and my disappointment was acute. The actual dress was . . . just a dress, and I grew impatient with the fuss being made over it.

The alcoholic's imagination, when it has few facts to anchor it, will conjure up possibilities far more potent and unsettling than the actuality of the co-alcoholic's thoughts and intentions. However clearly the co-alcoholic states that her sole design is to achieve a peaceful coexistence with a situation she cannot alter, the alcoholic will wonder if this does not mean that she is preparing drastic action. And her new freedom to refer factually to the drinking, the metaphoric but unmistakable gesture with which she opens her hands and turns loose the reins, will increase his apprehension. He is at liberty to drink, but, as much of a relief as this may seem at first glance, if he is free, she also is free. No longer grappling with him, no longer bound to him in a three-legged race in which, if he stumbles, she falls, she can take steps in independent, unknown directions. Where will she go? What will she do? His imagination may give him pause.

And while he speculates, perhaps unrealistically, on the future of her intentions, he may speculate with uncharacteristic realism on the future of his drinking. He has viewed drinking as something he does *now*. But the co-alcoholic, by refusing to argue whether or not he will drink and treating it instead as a foregone conclusion, has given de facto recognition to a life sentence. The alcoholic not only may drink; he will drink; he will always drink. That is her position. What is his? Does he believe his bondage is permanent? Since, like anyone else, the alcoholic hates to be told that he can do nothing but what he is already doing, he may set out to prove her wrong. Human beings are contrary; they dislike being pigeonholed; and there is no more certain way of dislodging a person from an entrenched way of being than by agreeing with his own argument that he can be no other way.

While this, in the describing, sounds like one more maneuver to bring the alcoholic's drinking to a halt, if it is only a gambit it will not be effective. The alcoholic is adept at unmasking attempts to manipulate him, and he will quickly call the co-alcoholic's bluff if he detects any ambivalence in her. Thus, the co-alcoholic must have no reservations about her acceptance of alcoholism. She should assume that any departure from routine, such as the alcoholic's being late in coming home, indicates that he is drinking, and she should not wait dinner, not grow fretful, not rehearse what she will say when he finally appears, but simply go on about her ordinary pursuits. She should steel herself to replace the customary question in her mind: "Is he drinking?" with the realistic statement, "He is drinking," so that she will not betray, by even the most momentary flicker of disappointment, that she has secretly expected him not to be. It is possible, of course, that he has been delayed by a flat tire, a train breakdown, or an unexpected appointment. If so, well and good and no harm done, for the co-alcoholic, at one glance, can tell that her assumption has been wrong and listen to the explanation with interest. If, on the other hand, he has indeed been drinking, her composure is proof enough that she views it as his problem, not hers.

The general law the co-alcoholic must embrace is this: If the alcoholic may have been drinking, he has been drinking. If he could be drinking, he is drinking. If he might drink in such and such a situation, he will drink. It is the keeping in mind of this maxim that is her armor, her support, and her key to the necessary detachment that allows her to see herself, not as coextensive with the alcoholic, but as coexisting with him.

Not long ago, I called a friend and asked if she and her husband would like to spend an upcoming holiday weekend in the country. "Oh, that would be lovely," she said. "Maybe Philip won't drink if we're with you." As it happened, Philip did stay sober, but he was surly and short-tempered and obviously found it infuriating that his wife's eyes were on him every moment, mutely reminding him of the promise she had apparently wrung from him. Like so many co-alcoholics, this wife feels agonizingly responsible for her alcoholic husband's behavior, as though they were one person rather than two individuals. When he drinks, it is her shame. She writhes with embarrassment when his speech becomes loud and repetitive. She says things in stage whispers like, "Philip, you *promised*," and, "Philip, don't you think you've had enough?" She follows the host into the kitchen to say, "Please don't give him another drink," and she apologizes for his drinking and wistfully pleads for understanding by explaining, "He can't help it. He really *meant* to be good tonight." She has asked the alcoholic to be responsible for his drinking, but then she takes responsibility for it. She makes it a joint burden, a joint failure.

Admittedly, it is difficult for the co-alcoholic to persuade herself that the alcoholic with whom her life is so closely linked is a separate person and that his behavior is no reflection upon her. I remember a scene from my childhood when my mother, much the worse for an afternoon's drinking, insisted on going for a swim in the town pool. She dived in, broke a shoulder strap, and laughed so hard that she had to be pulled, half-naked, from the water. She sat on the lifeguard's lap, ate the sandwiches that were to have been his supper, and, giggling, occasionally pointed at me and said, "Oh, dear, I'm embarrassing the child. She doesn't think her mother should have any fun."

In retrospect, I am certain that no one who witnessed the scene confused me with my mother. But I did. It was I whose breasts were exposed, I who was eating the purloined sandwiches, I who was the spectacle. In contrast, George Bernard Shaw has described a comparable scene from his childhood in which his father, a goose under one arm, a ham under the other, stood butting at the garden wall under the delusion that it was the garden gate. Of himself as witness to this, Shaw said that, instead of being overwhelmed with shame and anxiety at the spectacle, he was "so disabled by merriment" that he was barely able to go to his father's rescue. Clearly, he went on, he was not a boy "to make tragedies of trifles instead of making trifles of tragedies," and he added the observation that, "If you cannot get rid of the family skeleton, you may as well make it dance."

How much better it is to let the family skeleton dance rather than tug at its arm and plead, "Let's go home now, *please.*" I am not blaming the child I was, but I wish I had understood what Shaw apparently knew intuitively and what I learned only many experienced years later: one person, no matter how intimately related, is not another; one person is not responsible for the indecencies and indiscretions of another; one person's behavior is not a brush tarring the other person's very being.

But learn it I did, so solidly that now I never exchange a glance over the alcoholic's head, never let my attitude comment on his behavior, and never, never try to dictate his actions. I answer, "Ask him," when the host whispers, "Should I offer him ginger ale?" I answer, "Ask him," when the hostess draws me aside to inquire, "Should I put a wineglass at his place?" And when a friend inquires portentously, "How's he doing these days?" I refuse to understand that the query is about drinking and answer in other terms so that there will be no air of conspiracy. Above all, I don't watch the alcoholic, not even in my mind's eye—most particularly not in my mind's eye. If he drinks, it is his responsibility. If he becomes sloppy and a nuisance, it is that person over there, not me. If his behavior becomes execrable, I regret it for his sake, but not for mine. I can only answer for my behavior. His identity is not mine.

Circumstances make a person a co-alcoholic, but how she handles those circumstances determines whether she preserves an identity of her own or becomes a mirror image of the alcoholic's flaws. She need not react to every contretemps with merriment, but she can work at cultivating a sense of humor. Other people seldom take drinking mishaps seriously, nor should she, for if she is tense and apologetic, if she nags at the drinker or grows rigid to express her disapproval, she worsens the situation; she increases the tenseness of the atmosphere; and she is quite apt to goad the drinker into greater excesses. She need not be amused at his grotesqueries, but she can be uninvolved. She need not approve of his sallies, but she can be unprovoked. She need not ignore him, but she can ignore her own distress and concentrate on her contribution to the occasion instead of underlining his disruption of it.

Whereas the co-alcoholic often seems to feel that she must atone for the alcoholic's behavior by displaying her embarrassment over it, it is the very fact of her obvious humiliation that makes other people uncomfortable. They cannot help but be acutely aware of her distress, and they feel pity but also irritation for, while they might have absorbed the alcoholic's antics into the general atmosphere, they can scarcely do that in the face of her frowns, sighs, and figurative hand-wringing. The co-alcoholic, by being as glum and forbidding as the alcoholic is raucous and abandoned, polarizes the company. Are they to be light and silly with him or grim and disapproving with her? They wish to be neither, and they resent being forced to swing between the sides, now jollying the alcoholic along, now reassuring the co-alcoholic that they are not blaming her for his behavior.

To other people, it is usually a trifle that the alcoholic is drinking, and the co-alcoholic should let it be a trifle, not indicate that it is a tragedy by displaying a disapproving, despairing air. If she finds this difficult, she should perhaps question her own motives. Is she truly apologizing for the alcoholic's behavior, or is she bidding for sympathy? Does she want it appreciated how much she has to put up with? Is she anxious to convey the patheticness of her position? Does she want other people to shake their heads and remark to each other, "Poor So-and-So, he really gives her a hard time"? Does she want pity?

At a party I happened to be talking to the wife of an alcoholic when he stumbled and half-fell, half-slid down a short flight of stairs. She excused herself to help him to his feet, but as soon as she was satisfied that he was unhurt, she returned to our group and resumed the conversation. A fellow guest said tentatively, "Your husband seems to be a bit under the weather." "Yes," she said evenly, "he's an alcoholic," and said no more. That woman got something far better than sympathy; she got admiration. She did not make the other guests uncomfortable. She did not grope for reassurance by spouting apologies. She did not overexplain or excuse. She did not attempt to dissociate herself from her husband by remarking that she had no influence on how much he drank, but the very fact of her not doing so made her stand forth as a separate person, a valuable person in her own right, not merely the entangled alter ego of an alcoholic.

The co-alcoholic who wishes sympathy and support for the difficulties she faces in living with an alcoholic—and it is unremarkable that she should want these—must realize that the way to obtain them is not to seek them. What she cannot win by displaying her wounds may be freely offered if she behaves with dignity and restraint. The point she wishes to make about her helplessness to control his behavior is clearly made if she makes no attempt to control it. Their identity as two separate people is acknowledged if she confirms her own identity by simply assuming that she is not being judged on the basis of other than her own qualities.

In general, the attempt of a co-alcoholic to cope with the social behavior of an alcoholic falls into one of two patterns. Most common is constant attention to it, a preoccupation betrayed in eyes and voice and manner with what the alcoholic is saying and doing. Less common but frequent enough to be observed is a determined ignoring of the alcoholic, a turning away from him so complete that he might just as well be invisible for all the notice the co-alcoholic takes of him. Neither approach makes other people comfortable; both make the alcoholic the dominant figure in the group. It is a middle course—the same degree of attention accorded the alcoholic that is given any other person present but an attention free of watchfulness and apprehension—that is most effective in preserving the ease of the witnessing company. Perhaps the best comparison is to how one would be with a handicapped person: not hovering and over-protective, which calls undue attention to his disability (and, incidentally, to one's own seemingly generous but actually self-advertising solicitude), not, at the other extreme, pretending, eyes averted, that there is no problem at all, but able to offer help when that is indicated and able to stand back when to do otherwise would be an incursion on the independence of the handicapped person.

Just as it would be gratuitous to remark of someone in a wheelchair that he is crippled, so, often, is it unnecessary to call attention to the alcoholic's drinking, but if it is relevant to comment on it, the co-alcoholic should no more evade the use of the words "alcoholic" and "alcoholism" with other people than with the alcoholic. If an explanation is called for, if it would elucidate otherwise inexplicable behavior, the words should be used frankly, not shunned out of a wish to protect the alcoholic by keeping his condition secret. While it would be unkind to expose him unnecessarily, the co-alcoholic is under no obligation to lie for the alcoholic to try to save him from the consequences of his behavior. Indeed, she may best obtain tolerance and a suspension of judgment for him by naming his condition, since the concept of alcoholism legitimizes actions which might otherwise be socially unacceptable and cause him to be harshly rejected.

The middle ground is the best place for the co-alcoholic to stand, a position between the extremes of a brave and conspicuous total silence on the subject of the alcoholic's drinking and too unbuttoned a desire to spill out her problems and complaints to all available ears. By talking too much, which is an easy temptation, she courts the danger of becoming as great a nuisance as the alcoholic, while, by being utterly silent, she runs the risk of cultivating an unattractive air of martyrdom. Either extreme allows the alcoholic to jeer at her, whereas the ability to refer matter-of-factly to his drinking, with concern for him but without fear for her own image, further consolidates their individual identities and leaves him with no complaint except about his own behavior.

Although addiction to alcohol certainly exists entirely independent of the environment, the alcoholic is not unaware of his environment, and he is used to being the center of attention; even if it is a negative spotlight that is upon him, he is accustomed to it. He is used to restraints, and it is one of his pleasures to kick against them. He is used to cautious, careful handling designed to protect him from upsets. He is used to patient, agreeable treatment designed to placate him. Like a spoiled child, he is used to tyrannizing his company by the ever-present threat of getting out of hand. He is, in short, used to being infantilized, and however much he may purport to object to it, he counts on it; it defines his specialness; it gives him a prominent place and a way to be. He does not drink to obtain this definition, but if he drinks and does not obtain it, if the co-alcoholic, in her objectivity, exerts no gravitational pull on him, he may feel disconcertingly adrift. If life flows evenly on despite his drinking, if attention is not paid, if special notice is not taken, the spotlight is no longer a warm glow but a pitiless glare exposing him as exhibitionistic, troublesome, and sophomoric. And he will not be insensible of this. It will not necessarily change his behavior, but it will be one more piece of evidence that his alcoholism is his curse, not another's cross.

Although appreciative of the co-alcoholic's patience and loyalty, the alcoholic is not above nursing a secret contempt for her willingness to be long-suffering. As an alcoholic in an unguarded moment remarked, "My wife is a masochistic fool for putting up with me. If she was half a person, she'd tell me where to go." The fact that his wife did put up with him was a quality he not only took a certain amount of glee in exploiting but also used as a ticket to continuing irresponsibility and immaturity. He counted on her to cover for him, patch up the disasters he left in his drinking wake, fuss and fume and fret over him in an effort to save him from himself. Since the alcoholic cannot be saved from himself, he should be allowed to make a shambles of his life and his relationships, he should be allowed to cut a ridiculous, pathetic figure, he should be allowed to expose himself to perilous situations, he should be allowed to threaten his health, he should be allowed to reduce to shards those things he professes to prize, for the more successful the co-alcoholic is at protecting him, the more feasible she makes it for him to go on drinking. In attempting to save the alcoholic from himself, she postpones his recognition of the terrible cost of his drinking, a recognition that must come if he is ever to stop. For the drinker, the satisfactions of drinking are such that he will not truly consider giving it up until the penalties are so obvious and so severe that the cost of drinking, even to his eyes, begins to appear uneconomic, until the losses from drinking greatly overbalance the gains.

It is terribly difficult to stand by and do nothing to protect the alcoholic from jeopardy. But the eventual jeopardy from chronic drinking is greater, and often the day of reckoning, if it is allowed to come sooner rather than later, can be the turning point for the alcoholic. Just as in psychiatry it is becoming more and more recognized that a crisis in an individual's life is not only a time of great trouble but also a time of great opportunity for constructive change in that the old answers no longer serve the person and he must mobilize himself to find new and different answers, so, too, in alcoholism, a crisis, a thorough-going disaster, may be what it takes to bring the alcoholic up short. It may give him his first clear insight into the path he is on, his first intimation that he is not smart enough or durable enough to win at the drinking game. A crisis is a crossroads, and at a crossroads there is at least the possibility of taking a turn for the better.

Recently, I ran into an acquaintance on the street, someone whose professional path crosses mine occasionally, and I invited her home for a drink. She accepted but refused the drink and asked for a cup of coffee instead. "I've stopped drinking," she said, took a deep breath, and confessed, "I'm an alcoholic." I said, "Yes, I know," and she looked startled.

It turned out that, like many alcoholics, she had kidded herself that she held her liquor so well no one was aware that she was never entirely sober. "I suppose everyone knew it but me," she admitted. "Well, I sure do know it now," she said and went on to describe how she had gone to a restaurant one night, gotten drunk in accustomed fashion, and, leaving the restaurant, had entirely overlooked a short flight of steps, stepped off into the air, and crashed face-down on the sidewalk, smashing her nose and cheekbones so badly that a long operative procedure had been necessary to fit the splinters back together and there had been some question of whether she would lose her sight. "I thought it was the end of the world," she said, "but now I'm glad it happened. Only something as awful as that could have made me stop drinking."

But I know other stories as well, stories of alcoholics who have lost job after job, have been deserted by family and friends, have been in serious accidents, only to continue undeterred on their drinking path. There is no guarantee that a crisis will be a turning point for the alcoholic, and, certainly, no one can stand by and not catch the arm of an alcoholic who is about to fall, not get an alcoholic to a hospital if there are signs of liver failure, not lend him money if he is starving. But because the penalties of drinking must come to outweigh its compensations if the alcoholic is even to consider stopping, the co-alcoholic should think carefully on the limits of her intervention.

She can intervene to confront the alcoholic's denial mechanism. She can intervene to preserve a measure of kindness and generosity in their relationship. She can intervene in the ways that make coexistence possible. But perhaps she should not intervene in the alcoholic's drinking nor attempt to abort its consequences. Perhaps she should give him enough rope, not to hang himself, but to make it painfully, objectively clear that that is the danger he is running.

9

An Independent Existence

Because life with the alcoholic is highly charged, it may escape the co-alcoholic's attention how limited in emotional range it tends to be. The simpler but satisfying emotions which give variety and dimension to a life are usually lacking: uncomplicated companionship, relaxed fun, low-key exchange of thoughts, quiet pleasures. In the center of the maelstrom, the co-alcoholic may not consciously hunger for these, but if she sets out to find them, they can steady and enrich her life and make her far less prey to the alcoholic's moods and actions. It seems such a trivial thing to throw on the scales—a walk with someone else, a shared meal, a museum visit, an evening's ranging conversation—but even a brief disengagement from the alcoholic can be a welcome counterweight to the blindingly intense but curiously ungratifying relationship. The co-alcoholic needs simplicity in her life as well as complexity, casualness as well as closeness, mild feelings as well as strong, gentle affection as well as love.

And there is another necessity: stimulation. In all the immense amount of literature about alcoholism, one fact is never mentioned. Alcoholics are bores. Some are only boring when drunk, but drunk or sober, most have few interests outside of themselves, their immediate concerns and hair-trigger sensitivities. It is extremely time-consuming and mind-absorbing to be an alcoholic, and the person whose passion is drinking is rarely a person who involves himself in other pursuits as well. When he is drinking, every hour is occupied in getting drunk or trying to come off a drunk; he has neither the capacity nor the motivation to turn his attention to outside concerns. When he is not drinking—well, an alcoholic I know explained how his time was occupied. "What am I doing?" he shouted. "I'm not drinking, that's what I'm doing!" A person whose thoughts are circling obsessively on how to get or how to avoid the next drink has neither the time nor the energy to take an interest or to be interesting.

I referred earlier to an alcoholic whose conceit it is not to drink on weekends because he considers this to be proof that, despite his inordinate, compulsive drinking during the week, he is not an alcoholic. In order not to drink on Saturday and Sunday, this man spends the complete forty-eight hours in bed, reading incessantly during the day and watching television at night until the last movie ends at three or four in the morning. Apart from whatever comment might be made from this about his alcoholism, it is safe to say that his wife has a thin and uninteresting time of it. She is conscientious, devoted, and full of pity for his horrendous struggle with drinking, too conscientious not to be waiting when he staggers home on weeknights and too devoted and compassionate to leave him alone on weekends, and she is thus condemned to a flat, companionless, tiresome life without highlights except for the dubious drama of being threatened with strangling when he takes entire leave of his drunken senses.

The dimension of her life is his drinking. She has let her life contract to these narrow bounds out of loyalty to her husband. But what of loyalty to herself? It happens that he has an acute intelligence, but that does not mean that she can exist satisfactorily without stimulus to thought and reflection. It happens that he has several drinking buddies, but that does not mean that she can exist without social intercourse and friendship. It happens that he occasionally travels to Europe on business trips, but that does not mean that she can exist without the delight and refreshment of new sights. Her fealty to her husband, equally compounded of love and agonized concern, has led her to be false to herself, false to her own needs for enriching experience through wider encounter with people, ideas, and events.

Why should not this wife get a job as a means of broadening her horizons? Work, while not the end-all and be-all, in our society lends definition, and through conferring a sense of competence and accomplishment, it can provide an armature on which to fashion a strengthened self-image. This wife would argue that her husband's salary is more than sufficient for their needs, but money is not the only reason for working, nor is it always the most important one. A job would give her a separate identity, an area in which she would have to be herself and thus an area to discover who she is above and beyond being the wife of an alcoholic. She would also argue against it in psychological terms, anticipating that her husband's masculine sense of being the provider and support of the family would be affronted, undermining his self-image and subverting one of his main motives for continuing to function as well as he does. The argument that a husband's *machismo* must be protected is not very persuasive, however, since an alcoholic husband, even if he manages to protect his job, does not cut a masculine figure, and as far as disturbing his ability to function is concerned, the greater probability is that, by fearing to upset the status quo, she is preserving his ability to function as an alcoholic.

As it is, this couple is on dead center: she existing in patient passivity, awaiting some outside propulsion, like a threat to his health or his job, to move him toward a sane appraisal of the cost of his drinking; he existing in a balance, drunk enough of the time to satisfy his addiction, sober enough of the time to enable him to drink the rest of the time. Something, sometime, will happen to disturb this equilibrium, whether for better or worse, but why should his wife not disturb it now in a way that will preserve her ability to function as a co-alcoholic and threaten his to persevere as an alcoholic? Getting a job might do just this. Since employment would require her to be in a certain place at a certain time each day, instead of sitting up past midnight waiting to steer her husband to bed when he finally made his way home, she would have to go to bed herself at a reasonable hour, and the fact that she was sound asleep when he got in would indicate that her time and energies were not entirely at his disposal. The money she earned on a job, if put into a bank account of her own or used to buy stock, would give her a nest egg and invest her occasional threats to leave her husband with an authenticity they now lack. The fact that she had interests in addition to his care and feeding, other responsibilities, other loyalties, another area in which she was valued, would take her out of the second-class citizen category and would give her, as well, another world to think about and a person to be outside of their claustrophobic twosome. Their relationship would take its place in a broader canvas, remaining a paramount element, to be sure, but no longer so insistently to the fore that she as an individual disappeared into it.

Many co-alcoholics have young children or other responsibilities which might make it difficult for them to hold a job, or they may lack qualifications. In such instances, an alternative such as my wise friend, Ellen Gunther, found might be attractive. Ellen, realizing that her husband's alcoholism preoccupied her to the point of obsession, revived an old, rather casual interest in photography, enrolled in a mail-order course, and forced herself to study and experiment assiduously until a growing sense of accomplishment generated an honest enthusiasm for the work itself and carried her along. Her most available and favorite model being a neighbor's Persian cat, she became adept at animal photography, and soon she had a modest free-lance business going in the specialized area of portraits of pets taken in their own homes. Since it proved impossible to solve a lighting problem and at the same time brood about her husband's drinking, she gained hours of surcease from care each day which refreshed and revitalized her and allowed her to look forward to his homecoming without undue concern for the sort of mood he would be in. With assignments to think about and encounters to talk about, her life stretched satisfyingly beyond the confines of being the wife of an alcoholic.

Another co-alcoholic, in this instance the husband of an alcoholic, also decided to take a mail-order course. As an account executive in an advertising agency, he arrived home at the end of the day exhausted, wanting only peace and routine and relaxation, simple needs that usually went unmet because of the emotional climate created by his wife's drinking. He rightly guessed that his tiredness might be relieved by physical activity, hence he determined on reupholstering as something that would occupy his hands and empty his mind, as well as giving him the pleasure of creating handsome objects, and, indeed, he found it almost life-saving to have an hour or two's quiet work alone in his basement workshop to look forward to each evening.

Alcoholics, because they cling, because they are so highly vulnerable to upset and thus require massive infusions of ego support and reassurance, because they are emotional and irritable and jittered by discontent, are exhausting to stay in unremitting contact with, and some respite is needed, some neutral area to which the co-alcoholic can turn for relief and the recharging of her energies and spirit. One co-alcoholic has found this area in betting on the horses. She fills notebooks with data about bloodlines and past performance and works out her bets with all the science and care another person might devote to the stock market. What can one say: that gambling is a dangerous trap? But after one has said that, and perhaps clucked over this odd expenditure of intellect and energy, it must then be acknowledged that at least she is no longer the weepy, hand-wringing figure she was when she had nothing to engage her mind but her husband's drinking. The point may be not whether the co-alcoholic finds a job or volunteer work, takes a mail-order course in accounting, landscape gardening, or painting, becomes a specialist in dog-breeding or the raising of African violets, but that she find *something* to invest herself in to dilute her absorption in the care and tending of the alcoholic, both to keep the alcoholic and his problems in perspective and to place herself as a person with an identity of her own squarely in that perspective. The alcoholic must not be allowed to dominate, through weakness and need, and, often, sheer bad behavior, the whole of their life.

And this is equally true of their social life. Many a co-alcoholic, particularly in the years before there is awareness that the heavy drinking is really alcoholism, tries to keep up with the alcoholic, makes the rounds of bars and parties with him and drinks too much at home. The alcoholic praises her as a "good sport," but unknown to herself, the co-alcoholic is acting as camouflage, lending a veneer of normality to the drinking. If the co-alcoholic does not mind spending hours perched on a bar stool, if she does not object to always being the last to leave the scene of a party, there is no reason why she should not go on being a good sport; if it is not her pleasure to spend time in this way, however, there is no reason why she should. Her reason will be that she has to see that the alcoholic gets home safely, but delivering him intact to his own house and his own bed is tantamount to providing him with a license to drink. I have seen a wife stand up and walk out of a bar when her husband refused to go home, get in their car and drive off, leaving it to him to make his own way home however he could—in a taxi, on foot, through the kind offices of strangers—and this seemed to me a more sensible and admirable course of behavior than to nag and plead and pluck at the alcoholic's coattails into the small hours of the morning. Certainly it is one of the ways in which the co-alcoholic can refuse to be collusive to the drinking: by not protecting the alcoholic from its penalties while he indulges in its pleasures, as it is also a further way in which she establishes her claim to a separate identity.

To walk out on a group of friends and leave the unbudging alcoholic behind is a somewhat more daunting prospect, but an executed threat to do so can go a long way toward persuading the alcoholic that he cannot disregard the co-alcoholic's wishes and treat her merely as a chauffeur whose departure must be delayed until it suits his convenience. The co-alcoholic is perfectly justified in making the condition that, if the alcoholic does not come along promptly when she signals that it is time to go home, she will not hesitate to depart without him. Having made such a condition, however, she must carry it out ruthlessly so that he learns she will not draw back from roundly embarrassing them both if that is what it takes to convince him that he cannot behave as though only his wishes mattered.

A recent press report described a treatment approach to alcoholism in which institutionalized alcoholics were given free access to liquor but were subjected to electric shocks when they drank too fast or too much. The rationale behind this approach is to condition the alcoholic to more controlled drinking. While the co-alcoholic is in no position to emulate this treatment in its particulars, she can adopt the general method of conditioning the alcoholic to be less of a social embarrassment to her by administering the repeated shock of walking out on him at an time, in any place, when he refuses to be cooperative. All it takes is two sets of keys to the car and will power.

A few such episodes, delineated fairly in advance by the co-alcoholic's clear but friendly statement that, "If you do so-and-so, I shall do so-and-so," can go a long way toward persuading the alcoholic that he is dealing with an independent person and that he must be prepared, not for renewed pleading, but for firm consequences from which he will receive no help in extricating himself. The statements should not be threats; the actions should not be carried out in a retaliative spirit; but made they should be and carried out they should be, firmly and promptly, for weakness and vacillation will be cleverly and quickly exploited by the alcoholic to support his drinking patterns.

If the drinking has already commenced before an evening's engagement, if the alcoholic has started in the afternoon and it is predictable that the evening will be a messy one, the co-alcoholic need again not hesitate to go her own way. She can flatly refuse to accompany the alcoholic when he is drinking and either go without him or, if he is insistent on putting in an appearance, allow him to go without her, leaving it to him to make any explanation he can contrive for her nonappearance. As for her own explanations if she arrives alone, it is sufficient to say straightforwardly that her husband is an alcoholic, that he is currently drinking, and that, therefore, she has come by herself. In prospect, the co-alcoholic may cringe at the thought of arriving at a cocktail party or dinner party unaccompanied, but she should steel herself to carry it off naturally, head high, smile in place, and the moment she has given her matter-of-fact explanation, turn her attention to the other people present and set about enjoying herself. Her requirement is to be at ease so as to put her hosts and fellow guests at ease, and to do this, she must not trouble herself about what other people are thinking. She will be fearful of hidden laughter or pity or ridicule or criticism, but if she can summon any aplomb at all, she will receive five minutes of admiration for carrying off a difficult situation well and then people's attention will revert to their primary concern: preoccupation with the impression they themselves are making. It is a constant of human nature that people are far more concerned with what is being thought of them than what they think of someone else, and confronted with someone who is at ease, they will quickly become concerned enough with insuring her liking and approval that the question of whether to confer their own on her will go by the board.

When I have to go it alone, I remind myself of an incident in which an office acquaintance insisted that I come to a party she was giving. When I protested that she did not need an extra woman, she said that was exactly what she did need, several of them, because it made a party so much livelier. It was her experience, she explained, that a party of all couples ruled out chance and changing combinations, that extra men were inclined to think they had done everyone a favor by just showing up and made other men bristle to warn them against poaching, but that extra women put themselves out to be charming, made the men perk up, and prompted the female halves of couples to extend themselves to hold their own against competition. So, when I set out now by myself, I tell myself that I am going to be an asset to the hosts, that far from throwing the evening out of balance, I may be the one to make it jell. Whether true or false, it is a bit of harmless ego support that shores up my resolve to enjoy myself and reminds me that self-consciousness and self-pity are emotions the co-alcoholic cannot afford.

As for the alcoholic, who is probably out on the town himself, it is a nuisance to come home at midnight to a wife who is pacing the floor with worry, but it can be unsettling in a different and more acute way to meet at the door a wife returning happily from an enjoyable evening with friends. Let this occur often enough, let his wife set out expectantly on her own and return with stories of the pleasant time she has had, and the alcoholic may have a sense that he is missing something. He cannot rightfully complain about his wife's enjoying herself since it is by his own option that he has chosen to drink rather than to accompany her. He cannot claim that she should, instead, have remained at home in a state of agitation about his well-being, since he has often enough quarreled with her about doing just that. But neither is he likely to be sanguine about the changed state of affairs.

When he questions it, the co-alcoholic can be candid in explaining that she feels she must fashion a life for herself that extends beyond the bounds of their rather circumscribed relationship. He cannot meet all her affectional needs, nor her need for stimulating company, since, emotionally if not physically, he deserts her every time he drinks. He is not really there for her much of the time, and so she must look elsewhere for the concern and interest and support that are as vital to her as to him. Even more frankly, she can speak of the possibility that someday their life together will come to an end, either because she finds it too stressful to wish to continue in it or because he will destroy himself with his drinking, and she feels she must be prepared for such an eventuality by having a way she can go on alone. Said not as a frightening or threatening prediction but as a matter-of-fact appraisal of the realities of the situation, it is an unarguable proposition.

For herself, if she suspects herself of vindictiveness or disloyalty or has misgivings about the consequences of slackening off in her caretaking role, the co-alcoholic might think of it in this way. As long as she subordinates herself to him, she and the alcoholic are like two swimmers in the ocean struggling to keep their heads above water just at the point where the waves are breaking. As each wave crashes, the co-alcoholic grabs for the alcoholic to prevent him from going under or being helplessly tumbled in the turbulence, and in the relatively quiet intervals between breakers, she paddles anxiously around him trying to shepherd him back to shore. As her own strength is drained by the buffeting, as her own spirit flags from the realization that the alcoholic cannot or will not let them move out of danger, she cannot help but debate whether self-preservation must not take precedence over remaining at the alcoholic's side, whether she must not, so that at least one of them may survive, loosen his clinging hold on her and strike out for shore on her own. But there is, as the experienced swimmer knows, another alternative. Out beyond where the waves are breaking is quieter water. It is possible to dive through the breakers, come up beyond the surf, and conserve one's energy by floating on the swells.

It is this alternative that the co-alcoholic who makes an effort to enrich her life with work and friends and absorbing pursuits is electing. She has not turned her back on the alcoholic; she has not written him off. She is close enough to help when he must have help. She has simply moved a sensible distance away to hoard her own strength for the emergencies when it will be sorely needed.

The alcoholic, as complacent as a two-year-old in the certainty that he will be shielded from harm, will be outraged to discover that his life-preserver has gone out of his immediate grasp, and it is not in the least unlikely that he will cry wolf to bring the co-alcoholic hastily back to his side. The alcoholic wife of a golfer went into a panic when he announced that he did not intend to miss his Saturday afternoon foursome in order to hold her hand while she came off a drunk. She became so violent that he called an ambulance. At the sight of the ambulance attendants, however, she reverted to utter rationality, and because a rational person cannot be hospitalized without his own consent, the ambulance went away empty, at which juncture, thinking she had won and that her husband would not dare leave her, she poured herself a glass of whiskey. But her husband did leave her. He kept his golf date, not only because he felt it was important not to let her psychological warfare succeed, but for his own sake, for he knew that the knot of resentment inside him would spread and corrupt his entire feeling for her.

He returned home to find an empty house and a note that his wife had been taken to the hospital. The story he heard from the attendants in the emergency room was that his wife had taken an overdose of sleeping pills, but when he told his wife, by then considerably sobered by having had her stomach pumped out, that she now had no choice but to accept psychiatric hospitalization, she confessed that she had not taken the pills but had simply told the police that so they would come to her rescue. She had felt, she said, deserted and desperate, and she had had to have some indication she was not alone in the world.

She might have taken the pills. She might not have called the police. People make gestures, and gestures can turn into irreversible events. But this is a risk that must be run if the co-alcoholic is to put an end to the manipulations designed to keep him or her chained to the alcoholic's side. This wife learned that the fact that her husband did not intend to give up his life to her did not mean that he had stopped caring about her, only that he would not care *for* her beyond a reasonable point. He came to the hospital. He took her home. He understood her pain, and he did not put her through a verbal post mortem. But she knew and he knew that her bluff had been called, that he had made his point that there were two lives to be lived, and that when she could not or would not live hers, he nevertheless could and would carry on with his.

The weak, the immature, the dependent in general, and alcoholics in particular, employ need as a bonding agent to cement their partners to them. Just as hysterical women in Victorian times used invalidism as a way of enslaving their husbands, so do alcoholics exploit their seemingly stronger partners into coddling, protecting, and rescuing them. It is tremendously difficult to turn one's back on need, to refuse to submit to domination by weakness. There is always the possibility that this time the need is genuine, that this time it is not blackmail but the real thing. But the co-alcoholic must try to make an unsentimental distinction between a true and necessary cry for help and a fake cry for attention, just as a mother distinguishes her child's cry of distress from his cry of displeasure. And she must do so for the same reason: to wean the alcoholic from his dependency. A mother must have faith that her child can grow, can take responsibility for himself, can keep himself out of harm's way if she is not to perpetuate his infantilism. A co-alcoholic must have faith that there is, in the alcoholic, a core of strength, a will to live, a push toward health that will enable the alcoholic to pull himself back from the brink if she does not each time rush to his rescue. She must believe that, and she must let the alcoholic know that she believes it.

The evidence may be all to the contrary, in which event the co-alcoholic must ignore the evidence and proceed on the assumption that self-preservation motivates the alcoholic no less than other people. A woman who had repeatedly patched her husband back together after catastrophic drinking bouts began to wonder if there was not more manipulation than truth in his perfervid declarations that he would not be able to survive were it not for her selfless care. Deciding to hazard a test, at the obvious start of one of his binges, she, within hours, had packed their three children off to her mother's house and was herself on a plane to the Caribbean. She left no word where she could be reached; she did not even say which island she was going to; and she stayed away three weeks. When she returned, she found her husband had been sober and back at work for two of those three weeks. He was angry and hurt and accused her of heartlessness. Terrible things might have happened to him, he said piteously, while she was off getting a suntan. "But they didn't," she answered reasonably. "In fact, you seem to have pulled yourself together considerably faster than when I'm here, so now we know you're quite capable of looking after yourself after all."

Another wife, whose history was similarly one of slavish care for her husband when his drinking got out of hand, learned the lesson of devoted indifference and now simply retreats to their country place when a binge is in the offing. She refuses to reward his alcoholism by looking after him, and her actions make it perfectly clear that she considers him capable of looking after himself, which, since expectations have a way of being self-realizing, is indeed the case.

The co-alcoholic traditionally believes that it is the attention and support and encouragement she pours into the alcoholic that keep him going, but withholding these things may in the long run prove more strengthening. A term used in group psychotherapy is descriptive of how the co-alcoholic originally came to assume the caretaking burden. When one patient in a group, by emphatically exhibiting certain characteristics, pulls another into a complementary position, this is referred to as "role-suction." A seemingly independent member, for example, may seduce another member into taking up a dependent stance toward him. In the instance of the co-alcoholic, whatever her original propensities, role-suction has operated to draw her into a caretaking, nurturing, protective position. The role is obvious, it is almost irresistible, and it has the look of being necessary. The more successfully the co-alcoholic fills it, however, the more "successfully" can the alcoholic maintain his own role of being an alcoholic.

Since this is not the co-alcoholic's design, her problem is one of resisting role-suction. The apparent solution would be to have the alcoholic move out of his role of frequent helplessness and dependency and end the pull upon her. This would be equivalent to the group member's proposing that his vis-à-vis stop exhibiting independent qualities so that his own dependent ones would not be lured forth, and it would be no more effective. People do not alter their behavior on request; they begin to behave differently only when a change in the usual interaction forces them to or makes it more attractive for them to. The dependent member would have to grow more independent before it would occur to the other to back off from his self-assured ways and perhaps even let some of his own dependent needs come to the surface. Just so, the co-alcoholic cannot force the alcoholic out of his role; she must, instead, vacate her assigned role, leaving a vacuum which the alcoholic can only fill by assuming the responsibility for himself that he has hitherto thrust upon the co-alcoholic.

By whatever means possible—by cultivating satisfying and absorbing interests which can lay legitimate claim to her energies, by investing herself in friendship and maintaining a social life which includes both of them when possible but is carried on by herself alone when necessary, by undertaking, if feasible, a career which gives her both tangible and intangible rewards, by establishing directions of her own which allow her to resist the pull of the alcoholic's importunate demands, by setting and holding to worthwhile goals which can be realized whether or not the alcoholic continues to drink—the co-alcoholic must become an individual, a person with an independent existence parallel to, but not paralyzed by, the alcoholic's hazardous and empty way of life. She must be present to help the alcoholic, but not ever-present. She must be his lifeline to a saner existence, but not his life-preserver in his alcoholic existence. She must, if she is not to perpetuate the complementarity which supports him in his drinking role, break out of her supporting role and become a person in her own right.

She must, in short, cease being the conventional co-alcoholic.

PART THREE

The Treatment of Alcoholism

10

Treatment
and the Co-Alcoholic

If the personal equation of alcoholic and co-alcoholic is formulated as the alcoholic and his drinking versus the co-alcoholic and her opposition to his drinking, it can be appreciated that the two sides of the equation tend to remain in balance. Whatever energy the co-alcoholic invests in her side of the equation is simply met by equal, opposing energy by the alcoholic, and the steady state, although it may be raised to a higher power, is not essentially altered. Since equations are altered just as certainly by subtraction as by addition, however, what the co-alcoholic has not been able to accomplish by effort, she may bring about by a withdrawal of energy. To whatever extent she can cease being a co-alcoholic, she introduces disequilibrium into the relationship and forces the alcoholic to make compensatory adjustments.

This sequence can occur with surprising rapidity, for, as relentlessly and single-mindedly as the alcoholic dances to the music of his own piper, he is nevertheless acutely attuned to shifts in the atmosphere around him. Long before it would be perceptible to an outsider that the co-alcoholic has lessened the amount and direction of effort she is putting into the relationship, even, perhaps, rather sooner than the co-alcoholic herself is completely aware that she is thinking along different lines and beginning to act on different intentions, the alcoholic will sense it. He will intuit that her grip has relaxed, her control has slackened, her concentration has let up, her concern has shifted focus. While it is probable that he will react, as noted, with the type of behavior which has customarily alarmed her and drawn her closer in fear and guilty devotion, if she maintains her detachment, if she is not sucked back into the role of co-alcoholic, this behavior may subside, and the alcoholic, perplexed and a bit dismayed by her disengagement, may return inquiringly to home base.

He may seek to know what, if the co-alcoholic intends to look to her own life, she expects of him. Although the co-alcoholic must answer only in terms of her own life, in terms of the decisions she has made to seek and extend friendships, to establish the work and interests that will make of her own life a going concern, to carry on alone at those times when his drinking makes it necessary, her words will inevitably carry various implications about his drinking. She is indirectly offering him the reward of a companionable social life if he does not drink, the promise that her interest will not stray far from him, that she will not progress from sufficiency to self-sufficiency and come to have no further need of his need for her. She is implying acceptance of lesser goals: not an end to the drinking but more controlled drinking, a more thoughtful choice of when and how and how much he will drink. It is obvious that if she is saying to him, "I will not go to the party with you on Wednesday if you drink," she is not ruling out his drinking on Tuesday or Thursday, merely allowing him the option of postponing it to a time when it will be less disruptive. If she is saying, "I can't stay out with you until all hours to see that you get home safely because now I have a job of my own to think about," she is not refusing to let him drink, merely inviting him to consider the wisdom of drinking more moderately. None of this need be, nor should it be, stated explicitly, but the lesser goals will be there behind her words, and often the alcoholic will try to meet them. He can read the handwriting on the wall, and the modest goals of lessened drinking or better-timed drinking bouts are not as frightening as the potential alternatives of complete abstinence or complete abandonment by the person he needs.

He will try to meet the scaled-down goals, and if he is like the majority of alcoholics, he will fail. It is not as though this is the first time he has made an effort to control his drinking. For his own reassurance, to demonstrate to himself that he is in charge of his drinking, not that drinking is in charge of him, he has achieved any number of periods of abstinence, refused himself any number of first drinks because it was a dangerous time to drink, but none of his successes has been more than temporary, and the story is unlikely to be different this time. His resolution will be strong, the attempt will be genuine, and the outcome will be predictable: in weeks or months his drinking will have crept back up to its previous level.

A parallel process of slipping back into the old ways may also take place in the co-alcoholic. Observing how frightened the alcoholic is of losing her, witnessing the struggle he is making, and wanting to acknowledge and reward his efforts, she feels it would be callous of her to pursue the course she has set herself. Just this once, she decides not to go off without him. Just this once, she stands by to sober him up. Just this once, she postpones a plan, gives up a pleasure. Just this once, she lies to protect him, holds out her arms to him, lets him cling to her. Just this once. How can she do otherwise when he is trying so hard? But just this once becomes all the time, and the old habits of interaction are upon them again.

Perhaps it is not regrettable that the co-alcoholic experience the slippage, for it will bring home to her how fiendishly difficult it is to change by fiat, even one's own fiat. While change does not come about except by will power, will power alone is seldom enough to produce it. Knowledge and understanding are necessary, too. It is at this juncture of revisited impasse that the question of therapy may arise. But therapy for whom? It would seem evident that it should be therapy for the alcoholic, and, indeed, there may be an excellent opportunity to suggest it, for the alcoholic, having tried and failed to moderate his drinking, is apt to turn to the co-alcoholic and again ask what she suggests he do, providing the co-alcoholic with a tailored opening to urge him to join A.A. or go to an alcoholism clinic or seek psychotherapy. But she may be wise to sidestep the opportunity for several reasons. It is further encouragement to him to look to her for answers, which feeds his dependence, his passivity, his reliance on being given direction, while what would be infinitely preferable would be for him to decide on a course of action dictated by his own necessities, not hers. If given advice, he will rebel against taking it, or if he does grudgingly follow it, it will be to demonstrate compliance, not agreement. And because he is complying with her will, not his own, although he may dutifully attend A.A. meetings or present himself punctually for therapy appointments, no help offered him, no form of treatment given him will be effective because his volition is not involved and his commitment is shallow or absent. But that will not be obvious. What will be apparent is that he has done what the co-alcoholic has requested and that, too, has failed. He will ask what more can be expected of him, and the co-alcoholic will not have an answer.

Rather than risk playing her ace and having it trumped, the co-alcoholic does better to think back over the path she has followed to this point. She has divested herself of hope of changing the alcoholic and has, instead, looked for ways of changing herself. She has left off making choices for the alcoholic and turned her attention to her own choices. Why not continue? Why not resist this new attempt at role-suction in favor of such a simple declaration as: "I don't know what you should do. I can't give you answers. I can only look for answers for myself." And then why not consider the possibility that getting help for herself is the constructive way of looking for answers?

The pluses in a decision to obtain therapy for herself rather than urging it upon the alcoholic are these: It is unexpected, and thus it keeps their personal equation in the desirable disequilibrium that prevents the alcoholic from pulling out all the old stops. It is a generous departure from the chronic insistence that all difficulties in the relationship are entirely of the alcoholic's making. It is evidence that not all blame, all guilt, must be assumed by the alcoholic and that the entire burden for preservation of the relationship is not his alone. It emphasizes that there are two people, two individuals in the situation. It is further proof that the co-alcoholic is not pinning her hopes on reforming the alcoholic and has turned her attention away from eradicating the drinking toward a constructive living with it. It is an indication that the co-alcoholic can require as least as much of herself as she asks from the alcoholic. It suggests openness, willingness to change, a moving away from entrenched, defensive positions. It is disarming.

Like the medical researcher who establishes the safety of his drug discovery by first testing it on himself, the co-alcoholic, if there later comes a time when the alcoholic voluntarily begins to speculate on the desirability of obtaining help, will be able to be intelligent and reassuring about it. She has been there, she knows what therapy can and cannot do, and she can be realistic in talking over its promise and its drawbacks. She can be realistic, too, in her expectations of what therapy can do for him. The fatigued co-alcoholic is inclined to believe that if she can just deliver the alcoholic into the hands of a professional, her problems will be at an end and she can sit back and wait for the magic of cure to be wrought. But therapy can be a rocky road, and she will need all of the stability and empathy she can muster to stand by while the alcoholic attempts to negotiate it. If she has been in treatment herself, she knows that, and she will not be dismayed or disappointed when therapy does not prove to be a broad-spectrum panacea but just one step, albeit a pivotal one, toward recovery.

This said, however, there is a far more telling argument having to do with the co-alcoholic alone. She herself needs help. She is in a difficult, lonely, almost unremittingly stressful position. She needs to talk about it, to express her agonies and her rage and her fear and her despair. She needs to know if what she thinks she is doing is what she is actually doing and whether it is the most useful thing she can be doing. She needs to rediscover trust and respect for herself. She needs fresh insight into the person she is. She needs a place where it is safe to be herself and a person with whom it is safe to be herself, so that she can come to know and accept that self.

Alcoholism makes for exceedingly knotty problems in living,

and she needs objective counsel to help her to cope with them. She needs help in understanding what the alcoholic is going through and help in understanding her own reactions. She would like to handle their life more constructively and imaginatively, to preserve it if possible, to protect it from increasing deterioration insofar as she is able. She wants to understand her contribution to their problems, to increase her sensitivity to what happens between them when the alcoholic drinks, and when he does not drink as well. If there are children, she very much wants and needs help and guidance in protecting them from harm. She wants a place to go with her problems and concerns and insecurities which does not involve the eyes and ears of family or friends. She wants, not to tell tales, but for there to be a setting in which she can tell her tale and have the telling of it be a useful endeavor.

As unexceptionable as her reasons are, the alcoholic will doubtless find them threatening. He does not desire objectivity and rationality introduced into their situation; his ends are better served if their interaction remains emotional and unexamined. He does not want to be understood; his interest lies in being forgiven. He does not want the co-alcoholic to be clear-headed; the greater the muddle, the more assured is he of repeated second chances. He does not want his behavior examined, appreciating that, once looked at objectively, what sensible person would put up with it? Therapy for the co-alcoholic will be interpreted by him as the thin edge of the wedge prying open the door to her desertion of him.

A woman who wanted nothing more than not to have to leave her alcoholic husband began seeing a therapist for the single purpose of exploring ways to enable her to go on with their life. Her intention was to master her upset, to bring it under control by freeing herself from massive overreaction to her husband's drinking, and therapy, as it progressed, gave promise of helping her to achieve just that. She was beginning to understand that her dread of her husband's losing his job, which was one of the main scores on which she fought his drinking, was, in truth, grounded in memories of her poverty-ridden childhood rather than well-founded in present probabilities, and this insight was helping her to become less frantic about his drinking. But her husband, apprehensive that her unwonted calm was an indication of growing distance from him, became so vehement in his objections to her therapy that he coerced her into giving it up.

He could not abide the notion that he was being "dissected," as he put it, "sliced up like a muscle under a microscope." Since alcoholics are not innocent of paranoia, this is one of the provocative aspects of therapy that the co-alcoholic must be prepared to defend by insisting that the thrust of therapy is not toward the atomizing of the alcoholic. He may often be the subject of it, but he is not its object. There is no intent to dismantle him and render him something less than human. There is no intent to explore his guilt and return an indictment of incompetency against him. Therapy is not a weapon to be turned on the alcoholic but a tool to increase the co-alcoholic's comfort with herself.

In the beginning, when the co-alcoholic is contemplating treatment for herself, it is sufficient for her to state that it will be *for* her, not *against* him, but later, when she is actually involved in the situation, whether it be psychoanalytic or supportive or directive therapy, intensive or brief, individual or group, Al-Anon or counseling in a social work setting, she must be certain to act on this precept. Fresh from a session, her mind buzzing with the content of the session, she will be hard-pressed to resist citing chapter and verse, to resist speaking of old wounds reopened by remembrance, to resist quoting words of sympathy and support she may have received, but she should bite her tongue and hold it just as much as she is able. Stories heard in an Al-Anon or counseling or therapy group of co-alcoholics can be consoling to the co-alcoholic, for they put her own experience in a larger framework and reduce her sense of being uniquely tried by fate, but if retold to the alcoholic, even with the best of intentions, even with the thought that he will be heartened by hearing that other couples have found ways to survive more severe problems than theirs, that other alcoholics are in more stricken circumstances, he will nevertheless hear the accounts as an indictment of alcoholics and, therefore, since objectivity is a quality in strikingly short supply in the alcoholic, as an indictment of him. He will grow silent and depressed, and if prodded into speech, will erupt in a tirade about the futility of trying to do anything about his drinking since he has already been labeled and filed away in the category of "alcoholic," which is to say, "hopeless" and "worthless." To hear that other alcoholics behave more shabbily is, to him, a prediction, not a consolation. To hear stories of other lives means, to him, only that his own life is being exposed, perhaps laughed at, certainly clucked over and condemned. The relief the co-alcoholic experiences from finding that her troubles are shared is, to him, relegation to a scorned minority. A story simply repeated will, to him, be a moral tale, the moral being what happens to people who keep on drinking, and he will squirm at its implications.

His sense of being under attack is exponentially increased if the co-alcoholic quotes comments made about his behavior. He will greatly resent having an "outsider's" opinions passed on to him and will consider that, if critical, they are presumptuous, if sympathetic, they are patronizing. The only thing worse than being misunderstood is being understood. It takes a solid ego to withstand it, particularly if the interpretation placed on a piece of behavior does not jibe with the individual's own rationalizations, even more particularly if it is couched in terms of his unconscious motivations. Nothing infuriates an alcoholic more than to hear such a comment as, "The therapist says the reason you're so cussed is because you're really very dependent on me and you're trying to hide it." The co-alcoholic may feel that this is an enlightening observation which helps her to understand, and thus be less troubled by, previously baffling behavior, but if it is indeed an accurate appraisal of the alcoholic's unconscious need, the very fact that it is unconscious will send the alcoholic into battle to deny it.

So often, it seems that if a person could just be made to understand the causes of his behavior, he would be able to modify it, but, as a famous psychoanalyst once remarked, what a patient needs is not information but an experience. The success psychotherapy has in producing change in people comes about primarily through their experience in it, not through information gained in the course of it. Thus, although the co-alcoholic may be fascinated as the roots of his, her, and their behavior are untangled, it will do her no good to share her discoveries with the alcoholic because the information will not be useful to him, and he will be bitterly antagonized by the sense that it is being used against him.

Any benefit to the alcoholic from the co-alcoholic's assaying of therapy cannot be direct in the sense of imparting the information she gains. All she can offer him, in turn, is an experience. As she develops the ability to step outside their relationship and view it dispassionately, their interaction will change. Her lessened emotional reactivity to the drinking will allow her to preserve her equanimity and exercise her sense of humor. Her delighted rediscovery of herself as a person, as doer, not victim, will make her more generous, more relaxed, more unguarded. Her increasing sense that the alcoholism is his problem essentially, hers only tangentially, will redefine their areas of responsibility. The atmospheric pressure will be lowered, for the more unshackled she becomes, the less will she interact with the alcoholic in the sick ways that have bound them together but have also threatened to sink them entirely.

In the long run, her composure, the quiet confidence with which she handles situations that once reduced her to helplessness, will be a more potent advertisement for treatment than any words. The alcoholic will look and listen and wonder. He has known this person. He has played upon her. He has maneuvered and manipulated and dominated her. He has instinctively known which button to push to elicit which response, but gradually the responses take on a different character or do not come at all. The co-alcoholic pleasantly resists his artful tactics, or, unbelievably, she takes no notice of them. She understands more quickly and more clearly than he what he is up to, and she is not frightened by his twists and turns. She is walking on a higher and drier path, while he flounders in a swamp of guilt and pain and confusion. If therapy has set her on this path, might it not hold some promise for him? He cannot help but entertain the thought, if not to save himself, at least to prevent himself from being left behind.

But, again, this is not the goal of therapy for the co-alcoholic. If the co-alcoholic undertakes therapy only to arm herself with higher caliber weapons against the alcoholic or only to prove a point to him, therapy will neither benefit her nor be persuasive to him. Her commitment to treatment must be on her own behalf, an honest commitment toward the honest end of self-understanding. Certainly, in the early stages of, for example, an Al-Anon group or a therapy group composed of relatives of alcoholics, the talk will center almost exclusively on the abuses the members have suffered at the hands of the alcoholics in their lives. There is likely to be a can-you-top-this quality to the conversation as the group members vie with each other to see who can tell the most horrendous stories of what they have been through. This is cathartic, for it is good to unburden oneself and it is good to compare one's own experience with that of others'. One can come away from such sessions purged of heavy secrets and impressed by the resiliency with which people bounce back from dire events. But such sessions are little more than bull sessions, and it is only when this aspect of them palls, when the members grow tired of chronicling the transgressions of alcoholics and begin to turn to exploration of their own behavior, that the real work of the group begins.

This is true, as well, of individual therapy or counseling. The co-alcoholic cannot start out otherwise than by detailing the problems caused by the alcoholic's drinking and describing particular circumstances and events, adding information about how she has attempted to handle them, the measures she has taken, the type and amount of pressure she has brought to bear. This is simple communication, but part of her motive for the description will be to exonerate herself. Understandably, she wants to be told that she has done everything humanly possible. She wants sympathy for her straits and approval for her patience and forbearance. She wants to be relieved of the suspicion that there was something else she could have done, something she has left undone, something that she has not been kind enough or generous enough or selfless enough to have done. She wants to be relieved of nameless guilt, of a sense of inadequacy. She wants to be reassured that the failure has not been hers. Often, although it is not always a conscious desire, she wants to hear that she is justified in giving up; she wants a one-way ticket out validated by a professional.

If the co-alcoholic, while traversing this inevitable first phase of therapy, can hold in mind that she has sought therapy for herself, not to be let off the hook but to find out why she is on it, she can progress beyond self-exculpation to self-exploration, wherein lies the true value of any therapeutic endeavor. Keeping in mind that she is basically in therapy for herself, not as a stand-in for the alcoholic, she can move on to a probing of how she functions and of how she functions in relation to the alcoholic.

She is not alone in making the almost automatic assumption that she behaves by taking a reading of reality and appraising it in the light of rationality and experience, but judgment can be subverted and reality can lose its clear outlines when two minds are involved, as a psychologist demonstrated by requiring that husbands and wives whom he had tested individually retake the same set of tests together. His only instructions were that together they must appraise each task presented them and decide on a single, joint response. Rather than improving their test performance, as would be expected from the opportunity to pool their knowledge, many couples did more poorly together than one or the other had done separately. One partner might be certain that two and two make four, for example, but give in to the other's more insistently expressed conviction that three was the answer, and often it was the partner who saw things in the more distorted fashion whose opinion prevailed; the healthier one was more willing to entertain the notion that he might be wrong and thus could be led to deny his own perception of reality and his own judgment. If this happens in a testing situation, it certainly happens in life that it is not always the person with the greatest discernment whose view is accepted. Since it does happen in life, and perhaps with particular frequency in the interaction of alcoholic and co-alcoholic, one of the most useful functions of therapy for the co-alcoholic is to enable her to see where she has fallen in with the alcoholic's distortions, where she has been persuaded to deny or doubt evidence, where, together, they have befogged what one or the other of them alone might have been capable of seeing clearly.

Not all distortions will be the alcoholic's. Everyone wears the viewing lenses with which he was fitted in childhood: the set of beliefs and habits and expectations and motivations with which his experience of the world then equipped him. It is not the co-alcoholic's purpose in therapy to have her singular set certified as correct but to learn what they are, to deduce, insofar as possible, what the alcoholic's are, and to piece together an understanding of how the two sets interact, where the two people augment each other's vision and where they degrade each other's judgment.

An area in which this will be of prime interest is the drinking itself. It will be enlightening for the co-alcoholic to explore whether hers is a reasonable response to the destructiveness and waste of uncontrolled drinking or whether it is overdetermined. Is the alcoholic right in saying she takes his drinking far too seriously, or is she justified in reacting as strongly as she does? Does she handle it maturely or is she inconsistent, tolerant at some times, punitive at others? What, in her, dictates how she views it and how she copes with it?

As she explores her feelings, she may uncover an intense amount of guilt. She has tried to help the alcoholic, and she has failed. Therefore, she must have done the wrong thing or not enough of the right thing or failed to understand or added to his stress rather than alleviated it. In some crucial area, she must be inadequate, and that area, she senses, is her incapacity to provide enough love. Love is highly valued in our present-day society. Touted as the answer to most problems, if it does not succeed in solving a problem, well, then, it is not because it is not the right solution but because it is not the right love; it is not unstinting enough, encompassing enough, selfless enough, pure enough. Two things persuade the co-alcoholic to subscribe to this fiction uncritically. One is that a large part of the alcoholic personality's original attraction for her was the opportunity to prove her own lovingness, a quality which she has perhaps subliminally doubted throughout her life, for, did she not have hidden questions about her own capacity to love, she would not continue her attachment to a person who would constantly test it; persons who are certain of their affectionate natures can transfer their affections when the loving is profitless. The second is that the alcoholic's demand is for unconditional, limitless love, and when he receives anything less, he defines the affection as meager and stunted and grudging, a definition he is quick to apprise the co-alcoholic of. Since she has had a lifelong suspicion that she may not be a truly loving person, his accusation finds resonance in her, and she guiltily assumes that he is right.

This, in large measure, accounts for the seemingly masochistic willingness of the co-alcoholic to persist in trying with the alcoholic. She accepts a ration of hurt, disappointment, and frustration inconceivable to another person because the final admission of herself as unloving would be even more painful. The alcoholic accuses her of being cold and uncaring, she suspects but cannot accept that this is true, and the compelling necessity of proving herself otherwise holds her in subjugation to a situation which a more secure person would not tolerate.

As the co-alcoholic will come to recognize in therapy, she is not unloving. She appears to be so because she contrasts herself with the alcoholic, who, indeed, has an open and generous and amiable nature. But his love is indiscriminate, diffuse, and readily bestowed. In return for sunny warmth and indulgent approval, he radiates affection, but not because of admiration or respect for the object of his affection, not because he recognizes and cherishes particular qualities in the other, but simply because he is being accepted and humored. His is not a mature love. It is shallow, dependent, and made up in large part of need. But the co-alcoholic, dimly or not at all aware that there are ways and ways of loving, compares her doled-out, contingent feelings with his expansive ones and finds herself critically wanting.

Also undermining her ability to believe in her own lovingness is the fact that, in view of the circumstances of life with an alcoholic, there cannot help but be a heavy admixture of animosity toward the person who causes her so much pain, undermines her pleasure in life, tramples on her feelings, and torments her with his irrational and destructive behavior. In truth, her feelings for him are ambivalent, her love adulterated. While she presumes that this is because of some lack in her, some congenital incapacity, the defects are not in her but in the relationship. How could she love wholeheartedly and unequivocally a person whose demands for love are insatiable but who responds to it, as often as not, with pain-producing behavior?

Just as she cannot have confidence in her love because she also despises, so can she not even be quite certain that she hates because she also envies. It is simple enough, at one level, to be completely convinced that excessive drinking is wrong, but, at another level, who is one person to say to another that pleasure-seeking, tension-reducing behavior is bad, immoral? We have all become self-conscious about our puritan heritage, the ethic which proclaims that work, responsibility, and rectitude are the only worthy ways of life, that escape from burdens, interference with consciousness, and self-indulgence are reprehensible. We are no longer so certain that self-restraint and self-denial are laudable achievements in themselves. The mythology of our everyday lives conspires to persuade us that they are not, that mind-altering and emotion-tranquillizing and need-indulging and escape-inducing devices are not only acceptable but necessary expressions of contempt for a restrictive and repressive culture. Thus, unsure that the precepts we live by are enduringly valid and not merely the residue of outmoded traditions, we are not only hesitant about imposing them steadily on another but even perhaps secretly envious of the alcoholic's ability to be cavalier in rejecting them. We suspect that it may indicate a greater freedom, a greater independence. Is the alcoholic the emancipated one? Is the co-alcoholic merely too timid, too brainwashed by her upbringing, to dare forays into escapism?

Like emigrants from a foreign land who will never be entirely free of nostalgia for their place of origin, no co-alcoholic is without the remembrance of childhood when the demands were fewer and simpler and escape into irresponsibility was permissible. She intuits that the alcoholic still has what she has lost: the means and the defiance to go back, and some part of her travels with him, identifying with him and longing to be able to find the same surcease from pressures and care and responsibility. As a consequence, her censure is not steady; sometimes she is tolerant because she wishes the same regression for herself; sometimes she is punitive because she denies the same regression to herself. She is troubled by her inconsistency and baffled by it because she does not understand its sources. And that, of course, is where therapy can be of help: not in ironing out complexities and contradictions in feelings but in uncovering their source, and not in the alcoholic but in the co-alcoholic herself.

A co-alcoholic who sought therapy found herself remembering a childhood incident involving a younger brother who was her mother's humored favorite while she herself, as firstborn, was held to strict standards of behavior. Her brother had been too busy playing one afternoon to bother to go into the house to the bathroom and so had soiled himself. Their mother, washing out his underwear, had chuckled, almost lovingly, as she made a casual comment to a visiting neighbor along the lines of, "Boys will be boys." The girl, overhearing, well knew what a scolding she would have received for the same transgression and was, of course, resentful that she had to behave responsibly while her brother did not and jealous that, no matter how little trouble she caused and how much he caused, he was the one who was uncritically loved.

It was but a short step from recollection of this incident to an understanding of her resentful relationship to her alcoholic husband. He was irresponsible, uncontrolled, badly behaved, while she was conscientious, controlled, and impeccably well-behaved. Yet, he was the one loved and forgiven and watched over, while she received no praise or comfort or extra consideration. He made messes which were cleaned up for him, while it was assumed that she would both do the tidying up and make no trouble of her own. In repetition of a lifelong pattern, she behaved well and received no reward; he behaved badly and received no punishment. Of course, she was filled with resentment. Of course, she despaired of her own lovableness. Of course, she despised as well as loved her husband and was both scornful of his behavior and envious of it, as she had loved and despised her brother and been scornful of his childish ways and envious of his ability to get away with them. With this pattern unraveling before her eyes, much that had been inexplicable in her relationship to her husband ceased to be puzzling, including the frightening resentment that welled up in her when he drank and the shaming knowledge that she would not be entirely adverse to having some calamity befall him in retribution for his drinking.

When one is racked by vile emotions whose wellsprings are unknown, one dreads the presence of a meanness and malevolence in the self which seem as though they must surely be in-bred so tenaciously do they resist rooting out, and one remains unflaggingly on guard lest they escape into action and do irreparable damage. But when one is put in touch with the sources of behavior and feelings, there comes into existence the conviction that one is basically a loving and constructive person, and when that is believed, natural and spontaneous behavior becomes possible. No longer must feelings be fought down, words choked back, actions aborted. If they stream forth in attack, it is because that is the response the situation calls for. They are not an expression of a dark and terrible side of one's nature but a legitimate response to illegitimate provocation. Let the co-alcoholic come to trust herself, let her come to believe in herself as an essentially good and decent person, and she can end her self-censorship, not only adding immeasurably to her own self-respect, since she is now standing up for herself as a person entitled to express her feelings, but also, perhaps for the first time, revealing to the alcoholic the exact nature of those feelings.

The firmness of the hold the alcoholic has on the co-alcoholic commonly stems as much from her insecurities as from his persuasiveness. Doubting her capacity to care wholeheartedly, she attempts to prove it time and again with forgiveness and understanding. Uncertain of her innate decency, she demonstrates it with superhuman tolerance. Fearing that anger and envy reveal grave flaws of character, she speaks with tentative mildness. What therapy can do for the co-alcoholic, then, is to allow the real person to stand up. She may enter it hoping to find out how to handle the alcoholic, but if she perseveres, she will leave it knowing how to handle herself.

What type of therapy should the co-alcoholic seek? It does not really matter. All that is important is that she undertake it with the clear intent of understanding the needs of her own that she is living out in relation to the alcoholic: her identity needs, her caretaking needs, her aggressive needs. As therapy brings them to light, the co-alcoholic will find that not only has she been helped but that now she is in a far better position to help the alcoholic. Because she will need less from him, she will be able to do more for him.

11

The Co-Alcoholic
as Therapist

Psychotherapy has been described as the "assisted self-study of motivations," a definition which does not include the word change and carries no connotation that it is the intent or the responsibility of one person, the therapist, to change another person, the patient. It is a common misconception that an individual presents himself for therapy in order to have the therapist perform feats of psychic legerdemain designed to extinguish self-defeating traits and transform the patient into a paradigm of full-functioning normality. But the therapist has neither the means nor the power to weed out maladaptive behaviors. He can only assist the person in his own self-study of the motivations which dictate and maintain his behavior. To the degree that this endeavor is successful and the patient becomes familiar with the sources of his behavior, he may indeed change, but it will be because the motivations, exposed to his own scrutiny, wither and lose their influence, freeing him to seek new directions, not because the therapist has produced alterations by dint of psychic manipulations.

Were it otherwise, the saving in time and effort would be notable. The therapist, experienced in identifying unconscious motivations, could simply spend that amount of time with the patient necessary for him to gain a knowledge of the problem and then, as a physician does, having deduced the probable cause from the evidence of its effects, communicate a diagnosis to the patient and offer a prescription to right the cause of the patient's distress. But, unfortunately, it does the patient little or no good to be understood by the therapist. The patient must understand himself. And even the least disturbed of people have stubborn and complex defenses against this kind of understanding. The roots of behavior are largely unconscious, and before an individual can become aware of them, his defenses must be painstakingly unraveled. He must find his way, with the help of the therapist, through them and around them, picking his way through the thickets of his characteristic beliefs, rationalizations, and ingrained views until he has penetrated to their source, for only by retracing the way he has come to be like he is can he release himself from the necessity to be like he is.

How does a therapist assist an individual to study himself? Suppose, as an extreme example, a man is standing in front of his house systematically beating his head against a stone wall. A motorist might stop and intervene to restrain him forcibly, only to look back and find, when he started on his way again, that the man had resumed his pounding. Another person happening on the scene might use words alone, ordering the man to stop, again only to observe that the man returned to his destructive activity when the force of the injunction wore off. A third witness might attempt to reason with the man by asking him why he was beating his head against a wall, and the man might be at a loss to explain or might give an elaborate explanation but, in either event, be helpless to alter his behavior. A therapist, in contrast, might come and sit nearby and say little or nothing for a time and then merely offer an observation:

"That looks as though it hurts."

"Yes."

"You must deserve to be hurt."

"Why?"

"You tell me. You're the one who's doing it to yourself."

"I don't know why."

"If someone else were doing it to you, it would look as though you were being punished."

"Maybe."

"Could it be that you're punishing yourself?"

"I've done nothing wrong."

"Still, you're beating your head against the wall."

"I can't stop."

"What would happen if you did?"

"Something terrible."

"What?"

"I might kill someone else."

"Do you want to kill someone else?"

"No."

"Did you ever want to?"

"No."

"You're unusual. Most people want to kill someone some time or other."

"Oh, well, when I was a child, sure. I wanted to kill my father because he was hurting my mother."

"But you were afraid."

"Yes."

"Are you afraid now?"

"I might kill someone I love because she is hurting me."

"So, is it possible that you're destroying yourself to keep from destroying her?"

"I suppose it's possible."

"Is there any real danger that you might kill her?"

"No. I love her."

Since this is a hypothetical example, it can be granted a happy ending: the man, aided to achieve some insight into the heavy hand of his past on the present, gives a sigh of relief and abandons his self-destructive behavior. But in life a more probable outcome would be that his self-destructiveness would surface in another area, and another, and be manifested in relation to still other people, and it would be necessary for the therapist to prompt him repeatedly to the recognition that each fresh outbreak was traceable to the same old root: a fear of murderous impulses toward a hurtful person. An impactful time in childhood is hydra-headed· identify one form it takes in the present and it will pop up in another guise. And it will continue to do so until the bare bones of isolated memories have been fleshed out with the feelings that in all likelihood accompanied them at the time and those feelings have been lived through again and again until they grow attenuated and lose their power to drive to the forefront in every situation.

Being a professional archeologist of the mind, the therapist may need to see only the first exhumed bone to make an educated guess about the identity of the skeleton buried there, but for him to pronounce it a dinosaur is not convincing to the patient, who will have to uncover a very great deal more in the way of evidence before the past assumes a recognizable shape and its relation to the present becomes discernible to him. Knowing this, the therapist will not offer his patient a pat reconstruction but will encourage him to keep digging, now and again directing his attention to a promising area, commenting on something he is in danger of overlooking, and offering tentative suggestions on the possible fit of seemingly unrelated pieces, but otherwise leaving the spadework to him.

The therapist assists the patient to dig, not by asking *why*, but by asking *what*. He does not say, "Why are you doing this?" but "What are you doing? What are you feeling? What, in this time, is reminiscent of another time?" He does not volunteer information on what the patient is doing; he waits for the patient to tell him. And then he does not tell the patient why he is doing what he is doing: he helps the patient to study himself until the patient can tell *him* why, for only self-earned knowledge of the self is lasting and useful.

It might seem that any one person could ask another, "What are you doing?" and, indeed, it is perfectly possible for people to act as therapists to one another. Bartenders, hairdressers, teachers, confidantes, by listening, do it all the time. Why, then, is a therapist necessary? The answer is that he is not. Any friend or relative or companion can function in a therapeutic capacity. But interested parties rarely do, or they rarely do for more than a few consecutive minutes because, among other reasons, it is astonishingly difficult not to give advice. Any individual listening to another inevitably feels called upon to comment, to say something constructive, to offer a way out of a dilemma, and the advice he gives will be what he would do in a similar situation.

I have, when desperate over the problems of dealing with an alcoholic, spoken of my misery to friends, and I have gotten sympathy, which is momentarily consoling but of no practical help, and I have gotten advice, which has, almost without exception, reflected the friends' characteristic coping mechanisms. I have been told, for example, to take a trip, to go to Europe and get away from the problem for a time—by someone who is renewed and restored by travel, as I am not. I have been told to be patient and forgiving and wait for a better day to dawn—by someone whose capacity for suffering is greater than mine. I have been told to leave the alcoholic—by someone who is more of a loner than I. That I have gotten such advice is my fault, for I have said, "What should I do?" not, "What am I doing?" The latter does not occur to me because I take it for granted that I know what I am doing: I am trying to survive, and I am trying to find a way of bringing the drinking to a halt. But that is not the basic *what*.

Only one friend approached that. "Your mother died of alcoholism," she said. "Are you replaying that scene, trying to save someone else to prove her death wasn't your fault?" That was a useful comment because it at least posed the question of my motivation in being where I was and doing what I was doing. It would have been interesting to explore it further, but my friend and I were talking over coffee in a restaurant and it was midnight, near closing time, and we could not sit for another hour while I let resemblances between the then and the now float into my mind. Nor would she be able to listen noncommittally to my musings; inevitably, she would seize on a stray description to prove her thesis, for one becomes enamored of one's own insights, particularly if they seem promising, and a vested interest in substantiating them quickly develops. She was a friend, not a therapist, and I would not speak with absolute candor; I would censor what I said because I would not want her to think ill of me or because some matters might be too intimate or too revealing to share in such circumstances. And we could not long remain objective because I would soon, without being aware of it, shift from an examination of my needs to an acting out of them. I would, that is, try to lure her into meeting them. That is the way of people. If it was true that I needed to absolve myself of guilt over my mother's fate, I would so couch my descriptions that she, as a friend, would find it virtually impossible not to tell me that I was not to blame. And once she said that, we would no longer be studying my motivations but excusing them.

These are some of the factors that stand in the way of one (untrained) person's acting as therapist to another. As obstacles, they are not insurmountable, of course, and people do act therapeutically toward one another with some degree of success, but the success is limited, the exploration of motivations stops far short of full elucidation because it is extraordinarily difficult for even a wise and knowledgeable and personally secure friend to remain as detached as the assistant in self-exploration must be. Hence, while I have suggested that the co-alcoholic attempt to push back the bounds of her personal unknowingness just as far as she is able to by herself, and while there are occasions when friends can be of aid in this endeavor, it is obvious that professional help, if it is feasible and can be obtained, is the most effective means of release from the trapping aspects of co-alcoholism.

Since it is even more important that the alcoholic be released from his alcoholism, why is not the same unhesitating recommendation of therapy made for him? Therapy for the alcoholic can be, and is, the sensible long-range goal but, in all probability, the present positions of the alcoholic and the co-alcoholic are not the same. The alcoholic is an active drinker who may or may not be admitting to the problem of alcoholism but, in any event, is a long way from finding his situation intolerable and even further from desiring drastic alteration in it. The co-alcoholic, for her part, does find the situation intolerable, does want help with it, and is not threatened by the possibility of change. She is, in other words, motivated to engage in self-study, which is an absolute prerequisite of successful therapy.

Since the alcoholic is not only not motivated to attempt self-study but actively resists self-awareness and is characterologically antipathetic to the notion of looking inward, he is a poor candidate for therapy and is usually obstinately opposed to the notion of it. He identifies the locus of his problems as being outside himself, and thus he believes that it is externals which require adjusting, not his internal milieu. He is not interested in the nature of what he is experiencing, only, if the feeling is causing him discomfort, in being rid of it. He acts out rather than thinks out what is happening to him. He acts out rather than talks out his feelings, and since therapy is predicated on the basis of thinking and talking out problems rather than acting them out, there could scarcely be an approach less intuitively congenial to him.

Earlier, I suggested the probability that the stage is set for alcoholism in infancy, and infancy is a preverbal time of life. The infant experiences states of tension, the physical tension induced by hunger or other bodily discomfort, and his response is immediate: he cries. Because his brain has not yet developed to the point of employing language, he does not conceptualize the specifics of his distress and he does not communicate in words that he is hungry or cold or wet or has a pin sticking in him. There is no delay for thought between the experience and expression of a need.

For the majority of infants, however, there is some delay between the expression of a need and the arrival of relief, and as the maturing process goes forward, the child begins to fill in the time with thought. Questions form: Is she coming? Will she ever come again? Have I done something to cause her to stay away? The child grows accustomed to thinking about how he has behaved and how he should behave. As he gradually relinquishes his narcissistic, grandiose view of the world as an arena in which he occupies the catered-to, central position, words become a tool for structuring reality and identifying his place in it. Originally loved and cared for because of what he is, increasingly he realizes that he must also earn security and devotion by virtue of what he does. The environment, by reward and punishment, provides myriad clues as to how he is to behave, and as he grows less helpless, he becomes more deserving by responding to them. Behavior defined as bad by those around him is eschewed;

thoughts and wishes reacted to as unacceptable are suppressed; importunate demands are stifled because anxiety over possible loss of love and support is more unbearable than the tension of unmet needs. The child learns to formulate in thought his problem and the likely consequences of behaving in one way rather than another, and he learns to arrive at decisions which he can then communicate in words if he so wishes.

For a minority of children, among them those who later become alcoholics, this progression from the preverbal time of tension and action to a verbal time of thought and delay and communication in words rather than pure behavior occurs late and imperfectly because the environment continues to be over-solicitous, supportive, and devoid of demands for more discriminating response. Such children learn words, of course, but they are not the words of self-examination, self-questioning, self-doubt, and self-appraisal. They have no need of them, since the way they do behave gets them what they want. And when, as adults, the world is not always obliging in prompt delivery of ego-nourishing supplies of approval, acceptance, and applause, they turn to alcohol to provide them, again finessing the necessity for turning the spotlight of thought on themselves.

The alcoholic, never forced out of the security of the knowledge, "I am loved and taken care of because I am," into the questioning land of, "How must I be in order to deserve love and care?" honestly does not appreciate any need to examine his behavior in a systematic, intensive way. Schooled in a preverbal time, words are an unfamiliar medium in which to try to make sense of his life, his experience, his mode of functioning. He cannot credit that they might ever make an effective substitute for satisfaction. As a candidate for therapy, then, he is rather in the position of a medical patient who would be greatly benefited by reparative surgery but who would be an unattractive risk for such surgery because of a long-standing anemia.

Just as the physician can administer vitamin injections and oversee the patient's diet in an effort to correct an anemia prior to surgery, so also can the psychotherapist, confronted with a patient ill-prepared to withstand psychological probing and ill-versed in the use of the words which are its tool, undertake a period of pre-therapy training with the alcoholic. This he will do by attempting to establish an atmosphere of mutual liking and trust and respect and by encouraging the alcoholic to depend on him for support and some gratification of his dependency needs. He will try to build a firm relationship which the alcoholic places increasing reliance on and grows reluctant to jeopardize. He will try to fashion, out of the alcoholic's liking and need for him, the bonds which will hold the patient fast even after the pain of probing begins. When the bonds seem firm, he will slowly encourage the alcoholic to give expression to his feelings in words rather than actions and he will attempt to reduce the sympathy and support he offers in an effort to make the alcoholic more susceptible to anxiety than to his usual tension. If he succeeds and anxiety over losing the relationship replaces some measure of tension in the psychic economy, then, and only then, will the therapist proceed cautiously to the work of therapy proper.

All of this is a delicate and arduous process, and at any point the alcoholic may drift away, plausibly claiming that the therapist is not really helping him. He can label therapy a waste of time and money because, of all people, the alcoholic expects something immediate and tangible to be done for him. He can usually find or has available alternatives to the therapist's support and interest because, as readily as he invests emotion in one person, just so readily does he withdraw it and turn to someone else if the relationship is not satisfying along the parameters he defines as gratifying. Often, it is only when there is a literal barrier to his escape from the therapist, such as, for example, his being in a hospital, that he can be induced to continue seeing the therapist, and even then he may retreat into silence or a sham cooperativeness in which he is physically present but emotionally unengaged. Outside of a hospital setting, it is more than likely that, not being ready for therapy, he will ease out of the therapeutic situation before treatment as such can get underway and thereafter claim that he gave therapy a chance and it did him no good.

There is one person, however, whose loss would open an abyss in the alcoholic's life, to whom his attachment is strong and firm and whose love and support and interest he is already certain of. This is the co-alcoholic. Because the relationship which the therapist would have to build painstakingly before he could put any pressure on the patient to examine himself is already in existence with the co-alcoholic, it is she who is in the most advantageous position to undertake the pre-therapy training of the alcoholic. She is with him a great deal of the time; he can flee her, but only for short periods. She knows him; she sees him under all circumstances, and she is familiar with his moods and his reactions. She is aware of his drinking patterns and can explicate them with a high degree of accuracy. She obviously cares; she is not idly poking about for the pleasure of seeing him squirm, an indulgence the alcoholic quirkily suspects the therapist of engaging in. The alcoholic cannot accuse her of failing to cure him and use that excuse as an escape because their situation is not one in which there is an implicit promise of cure. He is dependent on her, and this gives her more leverage than a therapist would have: counting on the bonds between them to stretch rather than snap, she can confront him more directly and more frequently with the evidence of his behavior than an outsider would dare, and she has a weapon to produce anxiety in him; she can threaten him with loss.

As long as the alcoholic's chief emotional experience is tension, therapy holds no particular inducement for him. He can get instant, efficacious relief from a bottle, and the therapist has nothing to offer that can compete with that. Even if he could promise cure in the vague future, the alcoholic would consider the distant, and distinctly mixed, blessing of a life without alcohol inadequate compensation for present pain. Any person, not just the alcoholic, must experience intense unhappiness and have failed to find solutions to it before he is prepared to withstand the rigors of therapy in the hope of long-range relief. Since the alcoholic's solution to unease is to drink, this solution must fail him, and not only fail him but make an obvious contribution to the greater and less easily banished discomfort of anxiety before therapy has an appeal to make to him.

A considerable part of the co-alcoholic's task, then, in acting as pre-therapist is to foster anxiety in the alcoholic and to link it with his drinking. Since quarreling about the drinking, topped off with angry or despairing threats about the future, is a consistent feature of life with the alcoholic, it would seem that if the co-alcoholic were going to be successful as an agent of anxiety, she would already have been so. But the amplified volume of a quarrel gives even pernicious threats an unreal quality. Like the heated sparks a mother throws off to frighten a recalcitrant child into line, they quickly sputter out because the bonds are basically firm and the flurry is momentary. To be a stimulus to corrective anxiety, the bonds themselves must be called into question. And this is what the co-alcoholic does when she abandons efforts to cure the alcoholic. When she foregoes direct intervention to persuade or force him to stop drinking, when she focuses her attention on preserving and enriching her own life, when she moves out of the rigidified role of co-alcoholic, she demonstrates an impressive degree of detachment that steadily menaces the alcoholic's future and generates in him a sense of anxiety not lightly dispelled.

Whereas previously the co-alcoholic has taken some pride in her ability to be understanding and gentle and accepting and nurturant, and, in so doing, has acted as a surrogate mother, if she is going to stand *in loco parentis* to the alcoholic, that is but a part of the parenting function. To be fatherly is an equally legitimate and necessary function. The father is a representative of reality. He sets reasonable standards of behavior which he expects to have met, and he counters defiance or failure with punishment. He insists on efforts toward independence, and he utilizes his position of greater strength to encourage and enforce them. He threatens the child with rejection if the child weakly follows the path of pleasure over duty and responsibility. He uses his authoritarian position to tax the child with anxiety if the child is disobedient. He is both exemplar and executioner, holding up to the child what is right, cutting the child down when he is wrong.

As comfortable as it is to be motherly to the alcoholic, it can be difficult, even frightening, to be fatherly. A publishing executive had a colleague, a woman whom he valued as friend as well as co-worker and whom he had several times seen through alcoholic crises, and when she ceased telephoning in excuses after several days of absence from the office, he assumed another such crisis was upon them and prevailed on the superintendent of her building to let him into her apartment. He found her drunk and raging, near collapse from lack of food and determined upon suicide. After two days of hovering over her, expressing sympathy and support and ladling reassurance and affection into her in place of the practical nourishment she refused to take, he reluctantly concluded that hospitalization was the only recourse and called her (recently acquired) psychiatrist for help. The psychiatrist listened while Jim explained the seriousness of the situation, agreed with his estimate of it, but contradicted his proposed solution. "We'd be playing right into her hands," he said. "She wants to be hospitalized because that would prove she's helpless and has to be taken care of. She's blackmailing us, and if we give in, she'll never learn to take responsibility for herself. Now, my advice is this: leave her, go back to your office and be unavailable." Jim protested that they were playing ultimate games and that, if they lost, his friend would be dead. "I'm willing to risk it, and you have to be too," the psychiatrist said. "After all, if she is going to kill herself, there's not a thing you or I can do to stop it. She'll do it under our noses if her mind is made up. So, we have to give her a chance to find out that she's bluffing, that she really wants to live." Aware of Jim's desperate doubts, he added this: "Like Hamlet, we must be cruel in order to be kind."

The cruelty of being fatherly to the alcoholic in the sense of being firm to the point of harshness, of insisting that he fight his own battles, of refusing to rescue him from quagmires of his own making is not cruelty as it is ordinarily defined. No more than does a father, does one strike the alcoholic or lock him up or refuse to speak or look at him or sneer at him or write him off as someone too spineless to be worth bothering about. It is the cruelty instead, of being dispassionate. It is looking at an unwashed, disheveled alcoholic lying in clothes he has not changed in days and saying, "You are in a mess, aren't you?" rather than, "Let me help you get cleaned up." It is refusing to feel pity and, in its place, simply remarking, "What are you going to do about the state you're in?" It is answering his cry of "Help me!" with, "I can't help you. You'll have to help yourself." It is resisting the impulse to hide the liquor and fix some food which you then beg him to eat. It is saying, "What are you doing to yourself?" not, "What happened to make you do this?" It is refusing to sympathize or share his panic or believe with him that he is helpless. It is rejection of his self-pity and the calm insistence that whatever is to be done for him must be done by him.

It is, for the co-alcoholic on a day-to-day basis, leaving off attempts to keep the alcoholic unruffled, to placate him, to make his life run smoothly. It is replacing her tentative, eager-to-please, eager-to-agree manner with a cool forthrightness. It is switching from the hasty words designed to gloss over disturbance to the words that represent and may reveal reality. It is, for instance, asking the alcoholic who is threatening to quit his job, not why, but what. What happened today? What did your boss actually say? What made you feel you were unappreciated? And then summing up with: "It doesn't sound like sufficient reason to quit a job, but if you think it is, go ahead."

There is very little point in trying to argue the alcoholic into seeing the world in a different way, but there is a great deal of point in trying to make apparent to him the way he does see it. If he is asked why, he will build a case. If he is asked what, his case often crumbles. The facts, which tend to be trivial when they are brought out, should simply be allowed to stand, and his proposed solution, such as quitting his job, as extreme as it may obviously be, should simply be agreed with. When a person is argued with, he defends his position ever more heatedly; when he is agreed with, the wind goes out of his sails and second thoughts have a way of creeping in. A friend used to plead tearfully with her frequently disgruntled husband to remember his obligation to her, to their children and their education, to their mortgage and car payments when he announced his intention of walking out on his job; now she says, "Okay, let's go to Oregon and buy a peach farm," and it is he who becomes suddenly practical, who weighs the realistic considerations involved and decides that perhaps he is overreacting to whatever happened in the office that day. His rage subsides into grumbling, and his grumbling fades out in the course of the evening, and the evening becomes an ordinary one instead of another page in their calendar of fights and tears and insensate drinking on his part. What his wife has done is to preempt his unrealistic position and force him to move to a position where he can scarcely escape thinking realistically.

Confrontation with reality, which the alcoholic so sorely needs because he is given to distortions and exaggerations, is best accomplished in this indirect way: not by telling him how he should see the world but by reflecting how he does see it and taking his reaction one step further. This one step further interposes thought between feeling and action. "Okay, let's go to Oregon and buy a peach farm" introduces a delay between the alcoholic's feeling—induced by whatever slight, snub, or setback he experienced during the day at his job—and his action—quitting his job in a huff. And it has an added advantage: it allows the co-alcoholic to remain cool. She is not drawn into an argument by her apprehension over what he may do. She does not become emotional herself. She keeps her objectivity, and this objectivity permits her to recognize resemblances between what the alcoholic is reacting to this week and what he reacted to last week and what he reacted to a month ago. A pattern begins to emerge which she is able to identify. Instead of being panicked by his mood, she can venture a casual comment on it: "That sounds like last week when so-and-so said. . . ." Her questions can be friendly, her comments merely a passing observation. The co-alcoholic's task as pre-therapist is not to force self-awareness on the alcoholic but to begin to train him that there are patterns to be aware of: that each day is not a new day, that each affront is not a new affront, that each reaction of his is not a new reaction, and that there may be common denominators in all.

When her objectivity permits her to spot certain common denominators, the temptation will be great to insist that the alcoholic see them too, but if at all possible, she should simply let them be on display where the alcoholic can add them up when and if he is able to. To rush in with, "What you are doing is . . ." risks rousing his resentment and resistance. A question is less provocative than a statement, and when there are enough similar answers lying around, the alcoholic may begin to gather them into categories which he comes to recognize. Then it may come about that he remarks, "What I seem to be doing is . . ." and that is when self-awareness starts.

A phrase like, "Okay, let's go to Oregon," can be instrumental in prompting the alcoholic to see resemblances. He comes home aboil because something entirely unprecedented, to his mind, has happened. Let the co-alcoholic respond with a phrase she has used before, and the repetition in her response may point to a repetition in the event. Such phrases can become a private language, a shorthand form of communication by which a telling comment can be made in an unprovocative way. An alcoholic I once knew well used to come through the door in a black cloud of despair and announce that he was smashing his cameras because it was obvious that he was totally untalented at his work, was quitting his job because he was disliked by everyone in his firm, was giving up his friends because it was apparent that they tolerated him to his face but behind his back thought him a fool and dullard, and was probably going to commit suicide because life was a cheat and a trap. For too long a time, I reacted with hasty, soothing reassurances about his talents, his friends, his work, and the rewards of being alive, all of which he angrily rejected—understandably, since the words sounded empty and banal even to my ears. Finally, I came to understand that these outbursts were invariably set off by a single, real or fancied, critical remark by someone in authority over him, and that his reaction could be summed up in one word: snowballing. The first time I used the word, he demanded to know what I meant. "Someone says something that hurts your feelings," I explained, "and, like a kid with a snowball, you start rolling it around until it gets huge, and you can't see over it or around it. Everything in your life gets bound up with it." It did not immediately happen, of course, that I could say, "Snowballing," and have his anger and depression disappear, for both of us were far from knowing why he did it, but eventually we both knew *that* he did it, and the single word entered our personal vocabulary as a quick way of saying this time is like other times, this reaction is a chronic reaction, nothing is new here.

The *why* of it was a job for a therapist, but the *what* of it was something I could call attention to. By repeatedly asking: "What happened? What did he say? What did you say?" always some blow to his self-esteem emerged. And since we both knew that such episodes were apt to trigger drinking bouts, it eventually became apparent that his drinking was not an inexplicable compulsion which overcame him without warning but a specific response to an identifiable event. There was a pattern, a pattern that could be known.

If I have made the revelation of pattern sound easy, I have done so mistakenly. It is neither a simple nor a brief undertaking. The alcoholic will not answer one's questions willingly. It takes patience and detachment to repeat the questions in the face of his anger or silence, and it takes a degree of astuteness to persist in asking them through all the metamorphoses of his behavior, for he will not conveniently present the same reactions each time. He will quickly sense any unmasking of his behavior and unconsciously ring changes on it so as to obscure the common threads running through it. With a vested interest in maintaining his necessity to drink, he will confound the co-alcoholic with apparently shifting reactions, but if she maintains her calm, if she refuses to reward his behavior by becoming frightened or concerned, if she treats his reactions as logical and logically carries them forward to their illogical conclusions, a measure of reality will begin to make itself known.

All of this can be summed up in the single word *confrontation*. The co-alcoholic, by asking after the facts, is confronting the alcoholic with the facts. She is not interpreting them. She does not offer any opinion as to why he sees things as he does. She is simply making the point that he does see them in a characteristic way, and she leaves it to him to become curious, if he will, about why he sees them in this way.

When the co-alcoholic is comfortable with confrontation, she can add prediction to her repertory, that is, with her calm questions having elicited that the alcoholic is irritable or depressed or angry because the world has in some way denied him egogratification, she can predict that he will get drunk, and she can make this prediction, not silently in fear and trembling to herself, but aloud, to the alcoholic, remarking, "I expect you'll be getting drunk tonight." The reply is apt to be an explosive,

"You're damned right I will!" to which she can answer, "There's the bottle. Help yourself." Whether or not this stops him, it may deflect him long enough to ask a few questions, to which she can comment, "You don't have any other way of handling your feelings, so, obviously, you have to drink." This, without accusation or argument or blame, points out to the alcoholic that he has just one way of defusing his emotions, just one standard response, and, thus, again, he is forced into some self-awareness without having it forced upon him. He will necessarily wonder, sooner or later, whether he is actually so limited, whether the alternatives that other people apparently use to deal with mishaps in their lives are absolutely closed to him, and if so, why. If he becomes even slightly curious about himself, the co-alcoholic is succeeding in her role as pre-therapist.

Many a co-alcoholic will shrink from the prospect of telling the alcoholic to do what she hopes and prays he will not do, that is, drink, but it can be a most effective gambit on two scores. That she is able to predict when he will drink puts on display the cause and effect relationship between his tension and his drinking. He cannot deny that he is drinking because of what happened, since she is able to predict, from what happened, that he will drink. This takes his drinking out of the category of a curse, a weakness, an affliction, and demonstrates it to be a piece of coping behavior, inutile and maladaptive, to be sure, but not inexplicable and immutable since, if he copes in this way, obviously he can learn to cope in other ways, a telling argument in favor of therapy.

The second reason for doing what, in psychological terms, is known as "prescribing the symptom" is that telling a person to do what he knows in the back of his mind he is going to do acts as an inhibiting device. Ordering a child not to cry, for example, usually brings on a flood of tears, while if he is told to cry, to cry louder and harder, he gives a few gulps and stops. Similarly, the most effective way of putting an end to an attack of hiccups is to demand that the person hiccup, insist on hearing him hiccup; within moments he will not be able to produce a hiccup if his life depended on it. On the same basis, a psychiatrist attempting to deal with a patient whose communications make little sense may ask the patient to "act crazy, talk in a crazy way," because he knows that the patient will stop and think and then will find it exceedingly difficult to continue deliberately what he has been doing involuntarily.

With the alcoholic who is ferociously silent when asked to talk about the events of the day and his feelings, as so many alcoholics are both because of their antipathy to verbalization and because of their dim realization that the ballooning hurt or indignation or frustration which is to be their excuse for drinking will slowly deflate if examined rationally, the maneuver of prescribing the symptom can be peculiarly effective. If the alcoholic is encouraged not to talk by the co-alcoholic's saying some such thing as, "It's okay with me if you don't want to tell me what happened. It saves us from going over the same old ground," he is apt to be momentarily silent while he thinks over whether it is the same old thing and then to burst out with a denial. Since the denial must necessarily include a description if he is to prove that the events are virgin, the co-alcoholic has the information she needs and can go on from there with her questions.

It is not the alcoholic alone who is contrary enough to be immediately consumed with a desire to speak of what he has been requested not to talk about. It is all of us. There is no better way of eliciting a secret from someone who is hesitating than to remark, "Please don't tell me. I really don't want to know." Within seconds the half-impulse to confide will be aflame and the secret will be out. And this tends to be equally true about actions. Tell someone not to do something and he will counter with reasons why he should; tell him to do it and his reasons against it will pour out. This general knowledge about the psychology of people can stand the co-alcoholic in good stead, and it should convince her not to shrink from asking the alcoholic to keep his troubles to himself, and when he demands to know what he should do about them, suggesting that he get good and drunk. In each instance, he is forced to think; he must think about what it is he is not telling her, and he must think about whether getting drunk is the answer. And thought is delay. It is an interval of time between feeling and action, that interval he failed to learn the first time around and must be manipulated into learning now.

It is more than possible, of course, that the alcoholic will think and then drink. If so, so be it; he would have gotten drunk anyway. Nothing has been lost, and something has been gained because there is always a next time, and the next time adds a little more practice in thinking. It also makes the alcoholic think about the co-alcoholic: why is she suggesting that he drink? Does she want him to lose his job, ruin his health, destroy his life? The co-alcoholic can reply that, if he believes these are the risks of his drinking, why is he running them? If he answers that it is because he wants to, she can say, "Why should I try to stop you then?" If he answers that it is because he can't not drink, she can say, "Then the sooner you hit bottom and find out you can't go on this way, the better." She may sound cynical, and, indeed, she should. Cynicism about the fate of uncontrolled drinking is far more jolting to the alcoholic than any amount of piteous hand-wringing and tearful predictions. I am, in fact, in favor of a frankness that seemingly verges on callousness in speaking about drinking to the alcoholic. I have been known to say, "Go ahead and get drunk if you want to. Just tell me first whether your life insurance is paid up in case your liver doesn't hold out." I have urged an alcoholic to make a will and give me the telephone numbers of relatives to be notified in the case of his death because the bland assumption that this can be the outcome of a drunk disconcerts him in a way that a warning of what may happen to him does not. The alcoholic sweeps aside attempts to frighten him into stopping drinking, mumbling grandly that that sort of thing happens to the other fellow, not him, but speak matter-of-factly about what to do if he does not survive the drunk and it can be, both literally and figuratively, quite sobering.

By the same token, if I suspect there are hidden bottles, I hunt until I find them, not for the purpose of emptying them but of putting them within easy reach of the drinker, and when he questions what baleful purpose I have in doing so, I shrug and say, "You're easier to handle unconscious than half-drunk." The alcoholic is inclined to be paranoid, and, on the whole, it is more efficacious to feed that paranoia than attempt to reassure him that whatever you are doing, you are doing for his own good. If you agree that he is the best judge of his own good, he may have severe second thoughts about what that good is. And the paranoid suspicion that you might just possibly wish him out of the way will bring all his self-preservative instincts into play.

He has to mull over whether the oblivion of drink and the potential oblivion of death are really so enticing. Is it possible that he would prefer to save himself? Can he save himself? It is obvious that the co-alcoholic is no longer struggling to do it for him. She has looked at the future and recognized its two possible alternatives; he will drink or he will save himself, and she is only waiting now to see which it will be. The arguments are over, the jury is out, and she passively awaits the verdict. She is not even, to the alcoholic's knowledge, rooting for one verdict over another. She believes that the alcoholic, no less than anyone else, has a reservoir of strength he can tap to will himself into a fight against his addiction, but she knows that only he can tap it and she is standing by until it becomes apparent whether or not he will.

If she has acquiesced to his fate, will she ride it down with him or is her acceptance an indication that she is gathering her caring emotions back for reinvestment in her own life? He should not be told the answer to this, for the question mark surrounding whether their relationship will survive, plus the question mark of his own personal survival, are the two things that will make the alcoholic consistently and persistently anxious, hopefully to the degree that the relief of this anxiety will become more important to him than the relief of tension. The co-alcoholic holds in her hands a carrot and a stick, the carrot of her belief that the causes of his alcoholism are knowable and treatable and that he can find in himself the will to recover and the stick of a limit to her patience and involvement. Holding out now one, now the other gives him both the reason and the incentive for obtaining treatment.

In such fashion does the co-alcoholic carry out her tripartite task as pre-therapist. By confronting him with the repetition in his feelings and behavior, she makes it possible for him to understand, if he will, that there is a pattern in his repetitive drinking. She puts him in touch with himself as someone who can be known and whom he must get to know if he is not to be tossed from one disaster to another. By predicting the symptom, she reduces drinking from an irresistible force to a simple piece of behavior; by prescribing the symptom, she reduces it from a compulsion to a choice. And by a benevolent neutrality that conveys that her options are open while his are fast narrowing, she transfers the weight of anxiety from her shoulders to his. She is cruel in order to be kind.

How long does pre-therapy take? Until the alcoholic says, "I must do something about myself," not that this must change or that must be different or this must be done for him. When he becomes curious about the way he is, when he senses that it is possible that he can be different, and when he grasps that the responsibility for rehabilitation is his own, then pre-therapy has done its work and therapy can take over.

12

Treatment for Alcoholism

When the alcoholic arrives at the point of conceding his need for treatment and expresses, with whatever hesitation and misgivings, his willingness to assay it, since there is no specific cure for alcoholism and therefore no single indicated treatment, a choice must be made between the various therapeutic approaches. In general, the possibilities divide into two large categories: symptom suppression or symptom exploration. The symptom is, of course, excessive and compulsive intake of alcohol. Suppression of the symptom would involve inactivation of it by means of drug therapy, reconditioning techniques, aversion techniques, or exhortative, self-help, group-identifying and group-supportive approaches, while exploration of it involves use of a psychotherapeutic modality to uncover the causes of addictive drinking and permit realignment of the personality along more mature and constructive lines.

Theoretically, the decision as to type of treatment should be left to the alcoholic so that he cannot later claim that he was forced into a situation uncongenial to him, the failure of which he could have foretold. But, in practice, as well as the question of what is acceptable to him, there are the additional considerations of what is available, what is affordable, and what may perhaps be necessary, e.g., hospitalization. The need for the latter may become abruptly evident, as was the case with a friend of a

199

friend, a heavy drinker over a period of years who, on the heels of a casual remark by her brother-in-law, a physician, that she was undoubtedly an alcoholic, indignantly, to prove him wrong, set aside her glass and drank no more that evening. Mid-morning of the next day, primly dressed in a neat navy dress, white gloves, and small sailor hat, she sought out my friend and, sitting straight and spinsterish on a ladderback chair, poured out an obscene tale of an orgy she believed she had witnessed the night before, full of language foreign to her and scenes that would have done credit to a Times Square pornographer. The friend, through a ruse of taking her to file a complaint with the police, got her to Bellevue and committed her. To this day, he remembers the look she turned on him and her foul screams as she was placed in restraints and carried away, but, as it turned out, not only had he had no choice, he had done her a true favor, for the shock of finding herself in a psychiatric ward brought her out of her psychotic episode and has kept her abstinent since.

As a doctor, should her brother-in-law have warned her against cutting off her intake of liquor so abruptly? Not even a physician can foretell whether there will be a psychiatric emergency, a medical emergency such as alcoholic convulsions, or no untoward consequences of withdrawal. Still less can the co-alcoholic, and thus, although she should be prepared to act if the need arises, she cannot arrange for preventive hospitalization unless the alcoholic himself agrees to it, in which event the further cooperation of a physician and a hospital are required. The physician must accede to the necessity for hospitalization and arrange for admission, and the hospital must be one which accepts alcoholic patients for the purposes of "drying out." If a private sanitarium is within the patient's means, there is no problem, since it is usual that a large proportion of patients in such facilities are alcoholics, but a general hospital can be another matter.

A woman who lived alone and who felt she could not begin to get her drinking under control without the interim support of a protective environment called the alcoholism treatment unit of a general hospital in New York City and pleaded for admission, which was denied until, after repeated calls, she threatened suicide. Unfortunately, even though the unit was geared specifically to the treatment of alcoholics, she received only dazing amounts of tranquillizing drugs in the way of medical treatment and the perfunctory advice to stop drinking in the way of psychiatric treatment during her five-day stay, and she died a few months later of alcoholism. A similar story is that of a young man who presented himself in the middle of the night at the psychiatric division of a renowned hospital in New York. He, too, was refused admission until he spoke of killing himself, then was granted a three-month stay and given daily psychiatric treatment. After his alloted ninety-day time, he was continued in outpatient group therapy under the aegis of the hospital, but, nevertheless, returned to drinking and when desperately he pleaded for readmission, he was refused. The identical sequence took place in a university hospital in the southern city where he went next to be near relatives. To describe these incidents is not to indict the hospitals concerned but to illustrate that there is a gray area into which alcoholics fall who need hospitalization to withdraw from alcohol but do not present a psychiatric or medical emergency.

The executive president of the American Hospital Association, Dr. Edwin L. Crosby, in commenting on the reluctance of hospitals to admit alcoholics, has remarked that, "Many professionals believe the alcoholic patient will be disruptive, unmanageable, need special facilities, won't pay his bills and will require time-consuming and ultimately unsuccessful treatment," this despite the fact that studies by the AHA have shown that the care of alcoholics requires no unusual arrangements and can be carried out in any ordinary nursing unit. The AHA has undertaken an educational program with the aim of bringing about "a new 'open-door' policy for many hospitals reluctant to admit the known alcoholic," with the director of the program noting that, "A combined effort between the hospital and other community facilities is needed if the alcoholic is ever to find his way into the health care system." There is hope, then, that the situation will change, but, for the time being, the co-alcoholic who envisions a short stay in a hospital for the alcoholic as a means of his "drying out" would be well advised to investigate the local situation before attempting to persuade the alcoholic of the wisdom of this procedure, for it will only make the alcoholic despair further if, after finally admitting he needs care, he finds that a major avenue of help is closed to him.

The situation is different in the instance of an emergency, such as alcoholic convulsions. The general hospital will accept such a patient for treatment, and the co-alcoholic should not delay in calling for an ambulance. This also obtains if there is a question of the alcoholic's having mixed pills—an excess of tranquillizers or barbiturates, for example—with his alcohol. Alcohol potentiates the action of these drugs, and the combination can be life-threatening. If in doubt, the co-alcoholic can call the nearest Poison Control Center for advice. In my experience, they recommend erring on the safe side and getting the alcoholic to a hospital. In an emergency room of the hospital, again my experience, the alcoholic will have his stomach pumped out, be given an intravenous infusion of glucose, and without further ado, be released. I have pleaded with a hospital to keep an exhausted, disturbed alcoholic at least overnight until he was a little more able to navigate and a little less distraught or, failing that, to transfer him by ambulance to a private hospital, only to be told that there was no bed available for an alcoholic and that only his personal physician could arrange for private hospitalization. At midnight, it is difficult to obtain the services of a private physician; in the particular situation, it was equally difficult to lay hands on the six hundred dollar advance in cash the private hospital required, and so, rather than agreeing to the only alternative the hospital doctor offered—transfer to the psychiatric ward of a city hospital—I have found myself on the street trying to hail a taxi to return a slipper-shod, bathrobe-clad alcoholic to his home.

Not only are hospital personnel likely to wash their hands of the alcoholic as soon as the medical emergency is over, but even while it is going on, they may deal with him with scarcely concealed impatience and irritation. The attitude I have met is that the emergency room of a hospital has more life-and-death matters to concern itself with than the self-inflicted state of the alcoholic, and the doctors and nurses tend to be abrupt and contemptuous in their handling of the patient. I have had the experience of accompanying the same person to the same hospital emergency room twice, the first time because of a dangerous excess of alcohol and tranquillizers, the second because of a fainting episode which mimicked a heart attack, and the difference in the respect, kindness, and care accorded the patient was remarkable. The first time treated as a pariah, the patient on the second occasion was given prompt, ungrudging, and compassionate attention.

A nonalcoholic friend, returning home alone after an evening with friends during which she had had two highballs, slipped and fell on a patch of ice, fracturing her kneecap. The policeman who called an ambulance to take her to the hospital remarked, "I've picked you up before, haven't I, lady?" and the resident in the emergency room said, "You do this often, lady, get drunk and fall down?" If she felt humiliated and despairingly aware of their scorn, which indeed she did, how much more devastating it must be for the alcoholic, who already has his own weight of guilt and self-loathing to contend with, to be treated in this way. Although the co-alcoholic may be sharing some of the same emotions of impatience and repulsion, this is not the time to fail the alcoholic as a human being, and she should stand by to shield him as much as possible from the it-serves-you-right attitude of the people involved in treating him.

When the emergency is primarily psychiatric rather than medical, since the onset of delirium tremens or a psychotic break with reality is often abrupt, the most usual course of events is for the alcoholic to be taken to the psychiatric ward of a city hospital, and from there, if there is no remission in his symptoms within a reasonable period of time and if, in the opinion of the psychiatric staff, he is not capable of functioning in an unprotected environment, transfer to a state mental hospital will be recommended. If the alcoholic agrees to this course, his commitment will be voluntary; otherwise, it will be by court order. (There will be a hearing at which the alcoholic can fight the commitment proceedings, as a friend of mine did, successfully, by obtaining the services of a lawyer through the Legal Aid Society.) Or, alternatively, the co-alcoholic can arrange for hospitalization in a private sanitarium.

Private hospitals are excruciatingly expensive. Some families can, of course, afford them without question. Some families can unquestionably not afford them. But what should the family do who perhaps can find the money but only at the cost of great sacrifice? It is a difficult decision for the co-alcoholic to make: whether to let the alcoholic be sent to a state hospital or whether to drain every resource to obtain private treatment for him. It would seem that such a decision could best be made by investigating whether the state hospital serving the area is one of those which have excellent and aggressive programs of treatment for alcoholics or whether it offers little more than custodial care, but the situation is not so clear-cut because the critical variable in rehabilitation of the alcoholic is not the treatment but his own degree of motivation. The best designed and executed program of treatment will fail if the alcoholic cannot be persuaded to participate actively and to mobilize his own strengths, while inadequate or absent treatment may succeed if the very atmosphere of the hospital so revolts the alcoholic that he makes an effort toward sanity and responsibility to effect his release from it.

I have known a more than middle-aged lady fallen from elegance and ease because of her drinking who raged at the heartlessness of her nieces and nephews for refusing to step in to save her from state hospital commitment, but who, once she found herself inside the institution, established herself as benevolent duchess of the ward and set about revitalizing its occupants by prodding them to make slipcovers and curtains, to improvise a beauty salon in which they did each other's hair, and to agitate for improvement in the food. Having for some time prior to this lived in idleness and loneliness, without people or a cause to spend her energies on and consequently soaking them up in drink, she found both in the mental hospital and emerged considerably the better for her stay despite the absence of any treatment program worthy of the name.

In contrast is this revealing letter written by an alcoholic.

For a state hospital, this place is quite remarkable and makes [a private sanitarium] look like a hellhole. I am still on the general admission ward and do not have to put up with OT [occupational therapy], RT [recreational therapy], and all those other scandals. My doctor allowed me to stay here because I was lucky enough to move into a private room on the third day, and he knows that the privacy has therapeutic value in allowing me to paint constantly—and also to avoid the either permanently deranged or simply uneducated simpletons on the rest of the ward. . . . This hospital is the equal or superior of [a famous psychiatric clinic] and costs about half as much (although nothing to me because I am covered by the county's mental health emergency program). I feel I have accomplished worlds of good, progressing faster and redefining my attitudes toward life (from here on out, painting seems the most important task and my best current hope for happiness) more thoroughly than ever I did at [the clinic]. There's a great deal of truth in the maxim that some people just need to be let alone to think things out. . . .

Sad to relate, despite the writer's optimism about his ability to think things out, he has three times since the writing of this letter been returned to a mental institution. He is a young man, and he has received, by any standards, the best of both private and public care. The letter itself indicates, I think, why treatment has failed to alleviate his alcoholism and coexistent psychiatric disturbance. He is comfortable, he manages privileges for himself, and he escapes from having to look too closely at himself and his situation by taking refuge in painting. Since he is an attractive fellow and a talented painter (although, interestingly enough, he never paints except when he is in a hospital), he enlists the interest of hospital personnel, and this confirms his feeling that he is special and entitled to be spared the pressures placed on ordinary mortals. Like so many alcoholics, he sneers at such activities as occupational and recreational therapy; they are for the clods of this world while such as he deserve privacy for intellectual pursuits. What is implicit in the letter and explicit in his repeated hospitalization is his desire for a protected, nurturing, undemanding environment. It cannot be claimed that if he did not achieve it, if he found himself in a contemporary snakepit, he would marshall his resources and come to see his alcoholism as an addiction he was responsible for controlling, but neither can it be known that he would not.

Some hospitalized alcoholics, realizing that they have reached the end of the road, subside into total discouragement and resignation and give themselves up to an alien and awful environment, while, for others, finding themselves in a mental institution is the moment of truth and they set out to map the road back to normality. Thus, what for one alcoholic is the slamming of a last door may be for another the opening of a new door. If the hospital is a private one, some alcoholics respond well to the benevolent atmosphere, while, for others, it is a sojourn in a country club to which they are content to return periodically for "drying out" and an enforced abstinence from alcohol which enables them the better to drink when they are released. Depending on the person, the financial sacrifice to place an alcoholic in a private sanitarium is worth it in the case of one alcoholic, is wasted in the case of another. Obviously, no set recommendation can be made, no one course of action can be described as more likely to be effective than another. All the co-alcoholic can do when faced with a decision about hospitalization is to obtain the best professional advice available and weigh it against what she knows about the alcoholic. At the same time, she must be honest with herself about her own feelings, that is, that she is not allowing the alcoholic to be sent to a state hospital because she secretly feels he deserves this punishment or, alternatively, that she is not bankrupting the family to place the alcoholic under private care to assuage her own feelings of guilt at ejecting him from the family.

She must, if the need for hospitalization is equivocal, ask herself whether her view of the situation is being prejudiced by an unacknowledged wish to be rid, at least temporarily, of the burden of the alcoholic, to turn him over to professionals who will bring their formulas to bear on him and deliver him back a changed man or, if they fail in this aim, pronounce the sentence of incurability that will justify her own prior failure. The co-alcoholic cannot help but think longingly of the peace that will descend if the alcoholic is sent to a hospital, and if the alcoholic himself requests that he be hospitalized, the temptation is great to take this easy way out. Surprisingly often, in view of the fact that, to the ordinary person, hospitalization, particularly in a mental institution, is something to be avoided at all costs, the alcoholic will suggest it himself. Although not particularly sensitive to other people's emotional states, the alcoholic can be exquisitely perceptive about the immediate climate as it pertains to him. He may sense that he is scraping the bottom of the barrel of patience and tolerance, that he is near to exhausting the supplies of support and concern available to him, and rather than passively await ultimate and final rejection, he may attempt to preserve some credit in his account by proposing that he be placed in a hospital until he can pull himself together and make a fresh start. This has the lure of removing him from a situation the further deterioration of which he cannot afford, and it seemingly indicates a brave bowing to the need for treatment. What he does not acknowledge and often does not consciously know is that he wants to be taken care of, and he wants, as well, this tacit admission of his helplessness. He, too, wants to shift the burden of responsibility for curing him to the professional; it is a way of postponing, yet again, taking responsibility for himself.

And this is the danger of hospitalizing a willing alcoholic. It appears to confirm his powerlessness to wrestle with his addiction himself. Although presenting himself as an available target for therapeutic aid, he feels himself a presence there by default, not an active seeker willing to do at least his share if he is shown the way. In both physical and mental illness, the patient who recovers fastest is the one who fights against being ill, who struggles to free himself of the dependent situation of illness. A psychiatrist writing about the men under his care on the ward of a veterans hospital commented that the patients who did not adapt, who hated being in the hospital, who fought to preserve their initiative and individuality among the rules and regulations were those who gained release soonest, no matter what form of treatment they were given. By extension, if an alcoholic asks to be hospitalized, it cannot automatically be viewed as a first and positive step toward seeking cure. On the contrary, it may be one more dodge to perpetuate his dependent status.

Alcoholics tend to do quite well in hospitals, well, that is, in the sense of being untroublesome patients. The passive side of their passive-aggressive natures is gratified by being in a situation in which they are taken care of and relieved of stress. But they do not do well in terms of cure rate because their aggressive side leads them to evade any therapeutic impact the hospital program might have. They welcome a structured situation, as a child welcomes parental shelter, but, just as a child tests the limits to determine what he can get away with, so are alcoholics covertly rebellious. Like my letter-writing friend, while enjoying the benefits of a structured situation, they set about circumventing its restrictions. Used to having authority figures retrieve them from the consequences of their behavior, they quite willingly entrust themselves to staff care, but, equally resentful of authority, they are, in concealed ways, evasive and uncooperative. Willing to have anything done *for* them, almost anything done *to* them, they tenaciously resist the notion that anything must be done *by* them.

The best of hospitals make every effort to involve alcoholics in their own care by interesting them in ward government groups, in mutual help groups, discussion groups, A.A. hospital groups, educational groups, and activity groups, as well as in therapy groups composed of fellow alcoholics and, in some instances also, of relatives and friends of alcoholics. That groups are the favored modality of treatment is so for several reasons. Alcoholics, despite their conviviality, are inclined to be somewhat isolated individuals, in the world alienated from ordinary people by their addiction, in the hospital alienated from other patients by their sense of not being mentally ill, and groups bring them and keep them in social contact. By not allowing the alcoholic to withdraw into idle fantasy of the marvelous things he will accomplish upon his release, they prevent him from seeing himself as so very different and so very special. Forced to listen to the rationalizations of other alcoholics about their present situation, these may strike him as absurd and thus cause him to suspect his own. His denial mechanism can be shaken by the very fact of hearing other alcoholics reject or distort reality factors, and this plus educational lectures on the basics of alcoholism, about which alcoholics often contrive to know astonishingly little, can cause him to reevaluate his condition and come to see it as less benign than he has consolingly believed. Listening to the histories of alcoholics who have been hospitalized repeatedly may bring home to him the fact that dreams and resolutions are not the answer to alcoholism and persuade him to a true commitment to therapy rather than a shallow going through of the motions while he waits for release. In a therapy group, he will hear derisive hoots when he claims that he has his drinking problem licked. He will be subjected to scoffing by fellow members when he defends his refusal to look at himself by stating that, since he does not intend to drink again, it would be a waste of time to explore the causes of his drinking. Also in a therapy group, he may come to experience how rivalrous he is for the therapist's attention and concern, how automatically he looks to the therapist for direction and how instinctively he balks at accepting direction, thus gaining some glimpse into the problems with authority which may have plagued him on the outside. In self-help groups, he may acquire appreciation of the responsibility he must assume for himself, if only from the example of the defeated members, and in activity groups, he may find a new consciousness of how effective he can be, of how much genuine strength of his own exists to be called on. By repeatedly being confronted by and with others, he may ultimately confront himself and begin to strip away his defenses, unmask his pretenses, and dig for the essential person who became an alcoholic. If he then begins to assume responsibility for that person, he is on the way to recovery.

Motivation is the key. The hospital with a total push program can rehabilitate some alcoholics because it succeeds in motivating them. The hospital without a program can inadvertently motivate some alcoholics because they resolve never to undergo the experience again. The private sanitarium likewise succeeds or fails with the alcoholic, not on the basis of methods, but in accordance with his motivation. Treatment is better than no treatment, but no treatment is better than the motivation of the alcoholic, and all treatment must begin with motivation. It is impossible to say that an alcoholic will recover in one type of hospital but not in another. The only judgment has, of necessity, to be empirical; if it works, it was the right thing for that alcoholic. If five days of "drying out" in a general hospital only improves the alcoholic's health to the point of allowing him to drink again, the next time a longer stay in a sanitarium may be indicated. If that proves to be merely an expensive vacation, a state hospital may have more impact. If the state hospital is good, that is a plus; if it is bad, it may have the desired effect by default. The most feasible course for the co-alcoholic to follow in making decisions is to pursue the possible and search for alternatives only if the possible does not prove to be the efficacious.

This is equally the case when hospitalization is not being considered but treatment of some type is. How should a choice be made between A.A., an alcoholism clinic, psychiatric treatment, or one of the drug or vitamin or conditioning therapies that come and go on the tides of fashion? To a large extent, the alcoholic's preference for one or another is likely to be determined by how he unconsciously thinks of himself, whether he views himself as bad or as sick, whether he considers that he has succumbed to alcoholism because he is weak-willed or has been overwhelmed by it because of physiological deficits. If he thinks of himself as bad, of his drinking as evidence that he is weak-willed, and if he therefore assumes that what he needs is an infusion of strength to stiffen his spine, A.A. will appeal to him. If, again, he thinks of himself as bad and weak but despairs of being able to change by his own efforts, drug or conditioning therapy, a therapy in which he will be reformed by an agent given to him or a method performed on him which will require no effort on his part, will attract him. If, on the other hand, he believes his alcoholism to be an illness, depending on his further definition of it as a medical or psychological illness, he will seek physical or psychiatric treatment.

No one treatment modality is superior to others statistically. Claimed recovery rate seldom goes above thirty per cent for any type of treatment, and frequently is lower. A.A., however, may have the edge, and since it is by far the best known approach and access to it can be immediate, the majority of alcoholics think of it first when they think of getting help. No matter the personality make-up of the particular alcoholic, A.A. is always worth a try, and the co-alcoholic, if she is consulted, as it is likely she will be, should encourage the alcoholic to attend A.A. meetings or even take the initiative of requesting that the local chapter send a member to scout the chances of recruiting the alcoholic. By the same token, however, she should not be discouraged if A.A. does not "take" with the particular alcoholic, for the A.A. approach may not be congenial to his personality nor a suitable answer to his particular set of problems.

In the Twelve-Step program of A.A., Step One is an admission of powerlessness, of the alcoholic's helplessness to exert control over himself and his life. For some alcoholics, this humbling acknowledgment is purging; it sets them free to begin again. But for others, for those whose lifelong struggle against their dependency needs has necessitated an insistent claim to self-reliance, it can be deeply threatening, as it can be also for those alcoholics who are fighting to stave off imminent personality disintegration. The last thing some alcoholics can afford is to give up the shreds of strength they are clinging to. They must hold on to their self-esteem, not because it is intact but because it is so close to fragmentation that they sense catastrophe if they abandon the pretense that they are in control of their destiny. Such people seem touchy, proud, even arrogant, but they simply cannot let themselves be stripped of self-pride lest it be all the glue that is holding them together. For any alcoholic for whom this is so, A.A. does not represent help but danger, and when this is so, the alcoholic will rightly flee A.A. quickly. It is better to be drunk than to fall apart, and the co-alcoholic should understand this and not despair at what seems self-destruction but may be self-preservation.

Steps Two and Three suggest that the alcoholic substitute belief in a higher power for his belief in himself, that he turn over his life and his will to God. If God is not dead for the alcoholic, if he can believe, this is indeed a constructive measure. It is comforting and sustaining to draw on transcendental strength rather than have to rely on one's own very uncertain will. But too many alcoholics have had weak or absent fathers, or conversely, frighteningly powerful and indifferent ones, to envision entrusting themselves to a Father in heaven, and very many alcoholics who try A.A. balk at having to subscribe to a faith they cannot feel.

A.A. has attempted to *minimize* this obstacle by formulating Step Three as: [We] made a decision to turn our will and our lives over to the care of God as we understood Him." The "as we understood Him," according to A.A. members with whom I have discussed the point, allows any interpretation of God—as a deity, of course, but more simply, if not the Higher Power, any higher power, any belief in a force for good outside oneself. But such latitude of definition still does not solve the problem of faith for many alcoholics and they are doubly threatened: by the requirement of submission and then by the question of submission to what? To something they cannot convince themselves exists.

Since four more of the Steps specifically mention God and the alcoholic's relation to him, making six of the Twelve Steps religious in tone, for the alcoholic who is without formal faith and who is struggling to hold on to the vestiges of faith he has in himself, the A.A. tenets may disconcert and disaffect him. Their religious nature, no matter how broadly he is urged to interpret it, may be so unpalatable that he cannot bring himself to make use of even those parts of the program which might prove helpful to him. Like all converts, A.A. members are fervent; they have seen the light and they wish to bring it to others, and this cannot help but lend an evangelical tone to the meetings, which, again, puts off some number of cynical and/or sophisticated alcoholics, many to the point where they attend a few meetings and never return.

Another objection raised by alcoholics to whom A.A. does not appeal is to the confessional character of the meetings. Members tell their stories of the alcoholic road they have followed, and, striving for utter honesty, they leave out none of the degrading details of the long descent to their personal "bottom." This has undoubted therapeutic value for the confessor and cautionary value for his listeners, and for the new member, it can be salutary to find that his history is neither unusual nor unmatched and, indeed, may be rather tame and decorous in comparison. If this is so, well and good, and one day he will rise and tell his own story and be the better for it. But some people consider it indecent exposure and are appalled; others quickly grow bored by the repetitive nature of the accounts; and others suspect a secret vying among alcoholics, each to paint himself worse than the other so that it is clear their rehabilitation is an awesome achievement.

Perhaps a degree of extroversion is required to become a successful member of A.A. In my observation, and only in my observation which is limited to the New York, New Jersey, and Miami areas, alcoholics who embrace A.A. are people who are, by temperament, outgoing, friendly, warm, and nonintrospective. They tend to work in the area of sales or advertising or manufacturing, occupations which bring them more in contact with people than ideas. Accustomed to repeated and easy encounters with other people and the after-hours camaraderie of bars and cocktail lounges, they welcome the quick and unstinting friendliness proffered at A.A. meetings. A.A. meetings provide the ready companionship they can scarcely do without, filling the long, empty hours they formerly spent in drinking. They do not object to the self-revelation involved; they, perhaps simplistically but nevertheless effectively, embrace the faith required; and they immerse themselves in A.A. as they once immersed themselves in liquor.

The evenings of talk, the acceptance of their peers, the support and encouragement and release of pent-up feelings, the endless cups of coffee and glasses of Coca-Cola provide much the same outlet for oral-dependency needs as drinking formerly did, while the group itself, the nurturing ambiance of A.A., quite possibly acts as a mother-substitute. There is a maternal quality to the A.A. group. Dependency on A.A. is encouraged and fostered. Identification with the group, a sinking of self into oneness with it, with undemanding acceptance offered in return, recapitulates, as well as substitutes for, the original tie to the mother. The indivisible oneness of mother and child, never renounced by the alcoholic and repeatedly sought again in alcohol, is replaced by the "we-ness" of A.A. For the alcoholic who can find it there and accept it there, A.A. is a replacement for drink.

A.A. does not so much cure an alcoholic's addiction as provide him with another to take its place, as evidenced by the fact that recovered members continue to attend meetings indefinitely, remaining active years after their own sobriety has become habitual. A.A. meetings and Twelve-Step work with other alcoholics are their maintenance dose, as methadone is for the drug addict. The symptom, alcoholism, has not been cured but suppressed. Since the symptom is a devastatingly desructive one, addiction to A.A. is infinitely preferable to addiction to alcohol, and most co-alcoholics gratefully accept the substitution and are endlessly tolerant about accompanying their alcoholic to A.A. meetings several evenings a week and doing without his company while he is engaged in trying to help other alcoholics. They are equally tolerant of the interminable talk about alcoholism in the enforced company of other alcoholics and their spouses, being quite willing to trade the agonies of co-alcoholism for the single-theme existence of A.A. socializing. I must confess that I myself find it tiresome and consequently have never been able to exert consistent pressure on an alcoholic to stay with A.A., but I take off my hat to the accomplishment of A.A., most particularly to its insistence that the central issue in recovery from alcoholism is self-help.

Most alcoholics have a dimly perceived awareness that their recovery is up to them, but when they recoil from the unimaginable effort of grasping their own bootstraps and using only their own motive power as leverage, they may turn longingly to a search for a therapy which gives promise of releasing them from alcoholism without effort on their part, e.g., a drug, hypnosis, or an injectable substance which purportedly will return their body chemistry to normal and end the craving for alcohol. Disulfram, or Antabuse, is the best known of the drugs which make it impossible for the alcoholic to drink as long as the drug is taken because of the violent reactions it causes when alcohol is ingested. There is certainly a place for its use, particularly in conjunction with other therapies, where it can be employed as an artificial means of keeping the patient sober until he has learned more effective ways of coping with stress than drinking, but, alone, it can produce such side effects as skin reactions, headaches, cramps, and nausea, and, occasionally, psychosis, while in conjunction with alcohol, with which it is initially administered in order to condition the patient to avoid alcohol, it can cause, as well as vomiting, an increased heart rate, breathlessness, unconsciousness, and even death. Thus, it must be very carefully administered and the lowest possible dosage established for the particular patient. An additional drawback is that the alcoholic must willingly continue to take the drug indefinitely, and there is no way of insuring that he will do so since any surreptitious administration of it, such as its being slipped into his morning coffee by a wife eager to keep him sober, is too risky, for, feeling himself safe, he may take a drink and be precipitated into a severe reaction. Thus, this drug, or any one similar in effect, is at best only a form of temporary insurance and offers no long-range solution.

Since alcohol ingestion is a learned response to stress, it has occurred to a number of investigators to attempt to decondition the alcoholic by means of systems of punishment and reward, punishment for reaching for alcohol, reward for avoiding it. The methods have been varied, the results variable, with the short-term results—six months to a year of sobriety—being better than the five-year recovery rate. If there is an active program utilizing this approach readily accessible to the alcoholic, there is no reason it should not be given a try, but the results are not impressive enough to warrant a far trip in search of a facility which offers this type of treatment.

The same may be said for hypnosis. In the hands of a few practitioners, successes have been obtained, but this may be due more to the personality of the practitioner than the effectiveness of the method, as can also be true of the deconditioning therapies and even hormonal and vitamin treatments. The practitioner's enthusiasm for his method, his belief in its effectiveness is communicated to the alcoholic, and suggestion can play a large part in the results. A practitioner may credit his approach with splendid results when, actually, it is he himself, through his personality, his interest, and his conviction that he can help alcoholics, who is instrumental in aiding the alcoholic to recover. This is often evidenced by other researchers' failure to duplicate his successes although ostensibly using the same methods, an observation which has given rise to the saying that the man without his treatment may be better than the treatment without the man.

This is not to denigrate the role of suggestion or of personality, since both are important influences in any treatment. Even with a medical illness, the patient tends to get better faster in the hands of a physician quietly confident that he has the means to combat the illness, and when the condition has a large psychological component, it is doubly important that the therapist be calmly optimistic and communicate his conviction that over the long term he can be of help. This is as true of psychotherapy as of conditioning and hypnotic approaches, and to remark on it is only to caution against the indiscriminate pursuit of elusive cures rumored to be effective. What may work with one alcoholic may fail with another because the first is ready to be cured, has faith in the treatment, is confident that he has the therapist's understanding and support, and responds to the general treatment ambiance, while the second is perhaps skeptical, ambivalent in his wish for recovery, and unresponsive to the therapist's personality.

That hormonal approaches to the problem of alcoholism, such as the use of adrenocortical extract, and that the vitamin therapies, such as employment of massive doses of vitamin E, have enjoyed brief favor and been individually hailed as breakthroughs in the treatment of alcoholism is probably due to this same factor of the personality of the administrator and the credence of the alcoholic. Such treatments come and go, gaining quick currency and then falling from favor as initial successes prove inconsistently duplicatable. Alcoholics are drawn to treatments which hold out hope of recovery through administration of a substance which they purportedly lack, but, as of now, no such enticingly simple and nonstressful answer exists, and the co-alcoholic should neither delude herself that it does nor encourage the alcoholic to go in search of it. Neither should she, however, expose her own pessimism if such treatment is available to the alcoholic and he chooses to undergo it, for a "faith cure" is no less desirable than any other kind. In this instance, it is the end, not the means, which is important.

If it is his personal physician whom the alcoholic consults about his drinking problem, what help can be expected? Since the physician's area of special competence is his patient's physical status, he will concern himself first with establishing the presence and extent of liver damage and other possible consequences of excessive drinking, including the malnutrition alcoholics are often subject to. He may warn the alcoholic about the dangers of continued drinking, and, impressed by the extreme tension alcoholics frequently exhibit, their nervousness, irritability, and unusual vulnerability to stress, he may prescribe tranquillizers with the thought that such medication will smooth the alcoholic's moods and enable him to weather the daily insults of life without resorting to alcohol. The rationale is impeccable; in practice, however, it is the rare alcoholic who does not simply add tranquillizers to his drinking regime, sometimes using them in place of liquor but more often taking them in quantity and switching to liquor when the relief they bring is disappointingly mild or incomplete. It cannot be forgotten that alcoholics are addicts, and introducing them to tranquillizers or barbiturates means, at best, supplying them with a substitute addiction, at worst, and more commonly, adding a second addiction. Tranquillizers in sufficiently high dosage—and alcoholics are not temperate people —can produce the same slurred speech, unsteady locomotion, and befogged thought processes as alcohol, making it difficult to distinguish whether an alcoholic is drunk or drugged. The alcoholic may argue that all that matters is that he is not drinking, but the co-alcoholic may soon find herself wondering if there is that much difference and come to regret the fact that she now has not only the effect of alcohol to worry about but the even more dangerous effects of the alcohol-drug combination.

There was once a period of several weeks when I found myself mystified by the behavior of an alcoholic whom I knew to be almost certainly not drinking but who nightly gave a fair imitation of drunkenness. The explanation finally proved to be that he would take a powerful sleeping pill early in the evening and then force himself to stay awake, thus replicating the clouded consciousness and benumbed indifference to his surroundings of partial drunkenness. When this stopped because of my vehement objections, there was an interval of normality, then again a return to a drunken state that apparently was not being produced by alcohol. This time the answer was a cough medicine containing codeine.

If a physician is insufficiently aware that the alcoholic is an addict and, as such, is vulnerable to addiction to substances other than alcohol, he can do the alcoholic as much harm as good; if he *is* aware of the ramifications of the problem, there is little he can offer beyond the advice to seek specific treatment for the alcoholism. Preferably, he should offer that advice before he has tried—and failed—to help the alcoholic by medical means; otherwise, the recommendation will be made in a spirit of last resort and perhaps in an impatient atmosphere of dismissal. The medical man, accustomed, in relation to his patients, to having his orders followed and accustomed, in his own person, to self-discipline, decisiveness, and the automatic assumption of responsibility, is inclined to fall out of sympathy with the alcoholic, to become impatient, and to invite him, openly or covertly, to take his problems elsewhere. Since the times when the alcoholic is willing to take his problems anywhere at all are few, perhaps they should not be wasted by sending him in this direction unless the physician already understands the limitations of the situation and has volunteered himself as an authority figure to pressure the alcoholic to seek relevant help.

Not every physician considers psychiatric treatment relevant help. The majority of physicians share with the majority of laymen an almost automatic aversion to, if not all psychotherapies, at least psychoanalysis. Despite the seepage of psychoanalytic theories concerning the formation and functioning of the human psyche into every area of life and art, the mind trained in science mistrusts the imprecise nature of psychotherapy, the untestability of many of its hypotheses, and the unpredictability of its results. And the physician is no more immune than the layman to the belief that emotional difficulties can be handled by firm strictures to the self to behave well and stop thinking a lot of nonsense. I have heard the brusque counsel of a physician to an alcoholic to "stop all that talking about yourself, get a hobby, find a new job to throw yourself into, make friends, fall in love," this from a doctor who would not dream of saying to a diabetic that he should stop taking insulin, scorn medical aid, and overcome his chronic condition by making changes in his life

There is something about the notion of probing into the self that disconcerts, perhaps frightens, many people, and, in defense, they view it as unconscionable self-indulgence. They have solved their problems, their hurts, their failures by repressing them, pushing them out of consciousness and bracing the door against their reappearance by immersion in successive experiences. They do not wish to have their coping mechanism branded inadequate by someone else's choice to face the hidden reaches of the self. But just as aspirin is quite sufficient medication for the ordinarily healthy person with a transient indisposition but not for the more jeopardized person whose repair mechanisms are inadequate to contain his illness, so is a patent remedy not the entire or appropriate answer to pervasive psychological problems.

I make a point of this, not because psychiatric or psychoanalytic treatment is the entire or appropriate answer to alcoholism—all too often, for reasons to be considered, it is neither —but because not the least of the obstacles in the infinitely delicate course of attempting to lead an alcoholic to treatment is the well-meant but uninformed and prejudiced intervention of outsiders. I spent, for example, four long years breaking down the resistance of an alcoholic to psychotherapy, only to have a college classmate call, after an interval of fifteen years in which he had neither seen nor talked to the alcoholic, and exclaim, "What are you getting yourself involved in that nonsense for? You don't need that. Why, I remember you in college. You were the brightest, wittiest, most sophisticated of the lot of us. You can't have changed." His listener said in explanation, "Yes, but in the meantime I've become an alcoholic," and got back in answer, "So what? You don't need a head-shrinker. Just pull yourself together. You can do it." Incongruously enough, this from a man whose father had lived and died an alcoholic.

This kind of prejudice would matter little if one could set against it firm evidence that psychotherapy can be instrumental in aiding the alcoholic to recover. There is no such evidence. Self-exploration is a vexatious and onerous process, and alcoholics seldom have the staying power. They lack the habit of introspection, and they tolerate frustration, an inevitable part of psychotherapy, badly. They want an answer immediately, they want it to work as effectively as alcohol does, and they want it to be given to them, not painfully and painstakingly earned by them. The patient in psychotherapy must have the instincts of a detective and possess the detective's taste for the intellectual pleasure to be gained from the slow piecing together of clues, the unraveling of the seemingly unrelated bits of information that come to hand or can be ferreted out, and this is not the alcoholic's style. He may present the psychoanalyst quickly with much more information, and seemingly emotionally laden information, than the neurotic, but, having dumped the jigsaw pieces of his life into the therapist's lap, he settles back and passively awaits the return of the solved puzzle.

The alcoholic is not alone in misapprehending psychoanalysis as a quest for information akin to a prolonged and infinitely detailed history-taking by a professional who will, when he has gathered all possible facts, render a judgment upon them and lay out a course of treatment. But the neurotic is far easier to educate out of this view than the alcoholic. The neurotic can be led to understand that the intent of psychotherapy is to provide a corrective emotional experience by means of the reliving of important emotional relationships and attitudes in the therapeutic relationship. The vehicle of the corrective emotional experience is the patient's transference to the analyst, transference, as defined by the *Psychiatric Glossary,* being "the unconscious attachment to others of feelings and attitudes which were originally associated with important figures (parents, siblings, etc.) in one's early life." The neurotic, unconsciously viewing the analyst as mother, father, brother, sister, lover, spouse, as one or more of these important people at the same or different times, re-enacts the attitudes that have distinguished his relationship to them and re-experiences the emotions that have characterized them. He becomes profoundly involved with the therapist, but as this involvement is repeatedly analyzed, he comes to understand his feelings and attitudes as the structuring of present relationships to resemble past ones. He eventually appreciates that the repetitiveness in his experience with others is in himself, not others, and as he increasingly understands this, the compulsion to repeat past experience lessens and he tries out new ways of being and relating.

The alcoholic equally becomes involved in a transference relationship to the therapist, but since his most formative experience occurred in infancy when he was the passive recipient of total love and care, his attachment is undiscriminating, shallow, and highly demanding. His attitudes stem from the most primitive, undifferentiated time of life, a time when words and thoughts did not exist, when everything was expected from the other and nothing was expected of him, and the alcoholic carries this orientation with him into therapy. He cooperates to the extent of expressing his distress, as he expressed his distress as an infant, but he uses words minimally and he does not want words back; he wants to be ministered to; he wants his needs taken care of; he wants to be understood promptly and to be soothed. He experiences the detachment, the neutrality of the therapist as immensely frustrating, and since his attachment to the analyst is shallow, ending his frustration outweighs his need for the therapist's love and approval, and he flees to the comforting bottle.

There can be no analysis without a greater or lesser degree of frustration of the patient's needs, for if they are satisfied, they need not be analyzed, but an alcoholic never reaches for a drink quicker than when he is frustrated, and thus does he vitiate what would ordinarily be the motivation for self-exploration. The psychiatrist, then, may feel it useless even to attempt insight therapy with an alcoholic, being certain that the effort is foreordained to failure.

The psychiatrist who does accept alcoholic patients may do so only on the basis of certain conditions. He may make abstinence an absolute requirement of therapy, exacting a promise from the alcoholic that, if broken, will mean automatic termination of the therapy. He may require the alcoholic to join A.A. and to participate actively in its program while in therapy, and/or he may prescribe a regimen of Antabuse to prevent the alcoholic from drinking impulsively. He may insist that the treatment include group therapy as well as individual therapy or that it take place exclusively in a group context, both because the one-to-one relationship with a therapist can be too threatening for an alcoholic and because a group can provide peer support and encouragement to hold the alcoholic in therapy, as well as depriving him of the easy argument he may use against the therapist of: "You can't understand because you're not an alcoholic."

The alcoholic's agreement to one or more such conditions suggests that his motivation is reasonably strong and that therapy has some chance of success, particularly if the therapist limits his goals, which he may well do in the case of the alcoholic. Extensive insight into the causes of drinking may be theoretically desirable for the alcoholic but, in practice, unrealistic. It may be more feasible to aim for an awareness of when and how he drinks, and when this has been achieved, a further awareness of alternative methods of handling stress. This coupled with the eased marital and business relationships that therapy can also help bring about may be achievement enough with the alcoholic. If he can remain abstinent or even significantly reduce the amount and frequency of his drinking, the elusive goal of personality reorganization need not be pursued unless the patient himself desires it, which is almost never the case with an alcoholic.

Even if the psychiatrist sets no conditions about the circumstances under which he will treat an alcoholic, allowing him to drink or not as he will and relying on analysis of the times when he drinks gradually to make the compulsion less blind, he will probably alter his therapeutic technique in the direction of being more active than he would be with neurotic patients. He will speak more, volunteering a greater number of comments and observations than he ordinarily would, this for two reasons: the alcoholic's low frustration tolerance and his ready sense of rejection. Silence, the refusal of the solace of words, which are a symbolic feeding, can be too great a deprivation for the alcoholic. Whereas the neurotic, also finding silence painful, will be driven inward to explore his feelings about it, the alcoholic tends to experience it as a willful withholding of the supplies necessary to his life and will react with anger and flight; he will not be driven back on himself but away from the analyst. If not that, or before this extreme, he will fill the analyst's silence with fantasies of rejection, of critical disapproval, and he will grow unbearably tense. The analyst's delicate task is to ration the alcoholic patient's discomfort, not alleviating it enough so that the therapeutic hour is simply a warm and comforting interlude in the patient's day but neither allowing it to intensify beyond the alcoholic's limited capacity to absorb it. To this end, he will allow more of himself as a real person to be seen and experienced by the alcoholic. He will respond with advice when asked. He will express opinions. He will prompt the alcoholic to talk. He will ask for dreams and fantasies, and he will interpret them more readily, although on a less deep level, than he might with another type of patient. He will bring more outward effort to bear on the analysis because the alcoholic, with his impatience with words and abstractions, will bring less inward effort.

The friend mentioned earlier, the friend whose steering into psychoanalysis took four years, ended his first session by turning on the analyst and saying, "Okay, now you know my problems, you tell me this: why did Dr. — refer me to you instead of some other analyst and why did you agree to take me?" The analyst, a seasoned man in his sixties with an atypically forthright personality for someone in his profession, answered promptly, "Because I have a reputation for being able to analyze patients who are supposedly unanalyzable and because I can win out over your self-destructiveness." Since this exchange took place less than six months ago, it is too soon to guess whether he will succeed with this alcoholic. But it *is* almost six months and the alcoholic, despite a stormy time and many a threat to walk out of therapy, is still going—reluctantly, often angrily, and with two intervening bouts of drastic drinking, but going, which is a record of sorts when contrasted with his history of repeatedly joining A.A. and dropping out again almost immediately, his "cures" at psychiatric hospitals which never survived his discharge, his impulsive flights to distant countries, his religious counseling by a priest, and his psychological counseling by two different psychiatric social workers.

If alcoholics are unanalyzable, which in all likelihood almost all are in the conventional sense, why send them to a psychoanalyst? Only for the reason that finally was decisive for this alcoholic: all else had failed. This does not mean that psychiatric treatment is a last resort. On the contrary, it is the treatment of choice because it can not only be effective in relieving the alcoholic of his addiction but it can also open up new and effective ways of his being a person in the world, of living with more honest enjoyment, and of providing a realistic sense of self that does not swing between high grandiosity and abject vulnerability. It provides, that is, dividends beyond the cessation of drinking.

But since cessation of drinking is of first importance and because many alcoholics find the thought of psychotherapy anathema, there is no reason for the alcoholic not to try any other approach which appeals to him. No theoretical considerations are overriding; many practical considerations may be. A.A. offers the quickest help. A community mental health center may have a specific program of individual and/or group counseling or therapy. A local practitioner may be having success with a drug or conditioning approach. A psychiatric hospital may impose its own type of treatment. It does not matter. What succeeds in alcoholism is success. Whatever ends the alcoholic's addiction is the right treatment for him. What it is important to remember is that, if one method of treatment fails, there are alternative approaches.

13

The Alcoholic
in Treatment

A woman fell off her chair at her daughter's wedding reception. A man hallucinated the materialization of monstrous, screeching figures come to escort him to a hideous death. A woman stained the bathroom walls, floor, and fixtures with sticky green vomit after drinking the only remaining alcohol in her apartment, a bottle of creme de menthe. A man overheard his eleven-year-old son saying to his chum: "Don't mind my father. He's not a bad guy when he's not drinking." A woman found her pet cat lying at the foot of the wall she had flung it against, its back broken. A man staggered to answer the ringing of the doorbell and discovered his wife standing there with two policemen. A woman spent a night in jail, under arrest for drunken driving. A man woke with a broken jaw after a fight with a stranger in a bar. All were alcoholics. Each came up against an individual moment of truth, and each made a decision at that particular moment to get help.

Repeated studies of alcoholics have confirmed that it is almost invariably fear which drives an alcoholic to seek help, fear for his safety, health, or sanity, fear of loss of love, family, home, or job. An event ferocious enough, frightening enough, appalling

225

enough, or humiliating enough happens to breech his denial system. The dam of excuses, rationalizations and evasions surrounding his drinking gives way, and the future, that vague future of: "One of these days I suppose I'm going to have to do something about my drinking," is abruptly today. Chagrined, shamed, remorseful, the alcoholic takes a first step; he contacts A.A., consents to hospitalization, consults a physician or psychiatrist, or makes an appointment at an alcoholism treatment clinic.

But the defenses of the mind are like those of the body; they rush to wall off, to localize and repair damage. No sooner has the alcoholic faced the magnitude and malignancy of his drinking problem than the denial begins to build again and he begins to temporize. Listening to A.A. members describe their drinking careers, he is gratified that he has never sunk so low, that his drinking has never been *that* uncontrolled, his behavior *that* reprehensible, his morale and his life *that* shattered. He commences to find areas in which he is not like those people over there, the real alcoholics, and he allows himself to think that perhaps he is not, after all, a true alcoholic or that, if he is, he still has some more years of dedicated drinking in him before he hits their level. If he listens to himself describing his difficulties to a psychiatrist, he is struck by how much of his drinking is caused by the bad times other people give him, by his nagging wife, his unreasonable boss, his conventional friends, by the misfortunes and misadventures of his childhood and the plain bad luck that has fallen to his lot in a rotten world. If he hears from his physician that he has not yet managed to wreck his physical health but that he should begin to pull himself together and get his drinking in hand, he feels a sneaking sense of reprieve and an aggrieved sense that it is easy for someone without his problems to be moralistic about alcohol. If he finds himself in a hospital, he registers how different he is from other patients, how obviously out of place, and therefore how irrelevant the treatment offered him. If a clinic assigns him to a therapy group, he is ready to quit as soon as he has been sober for several weeks, for, although he may have gotten himself into a bit of temporary trouble, that is past now and he does not need the comments of amateurs to tell him how to think about himself.

This rebuilding of psychic defenses is just as automatic as are the body's reparative mechanisms, and it is no more characteristic of the alcoholic than of anyone else to gloss over the seriousness of a crisis once it is past and to have slip away the sense of utter necessity experienced at the time to find solutions. But the alcoholic is peculiarly vulnerable to this forgetfulness because, unlike the neurotic who remains haunted and hampered by the anxiety or depression which originally propelled him into therapy, the alcoholic quickly begins to feel considerably better after he has stopped drinking and his life tends to become much more manageable and rewarding. The people around him, in their relief, ease up in their pressures on him; his sobriety is so welcome that they gloss over other problems stemming from his immaturity. He himself grows optimistic, buoyant, confident, and it soon begins to seem a waste of time to continue in A.A. or therapy because he has his drinking problem licked.

As paradoxical as it seems, therefore, the first phase in any treatment approach to the alcoholic, even to the alcoholic who has specifically presented himself to obtain help with his drinking problem, must center on his being confronted with the inescapable fact of his alcoholism. He must be repeatedly reminded that he is an alcoholic, that he is no different from other alcoholics in his vulnerability to alcohol, and that his feelings of imperviousness to relapse are no more justified than theirs. Even with persistent confrontation, it may take three to six months before the alcoholic's efforts to rebuild his denial system taper off, and this will be the time of greatest danger that he will drop out of A.A. or back out of treatment. Thus, coupled with confrontation in the treatment situation must be reward, tangible, quick reward in the form of genuine interest and caring and empathy. The traditional treatment approach of neutrality and inactivity must be tempered vis-à-vis the alcoholic in the direction of expressed warmth and an active effort to persuade him of the sympathetic concern felt for him. His own disputatious nature will tend to garble this incoming message; the superficiality of his own emotional life will make him cynical about its truthfulness; and his passive-aggressive stance will render him simultaneously stand-offish and prickly. The therapist and/or other people dealing with him must be prepared for this and cope with it straightforwardly by both understanding it and prompting him to understand it by interpreting his responses as largely his own rather than situationally justified. Playing a waiting game with the alcoholic, waiting for him to see the roadblocks he is putting in the way of getting help and involving himself in treatment, is playing a losing game. Unless he receives immediate gratifications in the treatment situation, the long-range goal of finding that life can be better lived without alcohol will be too remote to hold him in treatment.

The alcoholic will not suddenly relinquish his denial system and achieve a commitment to therapy. Instead, if he is in A.A., there will be a slow erosion as he becomes increasingly aware of his similarity to other alcoholics. As he becomes conscious that their struggles are his, their defenses are his, their problems are his, he will begin to see himself in them and identify himself with them. This identification will lend him the strength to begin to confront his own attitudes and rationalizations. It will be a source of ego which he can borrow to cope with and examine his own life. If he is in group therapy, the same will obtain; and in individual therapy, it will be the therapist's ego he borrows and the therapist's view of his alcoholism he comes to subscribe to.

When this second phase of acceptance has gradually superseded and driven out the first phase of denial, the alcoholic often waxes exceedingly enthusiastic about A.A., the hospital program, or his individual or group therapy. He feels that the approach is special and invaluable. He views it as the answer, not only for himself but for all alcoholics, perhaps even for all troubled people. He talks about it freely and heartily, proselytizing on its behalf, bringing the word to the unenlightened and citing his new-found and energetic determination as evidence of its redemptive qualities. Grown fond of his therapist and/or fellow members or fellow patients, basking in the warmth of their tolerance, understanding, and acceptance, he considers them special people specially equipped to penetrate to and appreciate his real self. So positive does he feel, nestled in the cocoon of belongingness, of "we-ness," that he cannot conceive of a return of his old self. That tension-ridden, frustration-prone, tantrum-given, vulnerable and infantile self seems another person in another time, dead now and buried, never to rise again.

But it is a false spring, an early warm spell which does noι last, for, as he becomes freer, less defensive, and further from the surcease of alcohol, old angers arise, old disappointments come back to plague him, and old behaviors reinstate themselves. Although he feels that he has changed, and that, therefore, life and the world, in grateful recompense, should also have changed, he finds angrily that they have not. He is still being subjected to demands, to pressures, still being deprived of total love, total peace, still being forced to accept ambivalence, disappointment, indefiniteness, and uncertain rewards. He is, in short, still an ordinary human being subjected to the ordinary stresses of life. And he resents it. Having made what seems to him an heroic effort to stop drinking, he feels that he has qualified for a magical dispensation from the vicissitudes of life, and he is startled to discover that it has not been granted, that sobriety has been a step, but only an initial step, toward a different life. The phase of acceptance and enthusiasm is over. In its wake come irritation and disenchantment, and the treatment that was overvalued becomes undervalued because of keen disappointment that it has not solved all problems.

The possibility of flight is again strongly present, a return to alcoholism or, if not a literal drunk, a prolonged "dry drunk" of almost unrelieved fits of irritability and depression. This is a turning point, a time of harsh choice for the alcoholic. He can turn back into unknowingness, turn away from exploration of his problems and pursue satisfaction of his needs or turn toward them and try to understand them. He can abdicate responsibility for himself or shoulder it. He can come to accept that it is not enough to be sober; he must also behave well. It is not enough to exist; he must also shape his existence.

Unfortunately, his choice is not influenced by any objective curiosity about his own functioning. It is not that he does not find himself interesting but that he does not consider it interesting to find himself. He is impatient with the task, bored with its tedium, and dubious about its value. He cannot conceive of taking a delight in self-exploration for its own sake, perhaps because, unlike the neurotic, he has no great sense of inner conflict and unhappiness. Having always had his own permission to live according to the pleasure principle, his war is not with himself but with reality, and he has come this far only because reality has warred back so relentlessly that he is threatened with the loss of every pleasure.

If he goes on, assaying the middle phase of therapy in which his confrontation is no longer with his alcoholism but with himself, he will be satisfied with just that amount of self-understanding which will allow a truce to be declared—not peace, which is what the neurotic strives for, but a simple truce. Because of this, it is virtually never that self-exploration is pursued to levels of deep insight and pervasive personality reorganization. The alcoholic is content with far less, and so also must the change-agent be; indeed, the latter can take credit for a difficult job well done if the alcoholic gains enough insight into the ways in which he characteristically functions to enable him to remain sober and live a reasonably unabrasive life, for only a minority of alcoholics achieve even this much.

While, in practical terms, the undertaking of extensive psychoanalysis with an alcoholic is not necessary, perhaps contraindicated, and, with rare exceptions, impossible, theoretically it would be of great interest to know whether a classical psychoanalysis might enable the alcoholic to resume social drinking without risk of re-addiction. If the roots of the addiction were traced back, if the oral needs were relived and worked through, if there was regression to early modes of experiencing and being and then progression through the intermediate stages of growth to maturity, would the addiction be cured? Occasional instances of former alcoholics who have become normal drinkers are cited in the literature, but the overwhelming preponderance of opinion is that no recovered alcoholic can ever again risk a drink. Perhaps this is indeed unvaryingly so. Or perhaps it is because, given the personality of the alcoholic and the nature of his problem, treatment is necessarily incomplete.

Be that as it may, treatment is not only incomplete but in the long run ineffective if, in the phase of coming face to face with at least those aspects of himself which are linked with his compulsion to drink, the alcoholic does not also learn to adopt the technique of self-examination on a daily basis. It is not enough to understand what has happened in the past; the present, this moment, any moment in which tension threatens to build, must be a signal to the alcoholic to stop and think—not run, not act, not react, but think. Self-knowledge is of little value if it is applied only retrospectively. It is of interest to the alcoholic to be able to trace the course of his drinking career: "I started to drink when . . . I continued to drink because . . . I used drinking as . . . I had to drink whenever I felt . . ." It is of interest, but it will not protect him in the future. Only what might be called "instant analysis" will.

A friend of mine, an alcoholic in therapy but only at that point in therapy at which she believed that the therapist had the answers and could be cajoled into parting with them, turned aside from loading the dishwasher with breakfast dishes and rushed to the medicine chest for a tranquillizer. When I asked why, she said, "I felt panicky."

Again, "Why?"

"I don't know."

"What were you thinking?"

"Nothing. Just that I suddenly hated all the work." Since she was as aware as I that there is not much work involved in stacking plates in a dishwasher, she added, "Look, it happens all the time. I just happen to be subject to panic attacks. There doesn't have to be a reason. Now leave me alone!"

If she meant that there doesn't have to be a *good* reason, she was right, but there has to be a reason. Panic attacks do not come out of nowhere. One does not go about one's business normally one minute, only to be inexplicably gripped in tension the next. Something has happened. Taking the one thing my friend had said, as trivial as it was, and knowing her well, I could piece together what it was. The other people present were lingering over coffee at the dining table, chatting, laughing, relaxed and enjoying themselves. The alcoholic had gotten up to clear the table, no one moved to help, and suddenly she was the put-upon one, the one who was not given a place but had to earn it by doing a menial task, who had to demonstrate she was a "good kid" instead of being totally accepted and approved of no matter what she did or if she did nothing—a series of thoughts so foolish and fleeting that they barely registered on the surface of her mind but they sank like stones to that part of her unconscious mind which chronically saw herself as denigrated, exploited, ignored, and worthless. And the ripples set up rocked her always uncertain self-esteem.

When I suggested the possibility that this is what had happened, she said. "It doesn't matter what happened. The panic is still real, and I've got to do something about it. It's either take tranquillizers or drink."

Or hold still. Hold still, postpone relief, stand and accept the panic, and in the delay, turn and look at the self. Trace the passing thought. Pin down the errant feeling. Explore the blow, its direction, its force, its impact. Subject it to instant analysis.

Therapy can acquaint the alcoholic with his vulnerable areas, with those masses of buried affectivity which are likely to be triggered into an explosion, but psychological treatment does not produce a cure for them in the sense that physical treatment can be curative by ridding the body of the infection or disease which has caused malfunction. The individual's particular ways of functioning psychologically cannot be extirpated; they can only, by being brought to consciousness, be placed under his control. From then on, it is his task to maintain that control. He must, in effect, become his own therapist, that is, he must keep his finger on his own psychological pulse and be prepared, at the first hint of tension building, to screen a replay of the immediately preceding thoughts, sensations, words, and emotions so that he can identify and face the feelings aroused and disentangle the significance the events have had for him. Treatment provides the material for an early-warning system and identifies the quarter from which attack is most likely to come, but only the alcoholic can man the system and utilize it effectively to maintain what has been called the "preconscious vigilance" which permits trouble to be nipped in the bud.

When the early-warning system is operating reasonably well and the alcoholic is able to function therapeutically toward himself, he has the means of recovery within his grasp. But, curiously enough, he may yet again be tempted to turn back. This last high hurdle unexpectedly involves a sense of loyalty to an about-to-be-past self. With the road to recovery lying just around the bend, the alcoholic may hesitate and say to himself, "But if I take that road, I could always have taken it. If I can be responsible now for how I react, I was always responsible. My alcoholism was not an affliction, not a condition beyond my control. I could have done something about it at any time. And if that is so, I am guilty of it. The hurt and worry and harm I have inflicted are unpardonable. It would only be forgivable if I couldn't have helped it." Because it is devastating to indict oneself, the alcoholic may falter and turn away to demonstrate that he is helpless now and therefore was always helpless to alter the state of affairs. He may choose to be faithful to what he was rather than to what he can be.

The change-agent, whether in the person of fellow A.A. members, group members, therapist, or psychoanalyst, must be aware of this tendency of the alcoholic to bog down in sameness at the very moment when it would seem that real progress could be expected. And if the co-alcoholic, too, understands the nature of the alcoholic's loyalty to the past, she can, while offering discreet encouragement to him to try out new ways of being and behaving, also avoid placing him in a position in which he must feel defensive about the past. She can forgo mention of the wasted years, and she can soft-pedal her delight in the changes taking place so that the past is not indicted by implication. Such phrases as, "If you'd only done this years ago," or "I never lost faith that you could be different," although meant to convey encouragement and approval, may depress the alcoholic and drive him back to solidarity with that old self now being maligned. Better it is for the co-alcoholic to be saying in essence, "You can do it," than, "You could have done it," and whenever the alcoholic voices regret for what he has been and done, better that she say, "Without the past there wouldn't be the future," rather than agree with him that he has much to atone for. Guilt is a useful emotion when it provides propulsive power for change, but when it threatens to paralyze the alcoholic, it is more constructive to undercut it than to feed it.

Just as guilt over the past may seem to the alcoholic too heavy a burden to carry, so may high hopes for the future weigh him down and cause him to think longingly back to that old untrammeled self of whom the worst, not the best, was expected. Although he himself will speak glowingly of the future and deliver ringing affirmations of how rosy it is going to be, the co-alcoholic should not thoughtlessly echo his great expectations lest she produce a faintness of heart in him at the prospect of having never again to fail at toeing the line. The same refusal to hope that stood her in good stead during his drinking days can help her now to maintain encouragement but stop short of undue optimism.

If the alcoholic, despite nostalgia for that old self who knew how to get quick relief, who did not have to be *aware,* who could blot out reality instead of having to puzzle it out, who found oneness in a bottle instead of having to stand and accept aloneness in the world, if that alcoholic can keep going until he has made his own acquaintance and knows how to renew it whenever he senses himself threatened or frightened or angered, he is well on his way through the fourth stage of therapy, synthesis of what has been under analysis, and is beginning to look to its end: the separation of himself from the support of therapist, group, and/or fellow alcoholics. This does not necessarily mean literal separation, although this can follow naturally, but the commencement of a process in which he turns less and less to others for support and direction and more and more to himself. He begins to trust himself, to trust his ability to stand on his own feet, to trust his own powers of choice and discretion. He becomes, even, impatient at the "we-ness" which has been his support, like an adolescent who feels himself ready to move out from under his family's wing, ready to make choices and risk their being wrong, ready to accept the burden and the release of being an individual.

The adolescent will, of course, have made many small and large forays into the world before he cuts his moorings to his family, trial runs in which he tries out ways of being and behaving, and so, too, will the alcoholic. The alcoholic can use the semi-protected treatment situation as a source of feedback about what he is doing right and where he is still making mistakes, as a source of encouragement, and as a source of stimulation to further self-understanding. But the time will come when he will be ready to live, not talk about living, and he will face away from treatment into his own life, although not without anxiety and not without almost a process of mourning for what is about to be lost. There is the fear of aloneness, of isolation, of having to recognize that every human is, poets to the contrary, an island, surrounded on all sides by space, and that, no matter how close others come, there is no final bridging of the gap; there are only separate identities. It is a poignant realization for the alcoholic, who has again and again throughout his drinking life attempted to negate it through the spurious means of alcohol. It is his last hurdle—acceptance that he is alone, as all persons are alone, an individual, self-responsible.

There cannot help but be mourning, some sense of depression, some degree of fearfulness. But there can also be pride, a growing sense of strength, a quiet joy that there is a self and it can be relied on. Beyond self-blame and self-justification lies perspective, humor, playfulness, an openness to experience and a confidence that whatever experiences befall, they can be ridden out. The self is no longer helpless. It can turn outward to see, to feel; it need no longer turn inward to guard and to protect.

When the alcoholic has come this far, he can be said to be a recovered alcoholic. He cannot drink again, and there will be times when he will long to drink again, but the drinker he once was will be remembered by him as he remembers the child he once was: how nice to be that again when the answers were simple, but how impossible. He is grown now, and he cannot go home again.

Not being able to go back is not the same as going forward, however. The not-drinking state is an achievement, but a negative achievement. If the alcoholic is to have a worthwhile life, a life of some depth and richness, he has the same task of shaping it and using it to good purpose which faces anyone who wishes not merely to get through a life but to live it. Therapy, then, is not an end but a means, a means of freeing the individual to be himself, and that freed self must be invested. The investment will be in family and friends and job, of course, but more than that, there should be an investment in thought—in a philosophy of life—and in activity—in a framework of life. If treatment can be said to have provided the alcoholic with a rudder to steer by, he must still acquire ballast to insure his stability. He must care about more than immediate concerns. He must think about more than subjective matters.

To an alcoholic who swore convincingly, "I am never going to take another drink," I replied, "Fine. What are you going to do instead?" He was taken aback by the question and more than a little irritated, commenting acidly that he supposed I would like him to take up bookbinding or some other equally fascinating hobby. Since what he actually did when not drinking was to lie on his back and stare at the ceiling for hour after hour, bookbinding, or some other hobby, would have seemed not only preferable but indispensable to his goal of not drinking. The mind, when not engaged on some task, has a hobby of its own which it engages in tirelessly: it circles the self like seagulls over a beach, eyeing the debris of the day and picking out this small slight, that tiny hurt, that speck of threat and collecting them into a mound of self-pity and defensiveness. Therapy may make the process more conscious, may deprive the alcoholic of innocent belief in his obsessions, but it will not end them. Only other interests will distract him from lovingly minute examination of the wounds of the day, will divert his thought into the safety of more objective channels, and will prevent circuit overload of his emotions.

The most certainly recovered ex-alcoholic I know is a man who, after attaining sobriety through A.A., threw himself into the Twelve-Step work of recruiting for A.A. but eventually found himself growing bored and restless and dangerously vulnerable to the possibility of drinking again. He thought it was because he was going stale and, more out of desperation than interest, he signed up for an extension course in painting at the local high school. Finding that art gave him pleasure and solace but that his talent for it was negligible, he turned his attention to the history of art, studying and reading and, during vacations, traveling abroad to visit the great museums of the world. When he felt reasonably secure that he knew good painting from bad, he organized local art shows, and on the basis of their success, he sparked and led a drive to establish a regional museum, which he now, in retirement, heads and from which he frequently ventures forth to give illustrated lectures to schools and clubs. Asked if the thought of drinking ever tempts him, he snorts engagingly and dismisses the idea with, "I wouldn't waste my time on that nonsense!"

Speaking of "the value of impersonal interests," Bertrand Russell in *The Conquest of Happiness* comments that no one leads a life free of distress, threat, and setback but that, "At such times a capacity to become interested in something outside the cause of anxiety is an immense boon." While an interest or hobby that is in some way worthwhile is more likely to engage the attention in a lasting way, even trivial pursuits, such as reading murder mysteries or collecting matchbook covers, will serve well enough. It matters only that the pursuit provide the individual with something other than himself to think about. Physical labor can do it—an alcoholic who had spent an afternoon chipping old wasps' nests from the beams in an attic remarked, "Well, it's a stinking lousy job but at least you can't think about your troubles while you're doing it"—or mental involvement with a book or a jigsaw puzzle can achieve, not the obliteration of thought which the alcoholic formerly sought, but the distraction of it into realms other than preoccupation with the tender self.

If the goal of treatment for the alcoholic has been to render him capable of becoming his own therapist in the sense of being able to identify and face his true feelings, it may seem odd that, for the gains of therapy to be maintained, he must also become his own occupational therapist. Is not seeking distraction just another form of flight? In part, it is. But, at worst, it is honorable flight, and, at best, it aids the process of understanding rather than aborts it, for nothing so beclouds issues and distorts perspective as rumination on offenses to the self. The alcoholic stacking breakfast dishes could have poured herself a second cup of coffee and rejoined the conversation at the table, or she could have taken her camera and gone into the garden and become absorbed in taking close-up pictures of flowers, or she could have borrowed a bicycle and gone riding, or she could have taken a book out on the terrace. As it happens, she does not own a camera, she hates bicycle-riding, and in such a mood as she was in, the last thing she felt like doing was reading. But the point remains: What is the alcoholic going to do *instead?* The alcoholic must *know,* know himself, know where he is, what he is feeling, why he is angry, why he is anxious, where he is threatened. But knowing is not all the answer. He must also *act.* He must do something instead, instead of drinking, instead of letting anger and/or tension build.

Alas, the alcoholic is scornful of distractions. He scoffs at games, hobbies, lessons, crafts, and most sports, labeling them the trivia of children and deriding adults who throw themselves into spare-time enthusiasms. This is bound up with his impatience; he has not the staying power for the long haul, the time it takes to plan and accomplish a project or to become proficient at a skill; he wants to excel instantly and effortlessly, and if he cannot, he throws down his mitt and goes home. It is also bound up with his long experience of fast relief. How can the contented tiredness that descends after a day of gardening be compared to the easy magic of a couple of drinks? He feels there has to be something better, something more. He knows life to be essentially empty, boring, mundane, and if a distraction does not provide the quick glow which lights it up, for him it is a failure. He cannot be argued out of this. He can only learn, by forcing himself to continue through and past boredom and impatience, that relief can come in slow ways, and in small and unexpected ways.

To argue this with an alcoholic is to find oneself essentially arguing the alcoholic's characteristic view that life is not worth living. Whether he propounds the belief directly or not, it will be the burden of his resistance to diversionary activity: why, when all is meaningless, should I do meaningless things? The answer to his question is not a reasoned one but a philosophical one: life has meaning only when one has accepted that it has no meaning. One is alive simply because one happens to be alive, as a bird or a tree is alive. One has a time span as a clump of marigolds has a time span. There is no meaning to a clump of marigolds; it simply has an existence. There is no meaning to a life; one simply has an existence. But when that is accepted, that a life *is* but is meaningless, it takes on meaning. A day of gardening is without meaning, but straightening at the end of the day to the lovely sight of piled white clouds in a vaulting sky gives it meaning. The meaning is no more than that it is good to be alive. The moments are rare; they cannot be sought; but they come to the person who is not merely existing but investing himself in his life. He is not alive in order that he may make a garden, but because he makes a garden, he knows that he is alive and that to be alive is the meaning of existence.

The alcoholic is a firm believer in Murphy's law that everything that can go wrong will go wrong. And, he adds, it will happen to me. Further: I don't deserve it. That is about the extent of the alcoholic's philosophical baggage. For the rest, for the sustaining thoughts that allow other people to weather mishap, he has substituted liquor. Now, recovered, if he is to maintain his recovery, he must begin to piece together a set of personal beliefs to function as shock-absorbers whenever the going gets rough. They need be neither complex nor profound, but they must resonate deeply in the individual alcoholic and sum up a faith he can set against pessimism and cynicism. An acquaintance of mine has weathered severe losses in her life with a phrase learned in A.A.: When one door closes, another opens. The phrase, clung to when her husband died, when a best friend moved away, when a job ended, when she herself faced retirement, has turned her attention to the future and cut short her mourning for the past, even made her feel an excited expectancy about what was to come; and, indeed, there have always turned out to be other loves, other friends, other jobs, and, in retirement, a new and interesting life in a congenial climate.

Another friend has borrowed from Buddhism the insight that the origin of man's suffering is craving. When he feels unhappy, uncomfortable, uneasy, he asks himself what it is that he is craving. More often than not, the answer is love, recognition, approval, and once he has recognized that, it is a short step to inquiring of himself whether he needs to have love from that bare acquaintance at a cocktail party, recognition from that co-worker whom he knows to be something of a fool, approval from that small child who would benefit more from discipline than indulgence. Since the answer is no, the depression and anxiety that have begun to drift over him are quickly dispelled—and with them the long-range threat that he might have to drink to get rid of them.

A third alcoholic responded to E. M. Forster's phrase: the aristocracy of the plucky. Deciding that that was the class to which he wished to belong, he reminds himself of it when self-pity threatens to engulf him. Another alcoholic cautions herself more directly with the observation: self-pity is an indulgence I can no longer afford. Still another relies on two words: trust yourself. And another asks himself whenever anything threatens his equilibrium: a year from today will I even remember that this happened?

Catch phrases, all, and no substitute for reasoned thought, such phrases can nevertheless function admirably to buy the alcoholic time for reasoned thought. Karen Horney, in discussing the neurotic in *Neurosis and Human Growth,* observed that ". . . the potentiality for his special way of malfunctioning always remains with him. It is immediately activated when the patient succumbs to conceit, pride, or self-centeredness and retreats into his angry anxious isolation." Since this could scarely be more true of the alcoholic as well, the value of such phrases is that they allow the alcoholic to warn himself away from the trap of defensiveness or arrogance and obviate the need for retreat into the dangerous area of angry anxious isolation. A phrase, alive with personal meaning and summing up a wealth of individual reference, can open up some distance between himself and the scene taking place, shift it into a wider perspective, and drain it of much of its threat.

One man's banality can be another man's profundity. An observation of mild import to one individual can light another's life. It cannot be predicted which building blocks will be used by one person to construct a philosophy of life but be tossed aside by another as irrelevant. Thus, no alcoholic can be given a ready-made philosophy. Treatment cannot provide it. The co-alcoholic cannot supply it. It can only be achieved by the alcoholic himself. Just as he must find the activities in which he will invest himself, so also must he find the words which will allow him to pledge his allegiance to himself, to health, and to life—and to pledge it again and again, long after treatment has ended; indeed, until his life itself has reached its end.

14
Continued Alcoholism

There were three of us talking one evening, two co-alcoholics and an alcoholic, and what we were talking about was the wretched state of an absent alcoholic, a friend to each of us but the particular concern of the other co-alcoholic. As is usual in such conversations, we had been over all the explanations put forward by the absent alcoholic for his drinking and the motives it seemed to us he had for not drinking, trying to find the touchstone to sobriety left unturned. There was none that we could discover. The drinking was logically inexplicable, a monomaniacal trip to purest self-destruction. When offered any alternative course, however, the alcoholic immediately argued its impossibility. His view was so consistently and suspiciously negative that the co-alcoholic had recently remarked to him that, were he to be given an absolute guarantee that his life would magically be made perfect by something so simple as drinking a glass of orange juice each morning, he would refuse to do it. The alcoholic who was present smiled ruefully. "So would I," she acknowledged. "I'd think it was a trap to exploit me or destroy me, and I'd die before I'd fall for it."

That many an alcoholic would die rather than fall for the claim that abstinence has more compensations than alcohol is attested to by the depressing statistics on recovery rate in alcoholism. Only a minority of alcoholics manage to pledge their

243

allegiance to life and health by negotiating the quiet, undramatic, almost imperceptible internal shift from a chronic flirtation with oblivion to an affirmation of life. Only a minority rid themselves of avoidance as the organizing principle of their lives and turn to acceptance of life as it is. And thus, by unhappy extension, only a minority of co-alcoholics can look forward to release from the problems of coping with alcoholism via the infinitely desired route of the alcoholic's achievement of abstinence. The majority must consider the alternative of leaving the alcoholic.

It may be that the lucky ones are the co-alcoholics who settle the issue quickly. A friend of mine married a classmate the June they graduated from college. Within two years, it became obvious that the drinking which had seemed just a part of college social life was a necessity for him, and when he failed to meet her ultimatum that he stop or else, she packed up and left, on the straightforward basis that he had a perfect right to spend his life as he wished but that she had an equal right to choose to spend hers differently. A clear-headed person with firm ideas about personal standards of behavior, she perhaps was not lucky so much as not tailored to the role of co-alcoholic. She resembled the usual co-alcoholic, if generalizations can be made about so large a group, in that she was competent, capable, and self-contained. Co-alcoholics in general give the impression of being quite effective people, sensible, practical, reliable, and able, and she was no exception. But it is possible that in her this was a natural posture, the outgrowth of a secure sense of self stemming from confidence, security, and maturity, and therefore she was able to resign from the cast of this alcoholism drama early in the first act. There was certainly distress involved in resolving to disentangle her life from that of her alcoholic husband, but there was not the anguish that afflicts so many co-alcoholics.

This type of personal torture besets the co-alcoholic who presents the same outward aspect of strength and self-reliance but who suspects that her character traits of competence and composure stem from a basic inability to care greatly, to love generously, and to commit herself fully to another human being. Her effectiveness and her tolerance, she fears, are merely detachment, a reflection of an absence of real depth of emotion. More than adequate in the practical realm, she feels deficient emotionally, and the alcoholic plays on this concern by implying that, if her love for him is genuine, she will stick by him. In saying, "If you love me, you won't leave me," the alcoholic is implying, "If you leave me, you don't love me," thus roiling the co-alcoholic's hidden misgivings about her capacity to love. Since she wishes not to believe that she suffers this inadequacy, the co-alcoholic is maneuvered into staying, not primarily to convince the alcoholic that he is loved but to persuade herself that she is capable of love.

It cannot be denied that the alcoholic's unpredictability, his flights into single-minded unconcern, his dips into irresponsibility are inclined to exaggerate the co-alcoholic's stability. She is forced into a balancing posture of greater consistency, competency, and steadiness than she might otherwise display were she not obliged to act as counterweight to the alcoholic. But these are traits not foreign to her, and their exercising is not entirely distasteful to her. The need of the alcoholic to be cosseted and protected meshes with her need to be giving and protective. His weakness justifies and excuses her strength. But if she is at all ambivalent about that strength, it may be the force that binds her to him rather than enabling her to walk away from him.

The co-alcoholic can be in the position of a well-to-do aunt with an improvident nephew. The nephew wheedles for funds with the plea, "You have so much. Please help me to help myself," and the aunt sees the logic in the argument and generously agrees to a loan. When that hand-out has been spent, the nephew returns for another with the further argument, "You'll never miss it, and it means so much to me." And returns again: "People will say you're selfish and self-centered if you don't help me." And again: "You need me because you need to think of yourself as Lady Bountiful." And the ultimate argument: "But you can't refuse me now when you've always helped me before." An aunt who had no worries about her image, who felt that, whether she was rich by good fortune or good management, it was nevertheless not by her doing that her nephew was less well off and who considered that it was up to him to earn his own way would quite quickly have no compunction about turning her nephew down.

One or two hand-outs would be all he got; he could not return time and again to the well. And so it is, too, with the basically self-accepting, self-respecting co-alcoholic; perhaps originally attracted to the alcoholic because she is in a position to give and he is a person in need, she rapidly realizes that she is depleting her resources while not strengthening him, and since she does not need the evidence of self-sacrifice to prove her affectionate and generous nature, she can refuse him continued support. The aunt, and the co-alcoholic, who, in contrast, are insecure, misdoubt their own humanity, and cannot countenance the threat of revelation of themselves as miserly, whether with money or affection, can be exploited indefinitely. All it takes is charm, promises, and the subtle production of guilt, as the unscrupulous nephew knows consciously and the alcoholic knows intuitively.

It is not the self-sufficient co-alcoholic who could perhaps afford to stay with the alcoholic who does so but the self-questioning one. She will stay and she will try, until the time comes when she recognizes that she has failed and that the continued drain on her emotional capital is threatening to bankrupt her. Then she will feel herself faced with a major decision: whether to resign herself to the status quo or get out. When she begins contemplating this decision, however, the chances are that she will find that, like so many of life's choices, by the time it is seriously thought about, it has already been made. The early times when she did not say, "Either . . . or . . .", the middle times when she threatened but backed away from carrying out the threat, have been a series of small junctures at which she has acted selectively, and the choices, by default more than by design, have added up to a way of life. Now, in the third act, when the alcoholic's thralldom to drink remains unbroken, whether he has consistently resisted treatment, attempted treatment but could not maintain a commitment to it, or is apparently a treatment failure, and she debates her exit from the drama, she may feel that it is too late, that all the minor choices have summed to a major commitment that cannot be undone.

As an instance of how doors can soundlessly click shut, Carol, an alcoholic, met another woman, like herself middle-aged and alone, at A.A. meetings, and they became friends. Sharing a love of dogs, they decided to rent a country farmhouse and breed collies, with the second woman, Jenny, who had inherited a small amount of money from her husband, to live there and Carol to keep her job in the city and join her on weekends. It proved a passingly pleasant and successful arrangement despite the fact that Jenny resumed drinking. For a time the drinking was limited and discreet—beer and wine consumed mostly when Carol was not there—but eventually it became heavy and constant. Carol, as an ex-alcoholic, was not blind to what was happening nor fooled by the transparent excuses, but, having herself recovered from alcoholism, she remained tolerant, understanding, and hopeful. She tried to provide solutions to Jenny's litany of complaints; she agreed to close the kennels when Jenny blamed the responsibility of them for her drinking; she assumed Jenny's share of the household expenses when her inheritance had been dissipated. But still Jenny went downhill. Now she lives on in the farmhouse, frequently irrational, always drunk, raging at Carol for her isolation in the country, running up astronomical telephone bills as she tries to find a voice from the past to sympathize with her incoherent ramblings, depending completely on Carol but treating her as the villain in her life story. Carol finds the deteriorated situation almost intolerable, but she feels that there is no way out because, if she withdrew her support, Jenny would be homeless, friendless, and destitute.

Another co-alcoholic, one who had always presumed that, if there was no end to the drinking, sooner or later she would have to make the major decision about whether to give up, also found that later seemed to be too late. She has been married to an alcoholic for thirty-one years. A "controlled" uncontrolled drinker, her husband has never lost a job because of drinking, has never gone on prolonged binges, has never cracked up a car, and has never had a breakdown. He has also never allowed her freedom from worry, never allowed their home to be a place of peace, and never allowed her and their children to be secure in his love and affection, subjecting them instead to wildly swinging moods of elation, in which his behavior is silly and bullying, and depression, in which his behavior is corrosive and bullying. Elizabeth, his wife, has probably not spent a full week in their married life in which the thought of leaving him did not occur to her, but there never came a single time when her husband upped the ante for staying with him so sharply that she was forced into action. When the last child went off to college, she felt the time had come to make a decision once and for all, only to find that the question of whether or not to get a divorce suddenly seemed academic. Where would she go? What would she do? Was she not bound by thirty-one irretrievable years? If she hadn't left him early in their life, what was the point of leaving him late in their life?

Is, then, the co-alcoholic who has not walked out early in the first act doomed to stay to the bitter end? Not necessarily. Major decisions compounded of myriad small ones can be dismantled if the co-alcoholic has the courage and incentive. As enmeshed as both Carol and Elizabeth apparently are in their respective situations, either could get out simply because no one ever lacks the possibility of saying, "Enough." Elizabeth probably will not, but that is because she wavers at the thought of what will happen to herself, and her present troubles are not intense enough to drive her into the unknown. Carol, who has the greater incentive, would also have to have the greater courage, but, despite her despairing appraisal that she is living a classic locked-room puzzle, she too could break free if she willed it.

If she did not renew the lease on the house, had the telephone taken out, found homes for the two remaining pet dogs, put the local stores on notice that she would no longer be responsible for the bills, gave Jenny a sufficient sum to live on for three months, and, disappearing into the city, remained adamantly out of touch, their joint life would be liquidated. What stops Carol from doing this is, of course, the question of what would happen to Jenny. Her honest appraisal is that the consequences would be dire, and since she can foresee them, could she afterward live with the knowledge that she had allowed them to come to pass?

Years ago, in a comparable situation, an older woman, as gentle as cashmere and fond of my mother, commented that, if anything, her alcoholism seemed to be intensifying and asked what I planned to do. "Nothing," I said. "What can I do?" I expected a quiet nod of the head in agreement that my options were blocked. Instead, she said something more tough-minded than any unsentimental member of my own generation had been able to muster. Their advice was always to leave my mother to her own mercies until they met my mother, then it changed to acknowledgment that such a helpless woman could not be abandoned. But this woman was of a different opinion. "You've done what you could," she said. "Now you must save the healthiest." When I asked what she meant, she explained that it was like a physician arriving at the scene of an accident in which two people have been critically injured. He cannot help both, so he must choose between them. How will he choose? According to the unwritten rule of medicine: save the healthiest. Don't risk losing two lives in a futile effort to succor the fatally damaged one. Insure the survival of the person with the best chance to pull through, and then, only then, do what you can for the other.

It was true that my life, cored of its vital center by the depleting burden of looking after my mother, was withering. I did not lack the incentive to leave her to heaven, but I did lack the courage. I had only to think of the all-too-probable consequences to have a foretaste of the intolerable guilt I would experience, and I could not imagine how I would live with that. But that was because I thought of my emancipation solely in terms of desertion of her. When I began to conceive of it, instead, as saving myself, me, the healthy one, the one with a chance to survive and grow and go in new and useful directions, it was no longer an unforgivable default but an obligatory decision.

It can be argued that I would literally have survived. Carol would argue that now about herself, that she can struggle on, but one need not even question what price survival nor place a value on the two lives to answer that, for it cannot be known that Jenny would go under. My mother, seemingly in precarious health, as fragile as fine china, as lost as a wandering child, half in love with the thought of suicide, lived on for twenty more years. I would have given her twenty weeks or twenty days or twenty hours when I left her. I think I did give her the twenty years by leaving her.

The co-alcoholic who believes she has tried everything is mistaken. There is one thing she has not done, one thing she is afraid to do. Nothing. When I did nothing, I automatically eliminated the secondary gain in my mother's alcoholism. Her drinking was not designed to manacle me to her, but when it ceased to have that effect, it eased off, occasionally for long periods. I had unwittingly been rewarding the very behavior I wanted to discourage. Her drinking bound me to her to look after her; where, then, was the profit to her in ceasing to drink since it would bring about the very loss she feared. The same thing was true of her suicidal gestures. When I did not respond to the threats, they lost their usefulness and gradually disappeared.

I presumed, as Carol presumes, that to do nothing would be the last straw, but when the co-alcoholic who has been doing everything does nothing, the alcoholic may have to do something. Jenny would have to find room and board for herself. If she did not, the landlord would call in the sheriff's office to evict her, and that would be likely to bring in social service agencies and lead to their making living arrangements for her or obtaining a court order for hospitalization. If she found a room but could not or would not obtain a job to pay the rent, again she would come to the attention of the authorities. The co-alcoholic presumes that no one will intervene, but society will intervene if the alcoholic is helpless to help himself. The co-alcoholic is foolish to imagine that hers is the last of the helping hands and to conjure up images of a homeless alcoholic dying of starvation in an alley.

Astonishingly often, the helping hands may belong to someone much like herself. The appeal of the alcoholic is potent, the savior complex is widespread, and the alcoholic may be gathered into another compassionate bosom, or a whole series of them. Because she is at the end of her rope, the co-alcoholic imagines that everyone else will steer clear of the mess, recognizing the utter futility of trying to protect the alcoholic from himself, but another person does not know the long history, hears only the cry for help, and is seduced by it. My mother, with her brave story of trying to surmount the defection of her only child, enlisted a series of protectors, young and old, male and female, including a man, her junior by two decades, who married her and whose later convulsive desertion she also survived. The invariable first move by each of these *amici curiae* was to put in a long-distance call to me to let me know that my mother could not live alone and that she needed me. I thanked each, stated that I was un-available, confirming the contrast between coldly selfish child and loving mother, and encouraged each to proceed without me. Not a single caller backed off from becoming involved. Not one was alerted by my hands-off attitude to the fact that he might be getting into a quagmire. On the contrary, my detachment was a signal to rush to the rescue, on the basis, I have always supposed, of proving something about themselves and me. Lest this sound cynical, I hasten to add that, as must be apparent from earlier passages in this book, I too have rushed in where other co-alco-holics have ceased to tread, and with less excuse because of hav-ing had more experience. I also feel compelled to add, in ex-tenuation, that when a final telephone call came, this one from my mother herself in which she remarked in bewilderment that she could no longer get dressed because her clothes kept moving around, I did take over again and made the series of arrange-ments that were necessary for her care in the last devastated years of her life.

If I had it to do over again, I would not do it differently, but I would do it sooner for the reasons I have given. I was reward-ing her alcoholism by letting it function to bind me to her. She objectively was better off without a caretaker, as was evidenced by the fact that her periods of sobriety coincided with the times when she had no one to look after her and ended when she had lured someone into taking responsibility for her. And throughout the twenty years, there were other people; I was not the sole and single person who could help. At the end there was even society, for when her funds and mine were exhausted, the state main-tained her in a nursing home and a mental hospital.

I would not even have done it differently if the outcome had been twenty days instead of twenty years because her life was no pleasure to her and brought no pleasure to other people, and I cannot believe that an earlier death was something to be pre-vented at all costs. Dean Rusk, when he was Secretary of State, was once asked why this country was pouring more men, more money, more supplies into a rapidly disintegrating situation abroad, and he replied philosophically, "In for a penny, in for a pound." The co-alcoholic, in for a penny, is certainly in for a pound, for the penny of concerned help, so easily spared initially, swiftly pulls after it the pound of trying to fight the alcoholic's battles for him. But when it is apparent that no amount of aid is going to turn the tide, must pound follow pound follow pound down the drain? Must a strong life be sacrificed to prolong an enfeebled one? I think not. I think a choice must be made and that it must be to save the healthiest. Anything else is waste compounded.

Were I to do it again, however, I would handle the break as positively as possible. It is more than understandable that, when such a decision is reached, it has been born in despair and fed by anger, and the parting is often accomplished in a vitriolic storm of accusation. The alcoholic is told with ferocity that he is hopeless, beyond redemption, ungrateful, spineless, childish, self-centered, worthless, and intolerable, that he deserves neither love nor compassion, and that the bad end surely in the offing for him will be richly deserved. In a sense, the co-alcoholic has to believe all this in order to remain steely in the face of the pleas and promises and counteraccusations she will certainly hear, but to give tongue to her rage and disappointment, however satisfying it may be finally to burst forth, may destroy whatever flickering spark remains in the alcoholic. Perhaps the last favor she can do the alcoholic is to couch her reasons in affirmative terms. Rather than flinging his failure in his face by saying, for example, "You are beyond help," she might shoulder a share of the blame by saying this: "I am obviously not helping you, and I may be making you worse. It's time we found out." Rather than, "You're impossible," this: "I've become someone I don't like." Rather than, "I've done everything anyone could be expected to do," this: "Someone else may be able to do more." Rather than, "I'm at the end of my rope," this: "You have more strength than you give yourself credit for." Rather than, "I can't go on," this: "You'll be all right on your own. I'm sure of it."

Words? Yes. Lies? Perhaps. But people live by what they believe about themselves, and it is kinder to leave the alcoholic with some belief to clothe himself in than stripped of the last shreds of his tattered self-respect. The temptation to aim parting shots at the killing zone is great, but, resisted, it may save the alcoholic, and thereby save the co-alcoholic the guilt and remorse she will feel if he does go under and out.

When contact must be maintained with the alcoholic after the parting, there will be continued cries for help. I found that the best way to handle them was by the simple, firm statement, "You can manage." No matter how poignant the alcoholic's pleas for just one more rescue from one more desperate situation, "You can manage," repeated with conviction, makes them resistible. And eventually they taper off as he either does indeed manage or finds someone else to do it for him. Again, the difference between the negative statement of what one will not do and the positive statement of what the alcoholic can do seems slight, but in the long run it is more of a relief not to be cruel and it allows one to reject involvement without rejecting the alcoholic.

Perhaps the hardest of the alcoholic's maneuvers to handle are declarations that he has not long to live because of his physical condition and that he has not long to live because he intends to kill himself. The alcoholic sees no contradiction in applying pressure with both of these arguments, and he will use one or the other according to which is likely to have the greater impact at the time. Because alcohol does have such a deleterious effect on the body, he can in all honesty apprehend that he will not long survive, and because abandonment, or the threat of it, can be such a psychological threat, he can seriously believe in his intention to commit suicide. And there is not the slightest question but that alcoholics do die of physical causes and do kill themselves for psychological reasons. I have known both eventualities to happen, but, curiously, never to the self-identified victims. My mother, chronically protesting her imminent demise from any one of a lengthy catalogue of real and imaginary illnesses, ultimately died, literally, of bedsores, while a friend in hefty middle-age, suicidal but apparently physically strong, died abruptly of liver collapse. The alcoholic wife of a man who was himself a heavy drinker prevented him from leaving her by her proposal to kill herself but then fell down a flight of steps and sustained such a severe concussion that she became mentally incompetent, and it was her husband who eventually committed suicide.

That suicide and death do strike but not necessarily in the expected direction is not to suggest that the threats can be ignored but that they should not be allowed to be paralyzing. Acknowledged as possibilities, they need not be interpreted as probabilities but should, instead, be handled with calm common sense and realism. I have found it best to reply to the alcoholic's plaint that he is in such poor health that he must be cared for with the reiterated statement that, in such case, he should surely be under medical care. The answer to that is, of course, that a physician will tell him to stop drinking and he cannot, to which my answer is, "Then I can't help you either, can I?" Rather than argue either the drinking or the state of his health, I offer agreement: "Alcohol does destroy, and it may be destroying you, but I can't do anything about that."

Nor do I argue the question of suicide. I say, "If you feel you don't want to go on living, that is your choice. It's up to you." An alcoholic who was trying to prevent my leaving shouted, "You want me to kill myself!" "No, I don't," I said. "I'd very much rather you didn't, but it's your choice and if you've made up your mind, nothing I can do will stop you." He thought a moment and then burst out, "You know I can't! You know I don't have any sleeping pills!" I remarked that the windows were wide open, the river was only three blocks away, and, so far as I knew, the subways were still running, and added, "You don't lack the means. The only question is whether you want to, and that's up to you."

This sounds extraordinarily indifferent, but there are several arguments in its favor, not the least of which is not only did the alcoholic not commit suicide but several days later he announced that he had been thinking it over and decided that he basically did want to live and was going to stop hovering around the temptation of nonexistence. What happens when the person on the receiving end of the threat responds with anxious pleading and watchfulness is that the dialogue goes on and on, lending the thought a credibility it might not otherwise have. Each return to the discussion lends the proposal ever more reality, and what may have started as an empty threat becomes a valid possibility as the listener struggles and strains to avert it. The threats themselves must escalate lest the listener dismiss a fresh threat as just like other times, and the threatener may argue himself into a position from which there is no retreat except at the cost of being thought an empty bluffer; he may have to make good on his threat simply because there is no place left for him to go.

In the responder to suicide threats, two things can happen. A factor of fatigue may set in which leads to less and less heeding of the threats, to the extent that she may miss the one which is real. Or she can grow despairing of her ability to prevent the suicide and so turn away from the alcoholic, withdrawing her concern and inadvertently conveying to him that she feels the situation is hopeless. She, in a sense, comes to expect the suicide, concedes her defeat, and acts as though it has already happened, which, since this is the final rejection the alcoholic dreads, makes it highly likely that it will happen. Overreacting initially to talk of suicide tends to lead to underreacting eventually, and, therefore, it seems wisest to begin by handling the threat as seriously meant but the outcome of which must perforce be left to the alcoholic to decide in dialogue with himself. This neither dismisses nor minimizes the possibility, but it does make it his responsibility. It can be talked about, and it should be in order to make it clear that it is his right to live or die, but once treated respectfully and realistically, it should not be talked over. If the co-alcoholic does not cite all the reasons the alcoholic has to go on living, he, with no chance to argue the negative, may find himself marshalling the positive. He will live because, if the threat does not serve its purpose, what is to be gained by carrying it out?

If he does carry it out? Then, that is evidence that it was not a threat but an intention, and the co-alcoholic must make herself know that she could not have prevented it in any event. If one is not merely to be the manipulator of another's life, one must grant freely his choices, including this basic choice. The co-alcoholic made the choice to save the healthiest. It is not a wrong one. The alcoholic's tragedy must not be allowed to become hers.

Someone once wrote about his tour of Europe that he made it a practice, before leaving a sight, to imagine himself back home. What would he want to know about the cathedral or monument? What should he look at more clearly and carefully now so as to be able to answer his own questions later? It is not a bad course for the co-alcoholic to follow before she leaves the alcoholic: to imagine that she is back on her own and has learned that the alcoholic has died or committed suicide. Could she have done something differently? If so, there is still time to do it. Should she have made another choice? If so, there is still time to make it. Is the guilt unbearable? If so, it is not yet inevitable. Does the remorse go too deep? If so, she need not incur it. The emotions can be lived through "as if," as if the future had taken place, as if the events were over, as if there are now the feelings to be borne. Testing their power to devastate in anticipation, the co-alcoholic may realize that she will be able to live through the worst should it befall. Indeed, by living her feelings through in advance, she may sense that to some extent she has already lived them out. There is more resignation than apprehension now, more fatalism than fear, and she is able to entrust the alcoholic to destiny, knowing that her own fate will not be forever compromised should his prove tragic.

The question of whether one can live with oneself after walking out on an alcoholic is the paramount consideration, but many co-alcoholics are concerned as well with what other people will think and say. The answer is usually that their reaction is surprisingly uncritical. A man who went to the West Coast, ostensibly for a few days to investigate a job offer, failed to return and did not communicate with his alcoholic wife except to send a message through his lawyer that money for her support would be deposited monthly in their joint bank account. His wife had a breakdown, was hospitalized, and upon her release from the hospital committed suicide. Having to return to dispose of their property, the husband secluded himself, supposing that their friends despised him for what he had done and blamed him for what had happened. But one by one their friends sought him out to offer their sympathy and understanding, with a variation on one sentence running like a refrain through all that was said: "I don't know how you stood it as long as you did."

Friends, because their involvement with the alcoholic is less complex and more superficial than that of the co-alcoholic, generally have given up on the alcoholic long before the co-alcoholic is ready to concede defeat. They have fewer illusions about the alcoholic's corrigibility and less investment in remaining optimistic. While continuing to tolerate the alcoholic's deviant behavior, partially because they can afford to since they don't live with the alcoholic and only infrequently see him at his worst and partially, often, for the sake of the co-alcoholic, what they tend to say privately is that the co-alcoholic is a fool for being so patient. It is more common that the co-alcoholic is viewed, not as a saint, but a sucker. The decision to break away is usually met with: "It's about time. You should have done it years ago." And even if the outcome is as tragic as it was in this instance, people are apt to believe, not that it is the co-alcoholic's fault, but that the alcoholic was more disturbed even than they had suspected. In an odd sort of way, the tragedy that the co-alcoholic fears will bring condemnation actually is exculpating. When the end is known, hindsight makes it convincing that the alcoholic was rushing to keep an appointment in Samarra; how wise, in that event, was the co-alcoholic to refuse to accompany him to the inevitable end.

The supposed opinion of friends should not sway the co-alcoholic when she is considering whether to leave the alcoholic, but, by the same token, it is not especially useful to solicit their opinion in an effort to obtain help in making up her mind to do so. The most restrained, discreet, and scrupulously fair description of life with the alcoholic leads virtually any listener to comment that it is obviously intolerable and should be put a stop to, the sooner the better. The co-alcoholic, in airing her grievances, has no trouble sounding convincing, and the listener's reaction is: "For heavens' sake, do something, get away." That puts the co-alcoholic in the position of defending her inaction, and there she does have trouble in being convincing. It is next to impossible to convey the tangled skein of hopes, fears, feelings, and hesitancies which bind the two lives. The listener hears out her fumbling explanations and, still at a loss to understand it rationally, falls back on the one observation that seems to account for the incomprehensible: "What it must come down to is that you love him too much to leave him." But even that wide-mouthed net fails to catch the truth, and the co-alcoholic, having wanted advice, feels only that she has failed to find words for the many facets of her dilemma and has made herself appear something of a long-suffering fool in the bargain. While there is nothing wrong in talking to friends, although the fewer the better and one must be careful not to become a bore by endless shilly-shallying, there is usually only the temporary relief of ventilation to be gained from it, not the decisive guidance out of the maze one is hoping for.

There are two classes of people who should categorically be ruled out as confidantes, however. One is business associates of the alcoholic, whether superiors, underlings, or co-workers, and, as well, anyone not now associated with the alcoholic but who may someday be in a position to recommend him for a job or supply a reference. Even though his alcoholism is known, details which can only be supplied by the co-alcoholic about the extent to which it is affecting his private life should be rigorously kept from associates. The co-alcoholic should not solicit their view of how well the alcoholic is managing to function professionally, and she should not be lured into discussing her own problems by the offer of a sympathetic ear. Business associates are often genuinely concerned and they may telephone or drop around to ask if there is something they can do, but, without meaning to do harm, they can let fall a comment weeks hence, such as, "Even his wife is fed up with him," which slots into a growing picture of the alcoholic as a liability who perhaps should be gotten rid of for the good of the company. It is difficult to parry the questions of an employer or associate, particularly when prefaced by, "I only want to know for his sake so I can help him," but the co-alcoholic should remain as uninformative as possible, agreeing because it is obvious, "Yes, he's having some trouble now," but adding the positive note, "Bear with him. Cover for him if you can. He'll pull out of it." Never, never should she give a hint of her own worry, her own despair, and always, always she must resist the temptation to be appreciated for what she is going through. That her courage be admired is not one-tenth as important as that the alcoholic now, and in the future, not acquire an aura of troublesomeness and irresponsibility which may cause people to turn their backs on him. Many an alcoholic is so skilled at his work that his lapses are tolerated indefinitely if unguarded words do not tip the scales against him. Protecting his work has importance as a practical matter, but an even more central reason is that the area of employment supplies the alcoholic with an identity beyond that of being an alcoholic, which may be what his personal and social life has come down to, and he needs that identity to hold on to and, if he ever turns the corner to build on.

Even more strictly to be excluded as confidantes are children. If there is a wife of an alcoholic who has not at one time or another turned to her child and asked, "Should I leave your father?" I have yet to meet her. The wish to consult one's child can be rationalized in many ways. The child is desperately concerned in the situation; it is his home that will be broken, his parent who will be lost, his life that will be changed. He has, no less than the co-alcoholic herself, an intimate view of the situation; he knows, almost as well as she does, the cost of the alcoholism. He loves and is bound to the alcoholic. The co-alcoholic, believing she must know how stressful the child finds the situation, justifies her probing of his attitudes. Will he be happier away from the presence of the alcoholic parent? Does the alcoholism blight his life by causing him humiliation? Is he frightened by the alcoholic rages? Is he insecure because he can never be certain of the household's atmosphere? These are questions to which the co-alcoholic must seek the answers, but not directly, for, if directly posed, they are an invitation to the child to take sides, they almost invariably contain a concealed bid for sympathy, they require the child to be disloyal to the alcoholic parent, and they place an inordinate responsibility on the child. If he reveals his distress and his mother leaves his father, it will seem to have been done for his sake and he will bear the burden of it. If he hides his distress and his mother stays with his father, again it will be for his sake and he will be to blame for her continued unhappiness. The child cannot win however he answers, and he will sense that. Therefore, he must not be consulted. It is too great a burden to place on a child.

It is also unnecessary. The co-alcoholic who is not looking for something to make up her mind for her but is genuinely trying to arrive at the best decision can figuratively step back and study her child and find the answers to her questions by observing the expression on his face, the way in which he enters a room, the tenseness with which he carries himself, his eating and sleeping habits, his ability to make friends, how well he is doing in school, all the indices of his happiness or unhappiness, his anxiety or contentment, his fears or his mastery of the circumstances. The child will communicate to her in a thousand ways whether he is being damaged, and if so, to what extent.

This is not to say that she should not talk to the child or that she should hide her feelings. Indeed, it is important that she talk and that she express her feelings so that the child has implicit permission to do likewise. To pretend to a normality that is not present forces the child to play act also and deprives him of a chance to master his emotions by airing them. It also deprives him of the chance truly to understand what is happening and forces him back on his imaginings, which may be far more distorted and frightening than the reality. A child, even a quite young one, sees more than his parents realize and can understand and accept more than anticipated if it is explained in terms he can assimilate. If he asks, "Why does Daddy drink when it makes him do funny things?" he deserves the honest answer that his father is an alcoholic, that alcoholism is an addiction, with an analogy given to compulsive eating or smoking or thumbsucking, whatever will make sense to him, and that the alcoholic is not bad or sick or weak but a person with a problem which he has not yet figured out how to solve. How alcohol acts should also be explained, that it is a chemical which affects the brain, producing alterations in consciousness and therefore in personality. These two things, that the drinking of alcohol is a compulsion not under the immediate voluntary control of the alcoholic and that chemically it produces altered states of consciousness, can go a long way toward reassuring the child that the alcoholic is not being arbitrarily and deliberately destructive and that the effects of drinking, although they concern him, are not being targeted at him. I have observed children being extraordinarily tactful and helpful toward an alcoholic parent after they have been led to understand that they have not caused the behavior and need not identify with it. One child, a nine-year-old girl, for example, insisted to her drunken father that her heart was set on a swim before dinner and asked him to swim with her to make sure she would be safe. Her design was, of course, to sober him up, and she was able to accomplish it by an instinctive appeal to his pride without in any way damaging that pride.

The co-alcoholic who comments, "I sometimes get awful mad at Daddy when he drinks, and I expect you do too," gives the child a chance to express his feelings, and he may, if the conversation is carried on in an open, honest way, as though the child and his parent are just two people trying to be clear in themselves about their reactions, say more, and more in unexpected directions, than if he is asked leading questions. All the co-alcoholic can really do is to provide openings and try to keep her remarks free of pressure on the child to agree with her and see the situation her way. By giving the child permission to say what he feels and by straightening out any misconceptions he has, she can help the child, and this should be her aim, not to have the 'hild help her. Most particularly it should not be her aim to have the child side with her. The parent who is an alcoholic is still a parent, a figure looming almost mythically large in the child's life, and to tear down that figure by a cruel harping on the disappointments he has engendered is a double blow to the child. He is already having to contend with the reality of the alcoholic parent, and to be told that he must part with the ideal of parent and put contempt, derision, and rejection in its place is an additional loss. The most constructive thing the co-alcoholic can do for her child is to encourage him to distinguish between the alcoholic and his alcoholism, preserving his affection and respect for the person however disaffecting the behavior of alcoholism may be.

It will often seem grossly unfair to the co-alcoholic that she, having to be mother and father both to the child and discipline him and guard him and take care of all the practicalities of his care, may seem to matter less to the child than the alcoholic parent. The alcoholic, as mentioned repeatedly, is charming, and when sober, he may be so remorseful over his neglect of the child and over the unhappiness he has caused that he may treat the child with special gaiety and arrange companionable expeditions as a treat. And the child undoubtedly will respond in kind, not only out of pleasure but out of relief, making the co-alcoholic feel left out and unappreciated. But this is something that the co-alcoholic, for the child's sake, must simply swallow. It is a part of human nature to desire most fiercely the love that one is unsure of having, and the child who has to deal with all the ambiguities of a relationship with an alcoholic will be far more anxious to have the alcoholic's love, and will respond far more emphatically to signs of it, than to the steady supply of affection he takes for granted in the other parent.

However she herself feels about the alcoholic, the co-alcoholic must respect the child's positive feelings and give what help she can to his effort to understand and integrate his negative feelings. She should encourage his tolerance and discourage a judgmental attitude. She should allow him, without jealousy, to get what he can from the relationship, and she should try to supply what is missing. Her greatest care must be never to place the child in the middle, and to this end she must never ask him to share in her decision about whether to leave or stay with the alcoholic, and after the decision is made, she must never, in any way, shape, or form, suggest that what she has done she has done for the sake of the child. If she, as an adult, has intense difficulty in determining the right course to follow, has confusedly mixed feelings, and dreads any course, how much more difficult it is for a child to be made to feel responsible. The co-alcoholic must make the decision alone and, having made it, carry it out without a single bid for her child's understanding, pity, or approval.

It is a lonely decision, a searing crossroads to arrive at and with little to light the way when one is there. How can it be made? Some years ago a critic commented that every writer's work is informed by one basic view of life, a theme which runs like a flashing thread through his material, out of sight for some distance, perhaps, but reappearing and finally seen to be always there in some guise. For me, that theme, explicitly stated in an earlier book, is: the central relationship in any life is to the self. Other people are marvelously necessary, critically, blessedly important in uncounted ways, but not always the same people through all of a lifetime. They can take a different path and be lost, or they can die and be forever gone. But the self is lived with until the very end, and since how one lives with the self determines how happily and freely and creatively and generously one lives with other people, it must be looked to, not selfishly but sanely. If the self grows small and dry and hard and resentful and the scar tissue of hurt and failure makes it lose its resiliency, one, by becoming no good to oneself, becomes no good to other people. Thus, the crucial issue is not whether the alcoholic can be left without fatal damage to himself but whether the co-alcoholic can stay with him without irreparable damage to herself.

There are co-alcoholics who can purge themselves of tantalizing hope while not succumbing to the aridity of hopelessness. There are co-alcoholics who can appreciate the uniqueness and worth of the person behind the alcoholism and respond to that while forgoing the temptation to use the alcoholic as the target of their identity-molding, aggressive, and caretaking needs. There are co-alcoholics who can be *there* for the alcoholic while nevertheless recognizing that they cannot make decisions for him, cannot intercept the blows of the world, cannot meet his responsibilities, and cannot make his choices. There are co-alcoholics who are clear enough in their sense of themselves not to be threatened by the alcoholic's clinging attempts to merge and deny his separateness. There are co-alcoholics who have thought through their position and purpose and, while never cutting off discussion of their reasons for acting as they do, adhere to their position of honestly viewing the alcoholism for what it is and their purpose of proving more tenacious than it is without in the least believing that they can end it. There are co-alcoholics who know that their goal is to live with the alcoholic, not cure him, to bring the alcoholic to himself, not to themselves. There are co-alcoholics who, while recognizing that the alcoholic believes that not meaning to cause pain is the same as not causing pain, can accept the pain but let the wounds heal quickly and cleanly. There are co-alcoholics who, recognizing alcoholism as a form of suicide, nevertheless sense in the alcoholic a basic commitment to life rather than death and respond to that by trusting it and speaking to it, telling the truth about the present but always in the context that the alcoholic is strong enough to help himself when he so wills it.

Without these qualities, the co-alcoholic, however reluctant she is to fail another human being, must leave the alcoholic lest she fail herself and thereby lose all. With them, the co-alcoholic can accept life with the alcoholic if she chooses. Both, the co-alcoholic who stays and the co-alcoholic who goes, have done the only thing that one human being can do for another: given him room and reason to be himself.